EBURY PRESS

THIS BOOK WON'T TEACH YOU PARENTING

Riri G Trivedi is a psychotherapist, parenting mentor and trainer. She integrates the wisdom of yoga with evidence-based psychotherapy to support families in raising emotionally healthy and resilient children. Her corporate journey—across Japan, Singapore and India—shapes her unique, practical approach to her work.

As co-founder of Wellness Space, Riri integrates research-driven therapy, inner child healing and mind–body practices to empower parents with awareness and self-regulation tools. She conducts parenting workshops and teaches evidence-based psychotherapy, helping both parents and mental health practitioners create nurturing, emotionally secure environments.

Her doctoral research explored the long-term effects of childhood experiences on adult well-being, offering fresh insights into how parenting can shape future generations. With her team of globally trained therapists and a thriving online community of more than a million followers, Riri is a trusted voice in emotional wellness.

As a mother of two, she shares her parenting journey—embracing both the wins and the stumbles—with authenticity, warmth, honesty and heart.

Anagha Nagpal is an engineer-turned-educator. With a master of science degree from the US, she had over a decade of corporate experience when she decided to follow her interest in early childhood education and trained as a Montessori teacher. Anagha is now a certified parent educator and a life coach trained in hypnosis and psychotherapy techniques. She helps clients overcome adverse impact of childhood trauma, limiting beliefs, phobias and relationship issues.

As a consultant for Positive Parenting Matters in Singapore and a life coach at Wellness Space in India, she has conducted numerous workshops and consultations with parents. She has also published several articles in theAsianparent, a leading south-east Asian parenting website.

With extensive experience living and raising twins across four Asian countries—Japan, China, India and Singapore—Anagha writes from personal and professional perspectives. At the heart of her work is a commitment to helping people find deeper fulfilment and build joyful families where children thrive.

ADVANCE PRAISE FOR THE BOOK

'My heart tells me that I can't learn how to be a good parent from a book written by strangers. But my brain tells me I *can* learn from those who have dedicated years to researching how childhood is shaped and influenced by the actions of parents, those who have imparted their knowledge and real-life experiences from countless consultations into a seminal tome. It is not a manual as much as it is a judgement-free conversation, peppered with wisdom and practical tools to help you navigate parenting through the ages—be it toddler defiance, teenage self-harm or adolescent mood swings. This book won't teach you parenting but it will hold your hand and remind you that you are not alone'—**Soha Ali Khan, actor**

'*This Book Won't Teach You Parenting* offers a refreshing and deeply insightful approach to parenting. It begins by exploring how our own early experiences shape us as parents, bringing scientific depth and providing practical, heart-centred frameworks. The section on birth to 6 years stands out, addressing real-world challenges like toddler defiance, meltdowns, picky eating and more, with empathy and clarity. Thoughtful Q&A segments make it even more relatable. A must-read for anyone seeking to raise resilient, emotionally healthy children with wisdom and compassion'—**Guruji Dr H.R. Nagendra, Padma Shri awardee and president of Swami Vivekananda Yoga Anusandhana Samsthana (S-VYASA)**

'As a child psychologist, I often meet parents burdened with guilt—not because they didn't love their children enough, but because they weren't equipped to respond with emotional clarity. *This Book Won't Teach You Parenting* is not just a title that grabs attention—it's an honest and deeply insightful invitation into the inner world of parenting, trauma and transformation. What sets this book apart is its refusal to offer rigid how-tos or perfect-parent checklists. Instead, Riri G Trivedi and Anagha Nagpal provide something far more valuable—a compassionate, research-informed guide that gently leads parents inward, helping them understand their own childhood wounds and behavioural patterns before they attempt to "fix" their child. With case studies, cultural context, neuroscience and real-world parenting challenges—from meltdowns to teenage withdrawal—it offers a rare blend of psychological depth and practical empathy. It doesn't judge. It doesn't overwhelm. It simply illuminates. Whether you're a parent, a teacher or a mental health practitioner, this is a gentle but powerful resource that can shift generations. I wholeheartedly recommend it'—**Riddhi Doshi Patel, child psychologist and parenting counsellor**

'*This Book Won't Teach You Parenting* focuses on how childhood is shaped and influenced by parenting actions. It gave me insights on children's behaviour and thoughts on how to manage the classroom effectively. I will definitely recommend this book to educators and parents as it contains well-researched anecdotes that could be applied in real settings'—**Ramya Shyam, educator, curriculum design consultant and advocate for cross-cultural education and parenting**

'The book feels like a warm, honest chat with someone who truly understands the ups and downs of parenting—especially when you're still healing yourself. Backed by years of research and real-life consultations, it's full of practical tools, age-specific advice and a non-judgmental approach to tough topics like social media, self-harm and emotional resilience. It's not just a parenting guide—it's the kind of support every parent wishes they had'—**Kunal Jaisingh, TV actor**

'*This Book Won't Teach You Parenting* is an educational and informative guide firmly rooted in research on childhood trauma and centres itself on adverse childhood experiences, or ACEs, as they are known in mental health parlance. What I found most interesting is its focus on positive parenting, where the authors focus on the dos rather than the don'ts, empowering parents to look at what they can do right rather than only worry about what they are doing wrong. All in all, this is a comprehensive handbook that doesn't claim to teach you parenting but will certainly go a long way in making you a better parent'—**Samindara Hardikar-Sawant, co-founder of Disha Counselling Center, psychologist and psychotherapist, trauma-focused therapist and author**

'This book is based on real-world accounts dealing with childhood from birth to teenage. The scheme is based on positive parenting in an Indian context. It encompasses cultural, social and spiritual aspects. It is a must-read for young parents. I am sure they will get good insights into rearing children as good citizens and noble human beings'—**Bhavnaben Dave, former mayor of Ahmedabad, former member of Parliament and former vice chancellor of University Granth Nirman Board**

'A culturally rooted, research-backed guide every modern Indian parent needs. It doesn't preach—it gently holds your hand and helps you parent from within. This book made me pause and reflect. Its emphasis on self-regulation and healing generational patterns is invaluable. The real-life Indian family experiences with practical everyday tools truly resonate. A must-read for raising emotionally healthy, resilient children in today's world'—**Alankritha Chandru, Montessori-trained early childhood educator, curriculum designer and advocate for cross-cultural dialogue in education and parenting**

'This book was incredibly informative and eye-opening. It shattered many common misconceptions about parenting and highlighted how even well-meaning actions can unintentionally harm our children—sometimes in lasting ways. I especially appreciated how it explored the cycle of repeated mistakes passed down through generations. In today's world, where so many parents feel overwhelmed, this book feels more relevant than ever. The practical strategies were a highlight for me—not just showing what to do, but also what not to do. I also found the insights into adult triggers and behaviours really powerful. A must-read for any parent who wants to grow and break harmful patterns'—**Renu Bhojwani, primary educator**

'This book doesn't just speak to parents—it speaks to the child within us all. It was a truly enlightening experience to page through one of the first copies of *This Book Won't Teach You Parenting* by Riri G Trivedi and Anagha Nagpal. Drawing from their deep experience in the field of mental health, they've created a gold mine of insight and compassion. It resonated deeply with both the child and the adult in me. The opening chapters, which carefully unpack the layers of childhood trauma, are truly eye-opening. The subsequent chapters handhold a parent through growing stages of a child ultimately speaking of self-regulation and self-care which are essential for all, whether they are parents or not. Too many of us move through parenting in a kind of sleepwalk—unintentionally passing down generational wounds and missing the warning signs along the way. I wholeheartedly recommend this book to anyone who is a parent, or who has ever been a child. Because ultimately, the responsibility of raising children doesn't just lie with parents alone. Every child in the world is, in some way, the shared responsibility of every adult in the world'—**Shraddha Pandey, superintendent of police, Uttar Pradesh, Indian Police Service 2017**

'Childhood trauma and its impact on physical and mental health is often not discussed at length in an Indian context. While Western literature has many good books on the topic, the vast cultural differences between those societies and our culture make it difficult to apply and translate the context to our parenting atmosphere. Riri and Anagha have filled this huge gap in a lucid, informative way, using the simplest of language and real-life relatable examples. This book is going to sit on my bookshelf for a long time, acting as my reference point for my own parenting journey whenever I am clueless as a parent. Riri, Anagha, you have done us a great service by writing this book'—**Dr Ankita Singh, trauma-focused integrative dermatologist and regression therapist**

'In an era teeming with parenting tips, *This Book Won't Teach You Parenting* is unique in its soft but strong message: to raise children well, we need to understand ourselves first. This perceptive and introspective book does not merely concentrate on techniques to "fix" children's behaviours but rather invites parents to turn inward—to their own childhoods, inherited patterns and individual parenting styles. And that's where its magic begins. The authors, who are experienced parents and experts in their field, don't write from a pedestal. Rather than providing a checklist of dos and don'ts, they share their own parenting mistakes, uncertainties and "aha" moments. These raw stories—from school meltdowns to bedtime battles—make the book so relatable. As a reader, you never feel judged. You feel understood. What I love about this book is its mix of introspection and true-life anecdotes. Each chapter quietly walks you through the process of drawing the line from how you grew up to how you present as a parent now. But never in a preachy way. Whatever you call yourself—new parent, deep in teen trenches—*This Book Won't Teach You Parenting* is asking you to stretch along with your child—with compassion, clarity and much, much grace'—**Shireen Sultana, ex-founder of KinderPass, an award-winning parenting app**

This book ~~will~~ *won't* teach you parenting

but it will make you a better parent

RIRI G TRIVEDI
ANAGHA NAGPAL

EBURY PRESS
An imprint of Penguin Random House

EBURY PRESS

Ebury Press is an imprint of the Penguin Random House group of companies
whose addresses can be found at global.penguinrandomhouse.com

Published by Penguin Random House India Pvt. Ltd
4th Floor, Capital Tower 1, MG Road,
Gurugram 122 002, Haryana, India

Penguin
Random House
India

First published in Ebury Press by Penguin Random House India 2025

10 9 8 7 6 5 4 3 2 1

ISBN 9780143474104

Typeset in Adobe Garamond Pro by Manipal Technologies Limited, Manipal

www.penguin.co.in

To our parents, partners and children:
With our deepest gratitude for shaping who we are

And a woman who held a babe against her bosom said,
Speak to us of Children.
And he said:
Your children are not your children.
They are the sons and daughters of Life's longing for itself.
They come through you but not from you,
And though they are with you yet they belong not to you.

You may give them your love but not your thoughts,
For they have their own thoughts.
You may house their bodies but not their souls,
For their souls dwell in the house of tomorrow, which you cannot visit, not even in your dreams.

You may strive to be like them, but seek not to make them like you.
For life goes not backward nor tarries with yesterday.
You are the bows from which your children as living arrows are sent forth.

The archer sees the mark upon the path of the infinite, and He bends you with His might that His arrows may go swift and far.
Let your bending in the archer's hand be for gladness;
For even as He loves the arrow that flies, so He loves also the bow that is stable.

—Kahlil Gibran,
'On Children', from *The Prophet*

Contents

Introduction

'I wish I had worked on myself sooner. I could have been a better parent.'
'I wish I had known this earlier when my kids were small, I would not have made the mistakes I made.'

How It All Started

In the fifteen years that we've been therapists, this is the regret we hear articulated most often. As parents, we understand that this feeling cuts deep and is a heavy burden to carry. It usually stems from a pattern of fighting and arguing in the family, which the parents would like to change but find themselves ill equipped to do so. That is when they reach out to us for help. A common sentiment is *'I feel so bad about hitting my child, but I just couldn't control myself', or 'When I get angry at my child, I yell at her. But later, I feel terrible about it.'* We have worked with many parents who are well-read, well-informed and know which behaviours are helpful to the child and the ones which are not, yet they are helpless victims of their own triggers and past patterns of behaviour. They seem to know what they need to do but don't know *how* to do it.

As part of our work, both of us offer one-on-one therapy sessions and workshops to help parents understand their situation better and find ways to change themselves. Through the regular practice of self-regulation techniques, learnt through our workshops and personal therapy, many parents have been able to improve their relationships with their children and family. While we are thankful to be able to affect the lives of our clients positively, we know that many more parents may not have access to the same kind of help. We hope to make these lessons pre-emptively available to all parents through this book.

A Bit About Us!

Riri started Wellness Space with her husband, Dr Gunjan Y. Trivedi in 2010. The intention was to provide mental health support for people through yoga and psychotherapy techniques. Wellness Space has since grown from one therapist operating out of a single room to a team of ten therapists who have conducted more than 10,000 client sessions and published research in the areas of childhood trauma, depression, suicidal behaviours, stress management, post-traumatic stress disorder (PTSD)[1] and parenting. Her social media channels, which have a huge following, are used extensively to build awareness about positive parenting and mental health, and her insights on many topics beyond what is covered in this book are available there.

Anagha joined Wellness Space as a positive parenting coach in March 2022, bringing with her over thirteen years of experience in helping parents learn positive discipline techniques. Her certifications in the field and experience as a Montessori teacher guide her approach in showing parents how to tackle specific challenges. She had been conducting positive discipline parenting workshops before joining Wellness Space. Her decision to become a positive parenting coach came from the desire to help parents do what was best for the child. She is also a life coach trained in hypnotherapy techniques at Wellness Space and has worked with many parents in their therapy sessions.

Wellness Space has worked with thousands of clients to help them with anxiety, depression, PTSD, relationship issues, chronic health conditions, insomnia, addictions and other conditions. We have also published papers on the effectiveness of our interventions in leading mental health journals. In our 1000+ personal consultations, most of which were with people who have children, we found that behaviour patterns stem from factors in their own childhood. Whether it is heightened emotions, dysfunctional belief systems or poor self-esteem, their early experiences and in some situations, childhood traumas, have a role to play. These traumas are primarily associated with their parents, primary caregivers and extended family.

Echoes of the Past

Often, such trauma survivors, who become parents themselves, unknowingly pass on their behaviours to their children. Adults may not often realize that they experienced childhood trauma because, from an early age, they are taught Indian cultural practices and folk tales that elevate parents to a god-like status. This leads them to think that their parents are not capable of doing any wrong. So, they may even experience denial and guilt for judging or resenting their parents. This can stand in the way of being able to recognize unhealthy behaviours and how they are linked to their childhood. This is how trauma can often continue for generations, unless the pattern is broken. Overwriting this harmful programming can take time and conscious effort, and harm relationships before the person can work on themselves. Seeing this first-hand strengthened our resolve to prevent childhood trauma.

It is important to remember that several other factors can also contribute to incorrect parenting, including stress at work or in a marriage. For example, a couple always fighting is usually overwhelmed by dealing with their distress and irritation. Thus, it can be hard for them to understand their child's emotional needs or be patient with their tantrums or misbehaviours. Parents' mental health conditions or marital issues also make it hard for them to be receptive to their child's emotional needs or any alarming signs of stress.

Power of Resilience

Having said this, we want all our readers to remember that not everyone who has been beaten, scolded or abused as a child is traumatized. Many children and adults manage to stay functional and even thrive, despite childhood trauma. This is because each person's ability to adapt to stressful situations, known as emotional resilience, plays a huge role in how one remembers these experiences and processes them. We must help children develop emotional resilience because we can't always be there to protect them from environmental stress. We will explore this in more detail later in the book.

Trauma Triggers

Today, many parents read books and consume a lot of parenting content on social media, and they have some idea of what to do or what not to do. Yet, when their child triggers their anger or insecurities, they react in the most unexpected ways and then feel guilty about it. This is a common reaction for parents who have not worked on their own trauma triggers or do not use any self-regulation tools. Thus, when they need to be regulated the most (for example, when their child is screaming or throwing a tantrum in public), they cannot use the methods they have learnt and react from their unhealed selves, making them violent or abusive. Thus, this book aims to help parents understand that self-awareness and self-work are the most important pillars of positive parenting, and no tools or learning in the world may help if they cannot regulate themselves.

Well Meaning Mistakes

After working with many parents over the years, we've realized that, more often than not, they have the right intentions even when they use the wrong methods. Moreover, blaming parents never truly heals either the child who has suffered or the parent who lives with their guilt. It only causes more strife. When the children or the parents acknowledge the situation and try to heal, they can often mend strained relationships.

Riri began posting videos on social media in 2022 to raise awareness about this and provide helpful tips for parents to take the first step towards positive parenting. Today, she has over 1.4 million followers across Facebook, Instagram and YouTube. Since she began posting, she has received many direct messages from parents who resonate with her content and ask questions about their specific situations. Many of the questions and scenarios in this book are based on the queries parents commonly post on her videos.

As a regression therapist and parenting coach with Wellness Space, Anagha saw first-hand how inner child healing techniques helped clients work through their childhood experiences.[2] Many of these painful memories were created inadvertently by parents—the most important people in the child's life. Working professional women, in their thirties and forties, were still carrying the burden of their parents' comments about 'not being as fair or smart as their older sister' or not ever feeling important because the parents wanted a boy. Once the traumas were addressed, and they learnt to regulate emotions, their emotional health improved. Many of them also took parenting sessions to be more responsive to the child's needs.

Strength in Synergy

With the objective of protecting the next generation from trauma, and helping children grow up healthy—not just physically but also emotionally—we decided to collaborate. We created a unique workshop to educate parents about the impact of adverse childhood experiences and raise self-awareness about their own childhood and parenting styles. We realized they could combine our unique strengths—Riri's vast clinical experience and extensive research, thanks to her PhD work on childhood trauma, and Anagha's passion for providing parents with tools to deal with their children's challenging behaviours—with patience and understanding, not violence. While Riri helps build awareness on what parents should avoid and how they can care for themselves, Anagha helps teach them what they *should* do, providing practical tips for specific challenges.

When we received an overwhelmingly positive response to our workshops and had parents tell us how they had improved their relationships with their children, we knew we had to equip more parents with practical solutions focused on positive parenting. The book you hold in your hands is our joint effort, shaped by our own experiences and interactions with our clients.

Our work has also shown that there's a severe dearth of the right kind of information. That doesn't mean that there aren't enough books on parenting, but very few are based on research and talk about childhood trauma and how it affects parenting experiences. Most parents are also unaware how healing their own childhood experience can help them become better parents. Also, the books that are backed by research rarely consider the age-specific experiences and cultural challenges of Indian parents, something that we have covered in this book, based on all the questions parents had posed in our workshops and on our social media handles. The book tries to balance a research-based approach and practical solutions that parents can use for their parenting challenges.

Parenting Cannot be Taught in Books!

We believe parenting cannot be taught like other regular courses—hence, there are no curriculums or colleges on parenting! This is because parenting cannot be the same when we are dealing with unique children, unique parents and unique families. Even within the same family, we have children who are completely different—what worked for one child may not work for the other! But we can definitely help parents with some basic guidelines for them to navigate parenthood with joy and positivity. We can also help parents to understand what behaviours can harm and what behaviours can help and enable them to understand their own selves and their childhoods better so they can be more mindful about their own triggers and reactions to their children. And we can attempt to answer some basic questions on commonly occurring parenting challenges at every age—again, guidelines rather than a defined way of doing things.

This book aims to bridge that gap and promote a non-violent and positive approach to parenting. It will also clarify what parents often do incorrectly and what they can do to avoid unhealthy habits. This book also grapples with issues that are more relevant to children and parents nowadays, which didn't exist in previous generations, such as social media usage, self-harming behaviour and conversations about sexual orientation and safe sex—something that Indian parents struggle to handle due to a lack of reference points from their parents or their generation.

Through specific challenges, we will also cover how parents' experiences have been evolving over time. Earlier, joint families and older relatives provided support and guidance. Nuclear families lack that support, which can lead to the adults feeling additional pressure to get each parenting decision 'right'. At the same time, those living with joint families face different challenges, especially when handling children's misbehaviours. For example, grandparents may still favour traditional methods of discipline, such as spanking and yelling. So, some parents may face criticism when they follow positive parenting methods. At other times, grandparents and other family members pamper the children excessively, while the parents are trying hard to set boundaries and be firm with their children.

Today, we have very involved parents vs ever before. Over-involvement of parents in the child's growth and development is also a cause of concern because parents' own stress and anxieties coupled with micromanagement of the child's life and activities is leading to different types of challenges that previous generations have not faced. Understanding the right parenting style that is balanced and universally applicable across generations and cultures is what this book also aims to throw light on.

How to Read This Book:

Why is This Book Important?

The first chapter covers various childhood trauma experiences that tend to affect the mental health and subsequent behaviours of children and parents. It explains why parents need to recognize their own childhood traumas and why they must be mindful of their own behaviours that might be a cause of stress or trauma for the child. This part sets a framework for parents to understand their childhood and how it may affect their parenting style.

The second chapter helps parents understand the impact of chronic stress on the body, brain development and behaviour. It also helps parents understand how their own past childhood experiences can affect their parenting behaviours.

Where Do We Focus?

The third chapter is the parenting compass which provides parents with a broad direction for their parenting approaches based on global research. It maps out four parenting styles on the basis of warmth and control, helping them navigate challenging situations.

How Do We Do It?

The fourth chapter gives specific guidelines based on positive parenting approaches and equips parents with strategies and tools for every situation. It provides a framework within which parents can manage their interactions with children at every age.

What Can We Do?

In the next three chapters, based on our experience of conducting various parenting workshops, we dive into specific situations that most parents need help with. Parents' challenges vary by age, and each situation requires specific answers, which we will explore in depth. These chapters answer the question of *what* you need to do and *how* to do it—be it a challenging situation or a difficult conversation. As a parent, you can choose to read the specific sections related to your child's age and challenges and visit the other sections later as your child grows older.

So, What Can We Do for Ourselves?

The eighth, and extremely crucial chapter of the book, is on self-regulation for parents, which provides practical advice on how parents can de-stress, regulate their emotions and physiology and take care of themselves. This part is essential reading, and we firmly believe that parents will find it hard to follow the principles and advice from the earlier chapters if they don't practice the self-regulation techniques outlined in chapter seven. Parents need to focus on self-work before trying to fix their children!

And Finally . . .

Every chapter ends with self-reflection questions for parents—to help you understand your own childhood better and to reflect on your own deep-rooted behaviours stemming from those experiences that may be affecting your parenting journey or your child's behaviour. As mental health practitioners, we hope you find the tools and advice in this book helpful. Our aim for writing this book will be served if we can help even one parent build a positive connection with their child, based on mutual respect and love.

After all, we bring children into this world to grow, and as parents, we want to nurture them, so that they grow into healthy, happy and empowered individuals. This core belief guides our approach to therapy, and we find that the best way to explain it to parents is through the poem 'On Children' by Kahlil Gibran. The poem is an excellent reminder that to be a good parent, you must allow your children the space to develop their own beliefs, as they work to become the best version of themselves. This is why we shared it in the epigraph. We hope it serves as a guiding light in your parenting journey, as it has for us.

1

The Shadows of Childhood

> 'It may be unfair, but what happens in a few days, sometimes even in a single day, can change the course of a whole lifetime.'
>
> —Khaled Hosseini, from *The Kite Runner*

Parenting is more than just raising good children; it is about cultivating an environment or ecosystem that increases the probability of raising healthy, happy and fulfilled adults. This part of the book provides the foundational elements of such an environment and provides specific situations that parents can directly control or influence.

Usually, parenting is all about what we should do for our children and how to do it. However, this book starts with an understanding of what we should not do as parents! We are referring to Adverse Childhood Experiences, or ACEs. They include all our experiences from birth to age eighteen, which have a long-lasting impact on every area of our life, including parenting approaches! In common language we refer to them as childhood traumas.

This chapter touches upon all elements of childhood trauma, the resultant chronic stress that a child goes through and the impact on the child's mind and body. The chapters are based on three decades of existing research in the area of ACEs, as well as research done at Wellness Space over the last few years, spanning thousands of client interactions. It also touches upon how traumatized children, might continue some behaviours even as adults and parents which might further perpetuate the trauma patterns and behaviours down to their children!

By understanding the ACEs and minimizing their risk, parents can heal themselves and also create the framework for their child's future well-being.

What are ACEs

'I want to be a loving mother. I don't want to beat my child anymore. I want to heal myself . . .'

She came to us because she wanted to be a kind and gentle mother to her five-year-old daughter. She had grown up in a family of farmers in the village with a very violent and abusive father. He would verbally abuse their mother and beat her up regularly. She hated her mother for provoking the father—the provocation would make him more violent. She remembers crying throughout her childhood and being told that she was a troublemaker and an unwanted child. Her parents would beat her up every day—for speaking up during mealtimes or going out to play or asking questions. Her father's beating was very severe, and he terrorized them to the extent of not allowing them to cry during the beating. The fear, coupled with not being allowed to cry, would make the girls pee in their panties. At the age of five, she was caught lying so her mother hung her by her wrists and beat her. Her family was very conservative, so she was not allowed to meet or visit her friends after school. She was not even allowed to go out and play. She grew up listening to verbal abuse from her parents daily. By the time she was ten, she started answering back to them, which got her beaten up even more regularly.

As a teenager, she grew up with severe body image issues as she had many pimples on her face—her mother and aunt would slap her until she bled. The image of her face with blood and puss still haunts her as flashbacks. She was closest to her grandfather, who loved her, but when he died, she plunged into depression at the age of thirteen. She grew up feeling shame, fear, humiliation and guilt and because of this, she was unable to make friends even as an adult. *It's always my fault, I must have done something wrong* was the constant voice in her head when it came to friends and relatives, in front of whom she would be beaten and shamed. She felt cared for only when she was sick—so she would keep falling sick as a child to get love and attention. She was also sexually molested by a relative between ages twelve and eighteen. The family had financial difficulties, so she never had good clothes to wear.

She felt disrespected by all her cousins and relatives due to her parents' violent behaviour and constant fights, and she blamed herself for most of it—growing up in toxic shame. As a teenager, she was forced by her mother to attend spiritual discourses that she hated. So, till date, as an adult, she hates the idea of God, festivals or puja. Due to her financial situation, she felt inferior to her peers. She wore horrible, ill-fitting clothes to hide her body that she was ashamed of. At twenty-three, she fell in love with a boy. The parents didn't approve of it—they locked her up, and all her relatives beat her up for days, dragging her by her hair, kicking her in the stomach and emotionally blackmailing her to give up the relationship. She eventually married him—a very nice man who was kind and understanding. But she realized that her past didn't leave her alone.

After her daughter was born, she started beating her daughter out of frustration and rage. She feels disconnected and cannot express her emotions well. She has compulsive tendencies about food and money. She has severe trauma from the physical abuse and domestic violence she witnessed as a child. She has a distant relationship with her parents and sister. She also finds it hard to focus on her work. She reached out to us for help.

'I have constant self-doubt. I have difficulty getting up. I feel ill all the time and I have been depressed all my life. I have had severe body complex throughout my life. I have no self-love at all. I am fearful all the time and have absolutely no confidence. Even doing small things is difficult for me. I get angry when my daughter cries and I end up hitting her.'

ACEs: Understanding Childhood Trauma

'Trauma' is a word often used in conversations today but usually not understood very well. Simply put, it is a deeply disturbing experience. Every individual is likely to face some form of trauma in their life. However, the important part is that not every experience may be scarring. How you react to trauma and deal with it is linked to your emotional resilience, a concept that we will return to through the parenting guidelines in Chapter 4.

In this book, we will focus on a specific kind of trauma called Adverse Childhood Experiences, which are commonly referred to as ACEs in mental health research. As discussed in the previous section, ACEs are important not just to a child's upbringing but are also reflected in adult parenting behaviour. So, by raising awareness about ACEs, we hope to help both children and parents benefit and heal. This is also an integral part of our research and methodology for therapy with patients.

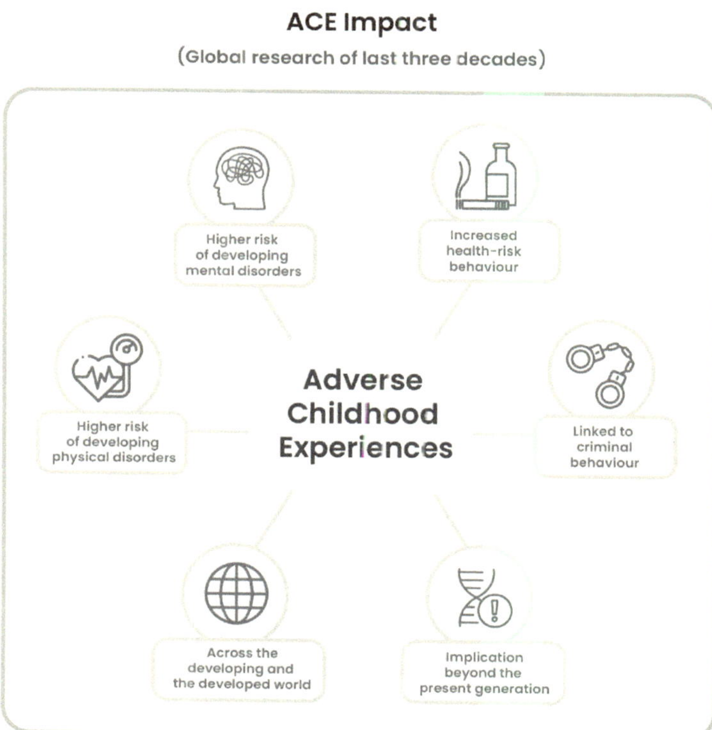

Figure 1: Impact of ACEs Based on Three Decades of Global Research

Research in the last three decades indicates that when there is any kind of trauma, especially if the trauma is severe, it may have an impact on a child's mental and physical development[1] (see Figure 1). Researchers have also been able to establish a dose–response relationship between childhood trauma and adults experiencing physical and mental health disorders. Simply put, this means that higher the degree or magnitude of the adverse experience, higher the impact on adult mental health.

Childhood trauma affects adult behaviour, including relationships and parenting. Research shows that parents who have been victims of childhood trauma or who have a high ACE score may not be able to maintain a balanced parenting approach as they tend to be affected by their own trauma responses as adults.[2] It is important to know about ACEs and understand their impact, not just for the sake of our children but also to recognize our own childhood wounds that may be affecting our behaviour, relationships and bond with our children.

In our work, we've found that there are commonly sixteen types of adverse childhood traumas, which can be divided into three distinct groups[3] (Figure 2). One group of trauma comes from household environment, another group is interpersonal trauma, which includes abuse and neglect experienced by the child, and the third is trauma in the external environment that influences the child's experiences.

Interpersonal trauma (Abuse, Neglect and Victimization) often has the most long-ranging impact on people's lives. Patients who come to us often experience physical, sexual or emotional abuse or physical and emotional neglect. Interpersonal trauma, coupled with peer isolation and bullying, has the maximum impact on adult mental and physical health because they directly harm the child's mind and body. In other forms of trauma, the child is a mute witness.

This section will explain the nature of such trauma and how it affects children. The following few pages are not easy to read, containing much information to digest, so we recommend you pause after you go through them. Some of the information might also hit very close to home and bring up pain. We want to mention details of multiple ACEs so that we can cover a broad range of people's experiences. If it resonates with you, we acknowledge your feelings. Rest assured that you are not alone, and we will try our best to help you work with these feelings as you keep reading the book.

Types of ACEs

ACEs include abuse, neglect, and household dysfunction, which often lead to behavioural and health issues in adulthood. Understanding ACEs and their effects is crucial for identifying patterns of abuse and preventing long-term harm. At the end of the book, there is a table outlining the ACEs and research-based outcomes for each ACE element for the benefit of those who are seeking validation from published research in this area. This chapter contains our qualitative insights based on personal interviews and consultations with 1000+ adults. As parents, it is important to understand the ACEs from our own childhood experiences that shape our lives and journeys. These experiences lay the foundation of our belief systems, relationships, coping structures and also automatic reactions to our children and the challenging situations in parenting.

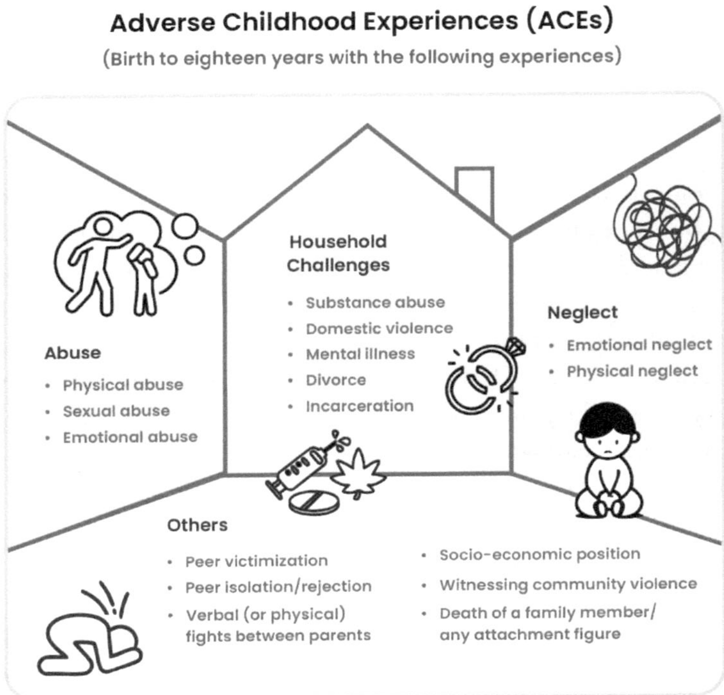

Figure 2: Types of ACEs

Beyond the Bruises: The Impact of Physical Abuse

Physical abuse includes pinching, beating, caning, pushing, slapping, spanking, hitting with objects and all forms of physically violent behaviour by parents or caretakers towards the child. Physical abuse makes the child feel unsafe from the very people who are supposed to protect and nurture the child. From an early age, the child grows up feeling unsafe and insecure and remains hypervigilant—constantly guessing when the next beating will come. Such children grow up in a state of chronic stress, which affects their hormone balance, immune system function and brain development. They also learn to normalize violent behaviour, both emotional and physical, including being violent towards themselves and others, as well as bullying and attracting violent, abusive partners. Children who grow up being physically beaten frequently can also become rebellious and show the same behaviour towards their parents, teachers or friends. They can also become completely numb or disassociated, feeling nothing.

After a point, they stop feeling any pain and fear. Then they keep doing what they want to do, knowing well that the beating will follow anyway. They don't learn any lessons from such methods but only get hardened and desensitized. This makes parents more frustrated and violent. Parents often see these children as stubborn, insensitive or rebellious. Such children may grow up finding it difficult to feel emotions of self and others. They may have difficulty in forming deep trusting relationships, especially as adults with their partner or child.

Parents who routinely abuse their children physically have usually been victims of childhood physical abuse and violent parenting themselves, or they may have PTSD (Post-Traumatic Stress Disorder) or other mental health challenges, which make them highly volatile and easily triggered or stressed. Many of them have displaced anger. Children become easy victims of the anger that parents cultivate towards their colleagues, bosses, spouses, in-laws or self, which otherwise remain unexpressed. Many parents, who have been victims of abuse at the hands of their own parents, do not wish to pass on the same violence towards their children. However, when they are triggered, or face an emotionally charged situation, they end up showing precisely the same behaviours they hated in their parents. Later on, they feel very guilty, which, sometimes, makes them give in to the child's demands.

What's worse is when parents convince the child that they deserve to be beaten and that the beating is for their benefit. 'Mummy has to beat you because you are a naughty kid' or 'you don't learn until you are not punished'. These force the child to believe that they deserve to be abused. They grow up with toxic shame and poor self-worth. When these children become adults, they continue to glorify their abusive childhoods or joke about it and sometimes even continue the same behaviour with their own children.

Beyond Violation: The Scars of Sexual Abuse

Sexual abuse involves forcing or enticing a child to take part in sexual activities, whether or not the child is aware of what is happening. The activities may involve acts like inappropriately touching the child's private parts or forcing the child to touch others' private parts, exposing private parts to the child, making a child perform sexual acts, forcing the child to masturbate or showing pornography or sexually explicit content to the child.

Sexual abuse is one of the most insidious forms of ACE because it often goes unnoticed or unaddressed. It can happen not just with strangers but also with family members, such as a parent, older cousins or relatives. Sometimes, parents never find out about it because their child is unable to communicate the experience or their pain. Moreover, in India, even when parents find out about it, sometimes they do not know how to deal with it or are unwilling to do so. They are often held back by the thought that it'll disgrace the family, or what the repercussions might be if they brought it up. Unfortunately, we've seen reluctant parents who choose to believe that it was somehow their child's fault. 'It happened because you talk so freely to boys' or 'You deserve it, the slut that you are' or 'It was a long time ago, so it doesn't matter. Forget, forgive and move on!'

Sexual abuse is also the cause of toxic shame which, in turn, is a major cause of self-harm and high-risk behaviours among teenagers and adults. It makes the person feel worthless, useless and undeserving of love or respect. This is seen especially among girls who are sexually abused. Sometimes, due to the abuse, children become sexually active at a young age and might display unsafe or irrational sexual behaviours or addictions and drug abuse. We have also seen a strong correlation between sexual abuse in childhood and compulsive behaviour in adults—especially obsessive-compulsive disorder, with prominent symptoms related to cleanliness and safety. The feeling of being violated or being dirty is so strong due to such abuse that, as adults, many of them have a compulsive tendency to wash their hands, clean the floor or bathe multiple times because they keep feeling unclean. It takes the form of a severe anxiety disorder that is associated with a constant feeling of being unsafe. So, they may check the lock multiple times or ensure they have switched off the lights or fans multiple times.

We have also that observed women, who are sexually abused as children or teens, also tend to have anger issues as adults—violent, angry outbursts or internalized anger—that they swallow and do not express. This, coupled with anger and hatred towards the parent who did not support or acknowledge them, also affects their relationships with their spouse, children or in-laws, and many have social anxiety or extreme distrust of strangers.

Research shows that sexual abuse among women is also strongly related to eating disorders and obesity in adulthood. The excess weight becomes a protective blanket against male attention that has caused trauma in the past. Work done by Dr Vincent Felliti in this area is highly relevant and gives lots of insights about how body responds to sexual trauma by overeating, binge eating or becoming morbidly obese.

In our experience, we have seen that boys who are fair, petite or cute are more vulnerable to sexual bullying, name-calling (*chakka, chikna, ladki, laado,* etc.) and abuse. Children who are sexually abused as children, by an adult male, may grow up with confusion about sexual orientation or might have homosexual or bisexual tendencies due to those experiences.

The Invisible Wounds: Emotional Abuse and Neglect

Of all the ACEs, emotional abuse and neglect are the least understood or acknowledged. Surprisingly, though, their impact may be far worse than physical and sexual abuse. Indian parents are often unaware that criticizing their children frequently, body shaming them, forcing the child to feel guilty and constantly nagging, taunting and threatening are all emotional abuse. So is isolating a child, withholding love, humiliating, comparing siblings and asking children to keep secrets or act as mediators in parental fights.

What is worse is that our culture can sometimes normalize and glorify this behaviour, considering it to be 'normal parenting'. Since emotional abuse is subjective, not all children who have been through the same experience will carry the trauma. Only those who have interpreted the emotional abuse as *I am useless, I can't do it right* or *I don't deserve any better* are the ones who grow up with the damaging effects—mostly, the highly sensitive children. Emotional abuse has the maximum effect when it is used constantly, over a long period. A one-off incident of any of these may not affect as much as repeated occurrences, over time, especially in the early years.

Most commonly used emotionally abusive words parents regularly use[4]:

1. Shaming the Child

'You should be ashamed of yourself for being so slow.'
'Because of you, every PTM, we have to listen to your teachers complain.'
'Because of you and your behaviour, our family's reputation has been washed down the drain.'
'Nobody in our family has ever failed any exam; how could you?'
'Tu hamare parivar pe kalank hai.'

2. Making the Child Feel Guilty

'Because of you, Daddy gets upset at me.'
'If only you weren't born. You have been so unlucky for us.'
'We never wanted a third child, but here you are . . .'
'We have such high expectations of you, but you never live up to those expectations.'

3. Comparison

'Look at your sister and look at you! Why can't you be a little more like her? She is so smart.'
'You are the only one who hasn't taken after your father and me. God knows from where you got that big nose/forehead/dark skin.'

'Your brother is so good at both sports and studies. You . . . I wonder. Will you ever be good at anything?'

4. Body Shaming

'You have become so fat, please stop eating so much.'
'Look at you, so fat and dark, who will marry you?'
'Tu hamesha hi moti thi aur moti hi rahegi, tujhse shaadi kaun karega?'
'Itni kaali shakal se kaun shaadi karega?'
'Itni lambi hai, ladka kaise milega?' (Riri grew up listening to this for twenty-one years!)
Calling names like *Golu, Motu, Lambu,* Bhim, little black bear, camel, etc.

5. Threats

'If you don't behave, you will be punished.'
'You will be thrown out of the house.'
'If you don't finish what is on your plate, you won't get any food tomorrow for lunch.'

6. Humiliation

In Indian families, parents also commonly humiliate their child in front of friends and relatives by taunting the child, using sarcasm to point out the child's mistakes ('Our prince here has come home with a trophy. Check it out!' *[sahebzaada exam mein kya gul khilake aaya hai, zara dekho to!]*—to point out the child's poor grades), making fun of the child's body ('doesn't she look like she has come from a prosperous family?' *[bahut khaate peete ghar ki lagti hai,' 'beta, mummy ne bahut pyar se khana khilaya lagta hai]*—to point out how fat the girl is) or behaviour, and it is routinely done without considering how the child feels. We have observed that children who are criticized in public *(tujh se kuch hoga hi nahi)* are the ones who feel traumatized more than children who are corrected in private. It is the humiliation and shame of being made fun of or corrected in front of people (classroom, family gatherings etc.) which leaves long-lasting scars of toxic shame.

7. Confiding in Children at an Inappropriate Age

It is not uncommon in India for mothers to confide in their children on matters related to their marital problems. This could include conversations about their distrust of their husbands, their infidelity and, worse still, details of their sexual problems. They forget that the partner they are discussing and bashing so brutally is the other parent of the child. Consequently, we have seen clients who hate and distrust the maligned parent. The emotional trauma runs very deep, following these children into adulthood.

8. Emotional Blackmail from Parents

Constant threats of suicide or leaving the house (abandonment), by a parent, amount to emotional abuse. The parent uses these threats to manipulate and influence the child's behaviour. These children often grow into adults who have trust issues, fear of abandonment, insecurities and fears. In our therapeutic practice, we have found that, most often, this kind of emotional abuse is perpetrated by the mother. In one extreme case, one mother actually doused herself with kerosene on numerous occasions and threatened to set herself on fire. In another case, the mother would make a noose around the ceiling fan and threaten to hang herself. One other mother would sit on the window parapet and threaten to fling herself off.

Children who have been exposed to such parental emotional blackmail—unfortunately, it happens more often than expected—grow into adults who have severe anxiety, suicidal ideation, and even attempts.

Emotional abuse makes a child feel ashamed and small. It has been linked to self-harm and suicidal behaviour among young adults. Children who have gone through these experiences often grow up to be perfectionists, high achievers and are highly critical of themselves and others, which might help them succeed at what they do academically, but it impacts their close relationships in the long run.

Emotional neglect, on the other hand, is when the parents have *not* been able to provide for the child's emotional needs—for validation and support. Most Indian adults do not understand or recognize it! It manifests as a lack of attention, responsiveness and affection from parents or caregivers. Emotional neglect, coupled with physical abuse, is linked with anxiety disorders and depression.[5] Emotionally neglected children may grow up as high-achieving adults or perfectionists or may seek solace from addictions like binge eating, pornography etc. They may also seek constant reassurance and solace from their partners. They may become very clingy and possessive in their relationships and always feel neglected and unloved throughout their adult lives in marital or romantic relationships. As adults, they may struggle with loneliness, depression and perceived lack of social support, which makes them vulnerable to self-harm and suicidal behaviour.

A comprehensive meta-analysis of 3,37,185 individuals demonstrated that physical abuse, emotional abuse and emotional neglect were significantly associated with higher suicide attempts.[6]

The Absence of Care: Physical Neglect

Damaging instances of physical neglect include not being cared for properly or not being taken to the doctor when ill. This is sometimes a result of a parent being ill, unavailable or unable to provide due to socio-economic conditions. Children who go through physical neglect feel there is nobody to care for their physical needs, such as medical treatment, clean clothes, timely food and the feeling of being safe and secure. As a result, their emotional needs—such as safety and security—are neglected. As adults, they may struggle with loneliness, depression and a perceived lack of social support, which makes them vulnerable to self-harm and suicidal behaviour. Other traits include emotional eating, and clinginess and possessiveness in relationships.

Physical neglect is usually seen among families from the lower socio-economic strata where parents struggle with financial difficulty in providing for the child's basic needs of food, clothing, medical treatment etc. It is also seen among families where fathers are alcoholic and mothers are busy earning for the family. In some families, where the mother has mental health issues or severe physical illness, the children feel physical neglect and, many times, the oldest child is forced to grow up and become a caretaker of younger siblings and the ailing parent.

The Shattered Home: Community and Domestic Violence

We worked with three siblings, all of whom had grown up seeing their violent and abusive father regularly beat up their mother. Even in their thirties, all of them had flashbacks of their mother's bruised face and hearing her screams from inside the room. All the three children, as adults, had different challenges—PTSD, autoimmune disorders, relationship issues, trust issues, severe anxiety and manipulative behaviour towards siblings. As adults, none of the three got married! People can experience trauma even if it is not inflicted on them personally.

Children who grow up witnessing one parent abuse the other one, learn to normalize such violent and abusive behaviours. As adults, they may become abusers to their parents or partners, or end up being lifelong victims of their partners' abuse. Many grow up living in fear of the abusive parent and end up with a lot of anger and resentment for that parent.

Children who grow up being rescuers or mediators in their parents' abusive relationship are prone to frequent anxiety or panic attacks coupled with physical symptoms like shivering, trembling, palpitations, fainting, having convulsions or panic attacks with high blood pressure and sweating. The anger and helplessness that they carry by seeing one parent suffer and not being able to do anything about it affects them very deeply. Some turn indifferent and others become caretakers of their younger siblings and victimized parent for life.

Instances of violence in their household have a deep impact on a child's psyche. It need not even be from their immediate family. Community violence, too, can lead children to either normalize these experiences or live in constant fear. This, in turn, leads to constant stress, hypervigilance and feeling unsafe. Children who witness their parents being regularly assaulted or see violence in their neighbourhood may report having PTSD or CPTSD (Complex PTSD), which can lead to extreme fear, panic, anxiety, personality disorders and dysfunctional relationships with themselves and others.

Priti, an IT professional in her thirties, says, '*I grew up seeing my parents constantly shouting at each other. My sister and I would curl up in the corner of our room in terror. Sometimes, it would go on until late night. I remember my mom abusing my father in the most horrible language and my father eventually losing control and hitting her. It used to be a routine in our house. Today, I cannot tolerate loud noises at all. Even in the office, if anyone speaks loudly or in an agitated voice, I freeze. I feel I need to run away from there. When my husband gets angry and raises his voice, I can't stand it, but for him, it's normal.*'

Isolated and Targeted: Bullying and Victimization

This includes bullying by classmates, cousins, neighbours or other children. The child may feel isolated and rejected because their peers gang up against them, often in schools or on playgrounds. Bullying also includes name-calling, body shaming and pranking the child. It can cause social anxiety, loneliness and self-doubt. This affects their confidence, and the fear of judgement or isolation sets in. Bullies themselves have often witnessed violence at home or in their surroundings and learnt to normalize it. Many children, who grow up as high achievers, always topping the class and being teachers' 'pets', also report facing peer isolation from classmates. As adults, they often struggle with insecurity of losing it all, extreme anxiety or depression and loneliness.

In India, girls are commonly shamed for being dark, too thin, too fat or chubby and called *'kaali, moti, lambu, chhotu.'* This is very common in conservative families where the belief is that only if a girl is fair and pretty, she will get a good groom. We have worked with so many young women—bright, educated and smart—who still carry inside them a deep-rooted inferiority complex and self-doubt due to the body shaming in their childhood and teenage years by cousins and relatives for being dark or too thin or fat or having a big nose or small eyes. It is worse when the child has a sibling who is pretty—the comparison also continues to make the child feel flawed and self-conscious. Boys are also victims of bullying, especially if they are fair, feminine or look slim/petite. They are not just verbally bullied and labelled as girl or 'chakka' but are also physically and sexually bullied.

The scars of bullying run deep. They affect the victim's sense of self, long after the child has become an adult and has become successful in life and career. The underlying feeling of toxic shame, embarrassment, feeling small and unworthy can play out in different ways. They also get easily triggered as adults, among colleagues or friends, due to the past trauma of bullying. They may also have social anxiety.

Riri grew up with a lot of inferiority complex due to her height—she was always teased and called 'lambu' or 'Amitabh Bachchan' and she used to slouch in order to look shorter. This permanently curved her upper spine and years later she had to work on it with yoga and physiotherapy! She also agreed to marry the first guy who showed interest in her at age twenty-one—she was always told she will never find a boy due to her height!

The Loss of Connection: Parental Separation or Death

The death of a parent or close family member due to accidents, natural disasters or illness can shape a child's life for decades and force them to deal with grief and hardship. While it is very different from being separated from a parent who has to take care of a severely ill sibling or family member, the traumatic impact is similar. Sometimes, parents let their child grow up with grandparents or extended family to have better access to education. On the other hand, for example, they send them to stay with an aunt because the mother is a single parent, has a transferable job or is unable to take care of the child for some other reason. In all of these situations, children may feel abandoned by their primary caregiver. They tend to approach all other relationships with this fear and are cautious about getting close to anyone else. Children with abandonment issues may become clingy and over-possessive as adults—with their spouse, child or friends.

Caught in the Crossfire: Parental Conflict

Growing up in a household where parents do not get along can affect children without them realizing it. They may adopt similar argumentative and aggressive attitudes, reflecting those of the parents towards each other. Moreover, their idea of happy relationships can be impaired because of the animosity they see between their parents. In the West, couples are likely to get divorced if they feel that the marriage is not working out. However, in India, even if couples don't get along or have an abusive marriage, they seldom separate or divorce due to societal pressure. This further makes the child's environment toxic, forcing them to be a part of parental conflict—physical, verbal and emotional.

In Indian culture, couples are forced to have children to resolve their marital issues. Families believe that once a child arrives, the couple will stay together, thereby avoiding a divorce. What they don't realize is that once there is a child, the already strained marriage generally breaks down completely due to the additional stress of raising the child and also due to the differences in parenting styles. This increases the fights among couples. The child is the one who suffers the most—not just due to the toxic family environment but also because of the guilt of being responsible for this. '*We are only together because of you*', '*If you were not here, I would have left long ago*'—this is what parents tell children who then hold themselves responsible for the situation.

It is worse when parents expect the child to be a mediator in their fights. We have seen this very commonly in families with a single child. The child ends up being a mediator or is forced to take sides and judge the parents who are fighting. We have worked with many kids and teens who suffer from severe anxiety and panic due to such situations in their home.

Medha, a twenty-year-old student, came to us with history of panic attacks. She had to be hospitalized once because of fainting in school when she was seventeen and recently she had a seizure. The root cause was her stress of always being the mediator between her parents. Her dad was controlling and violent and would abuse her mother, who would cry and turn to Medha for support. Her symptoms would flare up each time there was a fight between her parents. Even when she was hospitalized her parents kept fighting, ignoring her condition!

Her mother confided in her about her marital problems and dragged her into every fight with her father. She would threaten to leave the house and commit suicide after every fight. At a young age, Medha became her mother's rescuer and her younger sister's caretaker. She suffered from a lot of anger, helplessness, anxiety and panic attacks due to this.

Fractured Families: Divorce and Parental Separation

While these are two very different situations, children in both cases are separated from either one or both parents, which takes away their sense of stability. Not only do they face separation trauma, but they may also find it hard to deal with the attention and scrutiny they face from society, relatives and friends. In some families, after a divorce, the child is not allowed to meet the father or mother at all. This affects the child's psychological and emotional development much more than the divorce itself! Often, one parent poisons the child's mind about the other parent and keeps the child completely disconnected from him/her. This can be very damaging, and the child may grow up harbouring a lot of anger towards both parents, along with trust issues and a sense of not belonging anywhere. A complete disconnect from biological parents is not advisable, unless the parent is mentally unstable or harming the child. Even if parents do not get along with each other, the child must have rights to both parents and not take sides.

Emotional Orphans: Mental Health of Parents

When the mother or primary caregiver suffers from a mental illness or severe anxiety, children may feel the effect, too, because they have a close bond with the caregiver. In many cases, they are forced to mature early and take on the role of caregiver. Mothers, who are on prolonged psychiatric treatments or suffer extreme effects of postpartum depression, are often emotionally volatile or unavailable for their children. Sometimes, a child or older sibling is forced to become the caregiver for the family or younger siblings when the mother or father has mental health issues and is incapable of meeting the family's needs. The child may cope and become responsible and mature very early in life, but can be burdened with stress, anxiety and the constant need to take care of others. A child, who is forced to parent a parent or sibling, may become codependent and grow up with the need for validation by over-caring.

Shame, Struggle and Survival: Socio-Economic Conditions

Children may go through a combination of peer isolation, peer victimization and physical and emotional neglect due to their family's socio-economic condition. Children, growing up in families that face poverty and deprivation, feel inferior to their peers and also grow up comparing their families and parents with those of their friends or classmates, feeling unworthy and ashamed. Many times, due to caste or financial conditions, kids are isolated or bullied by teachers or classmates, further deepening the sense of isolation, loneliness and poor self-worth.

Pallabi reported that school was extremely humiliating and stressful because, every year, as she would grow taller, her mother would just add an extra patch to her uniform to make it longer, and her friends and teachers would point it out and make her feel ashamed about it. She also grew up with an alcoholic father who caused her a lot of embarrassment. In school, she was never able to attend extra activities or go out for picnics due to her financial condition. Each time the school sent a reminder for fees, there would be drama in the house, which caused her a lot of anxiety and stress. She couldn't complain as she saw her mother struggle to make ends meet, and she grew up feeling, '*Why is my family like this, and why do I have such parents?*'—comparing herself to her classmates. As an adult, she has a very unhealthy relationship with money—not being able to spend and always feeling insecure—though she and her husband are both earning very well in USA.

Beyond the Bottle: Impact of Parental Addiction

When a parent struggles with substance addiction, it invariably affects their family too. Prachi had an alcoholic father, and it had a huge impact on her entire household. In her words:

> *I have been terrified of my father all my life. He would have these cycles—he would hit my mother, then remain angry with her for many days and then show love and affection again. We would all always be anxious that the next episode was around the corner. All four of us (my mother and us three siblings) were all victims of my father's anger and substance abuse.*
>
> *I began to shut down when I was twelve. I numbed my feelings by overeating. I started putting on weight and doing badly in my studies. I felt isolated in school and college, I was called* moti *(fat) and hence, I never went out. I spent hours watching TV or on the computer. My mom would hit me for all kinds of reasons. She was disappointed that I was not studying and that I would barely express interest in anything.*

Today, Prachi has severe anxiety and compulsive behaviour. She faces depression, body image issues and insomnia. She has a dissociation issue and reports seeing herself from a distance. She speaks as if she is a distant observer of her voice and speaks about herself in the third person. Because her father's behaviour constituted a repetitive pattern, leading to severe trauma, she now needs to put in a lot more effort to overcome the issues. She could not deal with her feelings of fear and stress early on, and it now shows up in her own behaviour. Her sister, who came to us later, also has severe scores on depression, anxiety and is struggling with suicidal thoughts. Both sisters have no relationship whatsoever with their father after they became adults. As therapists, we can confidently state that the father must have also experienced some childhood trauma to have become an alcoholic and abusive.

A table at the end of the book lists the types of abuse a child may suffer, the adult behaviours that qualify as abuse and their outcomes based on three decades of global research.

When Trauma Stacks Up

Hundreds of adults who have sought help from us for mental health issues have wished that their parents were available to prevent ACEs or help them cope. Parents also need to understand that these ACEs don't happen in isolation. It is important to note that:

- Nearly eight to nine out of ten adults, who are physically abused during childhood, also feel the emotional abuse and emotional neglect. Emotionally abused or neglected children are more likely to feel lonely and perceive that they

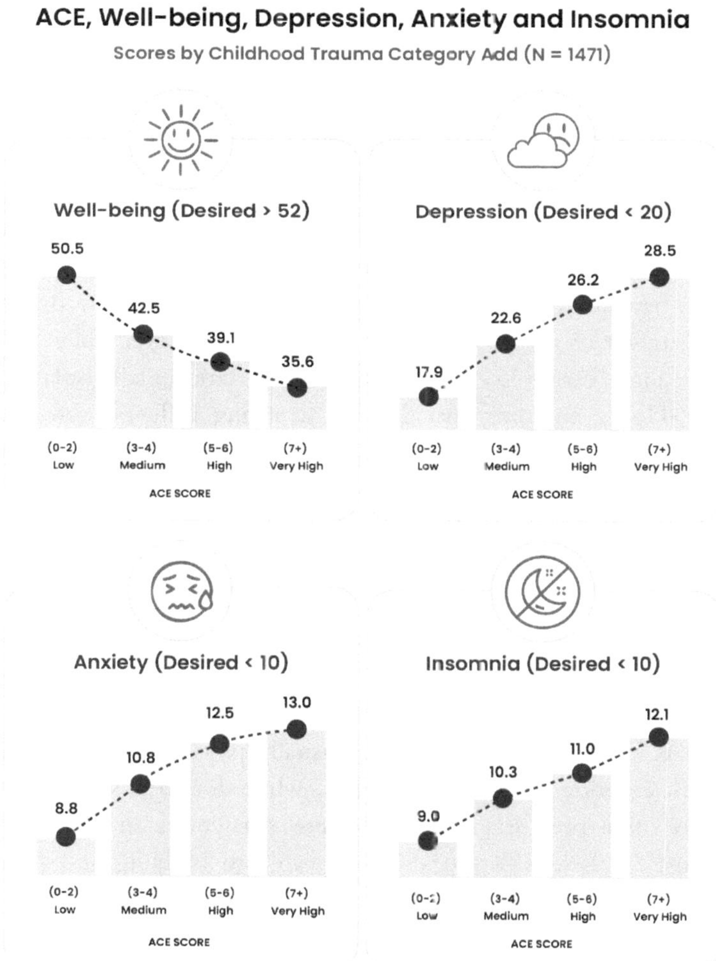

Figure 3: ACE Scores and Mental Health Outcomes (Based on Research Conducted at Wellness Space)

have no social support. Hence, parents must be careful about being available for the child and recognize that children are less likely to seek help when they experience such abuses or neglect.

- Nearly nine out of ten children, who have experienced frequent verbal fights between their parents, feel that their needs are not important, or they experience emotional neglect. These children continue feeling the emotions beyond their childhood. Even if the child is not a direct target of the parents' fight, the child and, eventually, the adult, carries low self-esteem and feels emotionally isolated.
- Home environment also has a strong influence on the child's mental health. For example, most children, who have witnessed domestic violence, have also experienced emotional abuse. The data is similar for physical abuse and domestic violence.[7]

The Compounding Effect of Multiple ACEs

Unfortunately, children may be exposed to more than one type of ACE in their household and usually physical abuse occurs with emotional abuse and neglect, while domestic violence is very often present in families where a parent is an alcoholic. Most of these kids are also vulnerable to bullying and peer isolation in school.

When a child experiences multiple ACEs, there is a high chance of developing physical health issues including autoimmune disorders, chronic health conditions, like Irritable Bowel Syndrome (IBS), heart disease and mental health issues like anxiety, depression and PTSD.[8] A high occurrence of ACEs is also linked to irrational behaviour, addictions and criminal behaviour. Research shows a dose response relationship between the number of ACEs and Mental Health outcomes. Our research at Wellness Space also matches the global research. Figure 3 shows that when ACE score goes up from low to very high, the severity of anxiety, depression and insomnia also goes up and well-being goes down significantly.

The Myth: 'Time will Heal All Wounds'

Very often, we are told, 'It will all be okay over time. Time will heal all wounds.' However, the reality is that time does not heal trauma. This is because trauma is stored in our long-term memory as explicit as well as implicit memory (more on this in the upcoming pages). The explicit part can change over time or be forgotten, but the implicit memory, which is non-verbal and somatic, does not change over time and remains in the body. This forms the base for subconscious automatic reactions and triggers. This is why, despite not wanting to act in a certain way, parents cannot control their reactions. They are triggered due to the deep-rooted automatic reactions created by their past experiences.

Sadly, due to the lack of research and awareness in India on these topics, many adults have grown up normalizing traumatic experiences or suppressing them. But the truth is, childhood trauma is not something that 'happens to other people'. It is the reality of families worldwide, across socio-economic strata, levels of education and cultures. The pattern of trauma tends to repeat across generations unless it is recognized and broken. This is why it is crucial that parents become aware of their negative behaviours.

Unfortunately, even parents, who acknowledge that they went through abuse as children, often argue that, just as they turned out fine, their children would also be okay. This is a flawed approach because not all children are equally resilient, and again, we cannot compare the previous generation and its challenges with the new generation; as the times and the environment change, the approaches to existing problems also need to change. Most children give up or give in to the abuse and become dysfunctional as adults, while others, who seem to have survived, often do so by numbing themselves. This affects their ability to develop deep connections with their family and close relationships. Many others survive trauma by resorting to addictions—becoming workaholics, alcoholics, drug or porn addicts.

Understanding ACEs is crucial to not only preventing our children from carrying forward our legacy of trauma but also to recognizing that not all children are equally affected. Many children are resilient. Despite a trauma history, they survive, succeed and thrive. This is because of a sense of support from their family or community. Many are able to channelize their anger or helplessness in other activities, such as sports or community service, which makes them functional. However, more research on emotional resilience is required to understand this further.

Self-Reflection for Parents

1. Did you have any ACEs and how frequently did they occur?
2. How did you experience those ACEs as a child, and what did that do to you as a person?
3. Did any particular ACE affect you the most?
4. Do you find yourself continuing some of the behaviour of your parents that might be contributing to your child's ACEs?
5. Has any ACE created strong beliefs (positive or negative) in you that you continue to hold on to as an adult?

2

The Neuroscience of Childhood Trauma and Parenting

'The architecture of the brain is shaped by early experience, and trauma profoundly alters that architecture.'

—Bruce D. Perry, MD, PhD
American child psychiatrist and co-author of
The Boy Who Was Raised as a Dog

Why Do We Need to Understand Stress?

As parents, we go through stress, and it affects our physiology and reactions to our children's misbehaviours. At the same time, children also go through stress, which affects their body and developing brain in many ways. As parents, it is important to understand stress not as a concept but from the physiological perspective, so that we may understand ourselves better and help our children manage stress. We have tried to explain the physiology of stress in the simplest way so you can recognize the symptoms of stress in yourself as well as in your child. It is important to note that repeated trauma can also result in chronic stress in the body and that has long-term implications on the body and health of the individual that may last a lifetime! Recognizing signs of stress in yourself and your children is important. Then you can learn techniques to reduce stress and teach them to your children as well. This is because, today, more and more young children are showing signs of chronic stress, and are prescribed medications for it from an early age.

ACEs and stress are closely linked. Understanding how stress affects our physiology is the first step to understanding the impact of chronic stress, which is the outcome of high childhood trauma. When the body perceives danger, it triggers an automatic response to fight that danger or run away from it. This is our stress response. It is known as 'fight or flight', and every species uses this response in order to survive.

How Your Body Prepares for Danger

Our Autonomic Nervous System (ANS) is responsible for biological functions, such as respiration, digestion, circulation and excretion, and for keeping us safe by protecting us against danger. It is called autonomic because we cannot voluntarily manipulate it, and it happens without us putting intentional thought and effort behind it.

This system has two modes, and it switches between them based on a given situation: the sympathetic nervous system (SNS)—we call it Fight and Flight mode—and the parasympathetic nervous system (PNS)—we call it Rest and Repair mode. (See Figure 4)

The Stress Mode (SNS): Fight or Flight State

When the body is under extreme stress due to fear, anger or a sense of danger (real or imaginary), the sympathetic nervous system (SNS) is activated (Figure 4). The body goes into the 'fight or flight' mode, preparing the body to fight or run away. All bodily functions become focused on this response. Blood flows to the extremities and away from the digestive system. The muscles in the arms and legs tighten, and glucose and stress hormones, like cortisol and adrenalin, are pumped into the blood. The pupils dilate, heart rate goes up and breathing becomes rapid. (See Figure 5)

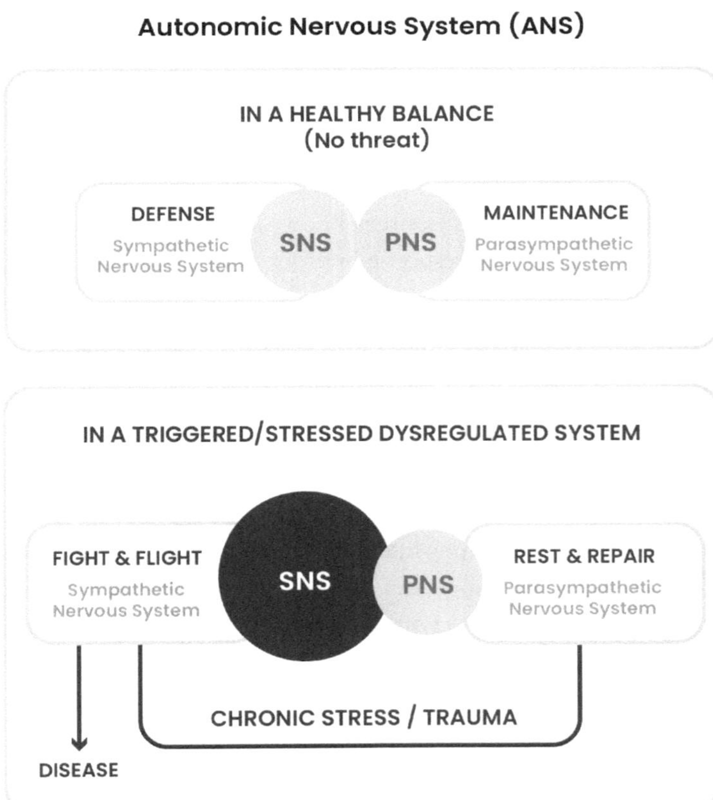

Figure 4: The Autonomic Nervous System That Is Healthy vs Triggered or Stressed

At this time, the body deprioritizes functions like digestion, reproduction, repair and sleep. The focus is only on fighting danger. In this state, there is a reduction in the flow of blood and secretion of digestive juices in the digestive tract in order to prioritize survival. In such a situation, sleep and appetite are affected. The body goes through this response during stress, fear or anxiety. Even imagined danger can trigger this response—like witnessing violence on screen.

Therefore, when the body is in the 'fight or flight' mode, the ability to think rationally, digest food or repair itself is compromised and all responses are based on surviving danger. When parents are angry or stressed, or when children are scared and throwing tantrums, they are in this mode. Hence, force-feeding a child or giving rational explanations when they are throwing tantrums, does not help. When children are in a stress mode, their ability to digest food and absorb the nutritional value of that food is significantly compromised. We'll discuss this in detail in later chapters.

What Happens When You Experience Stress?

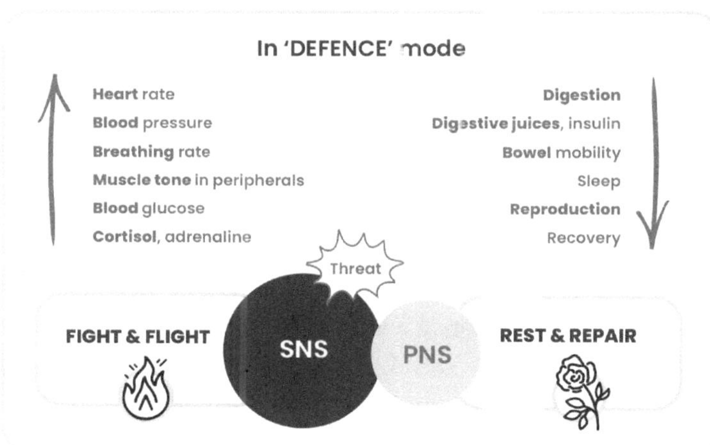

Figure 5: Nervous System During Stress

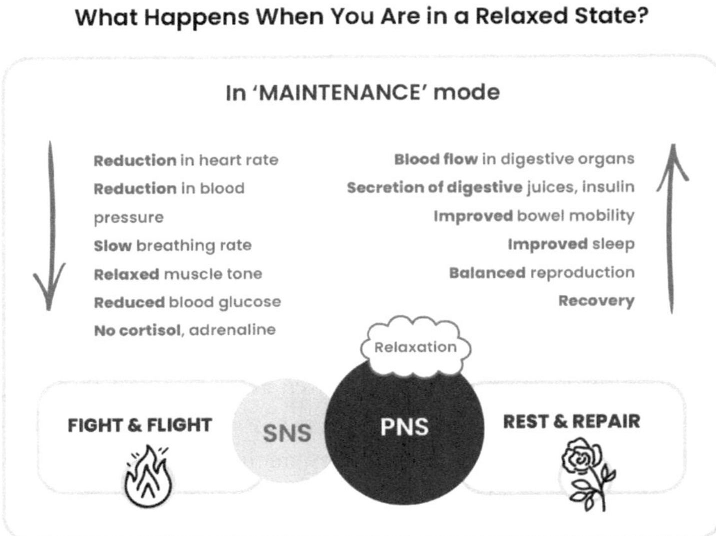

Figure 6: Nervous System During Relaxation

The Rest Mode (PNS): Rest and Repair State

Once the danger is gone or perceived to be gone, the body switches on the PNS and goes into the rest–repair mode. The system focuses on digestion, sleep, repair and relaxation. The heart rate reduces, breathing slows down, muscles relax, digestive juices are secreted and blood flow is directed towards the digestive organs. This is the state of rest and recovery, and the body goes into this state during rest, sleep or meditation.

In this state, the parent and child can be calm, think logically and rationally and be sensitive to other people's reactions and feelings. This state allows the body to stay balanced and aware and heal itself. It helps with sleep and improves appetite. (See Figure 6)

The Freeze Mode

The third extreme response to stress is freeze mode, which is the body's way of shutting down to protect itself. Heart rate goes down, the blood flow is diverted from the extremities to the essential organs for protection and the body becomes unresponsive or rigid. But the mind is hypervigilant and highly alert. While the body is rigid and unresponsive, the mind dissociates. The person may appear spaced out, frozen or unresponsive to anything being said or done. Many children develop this response due to extreme abuse and trauma and may continue to live in this state leading to chronic health imbalances. Imagine a car with accelerator and brake pressed at the same time! This causes a lot of internal stress and imbalance which leads to long term health implications.

Hence, we see that the ANS is a well-balanced system meant to keep us safe during danger. The SNS helps us fight or run away from dangerous situations, while the PNS helps the body regain normalcy and continue daily functions of eating, sleeping, rest and repair. The freeze state shuts down the system, preventing it from fighting or fleeing, and makes the mind numb to pain or discomfort. All three systems are geared to help us survive.

When a child experiences ACEs, their body goes through the SNS response. When they are beaten, threatened or made to feel fear or dread, their body goes into the fight or flight mode. Even when they are shouted at or witness violence between their parents, their system perceives danger and goes into SNS activation. This is not harmful, if it happens for a short duration and the body can go back to the PNS. However, when the body endures a prolonged activation of the SNS, all systems are affected, leading to imbalances in the hormonal, immune, digestive and cardiovascular systems.

> As a parent, think about what your stressors are. Have you noticed some of the signs you have just read about in your body when you are stressed? Have you noticed this in your child? In what situations does your child seem to be stressed?

Parents often ask: 'Should our children not go through stress at all? If everything we say or do seems to be causing some sort of stress to the child, then how should we discipline them? How will they manage when we aren't around?'

The Stress Spectrum

To readers who have the same question, we want to remind you that not all stress is harmful. (See Figure 7) Some amount of stress is helpful and is required for the child to learn new skills, build confidence, cope and become resilient. This is positive stress, which can come from learning how to eat by oneself, how to write, how to walk or how to ride a bicycle. Positive stress temporarily elevates the stress hormones in the body, but there is quick recovery.

The second kind is tolerable stress, where the stress system is activated for a prolonged period. It usually has an impact on the immune and cardiovascular systems but causes limited damage. This is because the stress eventually abates, usually due to the buffering presence of a comforting adult. They help the child with crucial warmth, comfort and recovery.

The third and worst kind of stress is chronic and toxic in nature. One sees this type of stress when the child is constantly anxious or threatened by their environment. The child cannot run away or insulate from this and there is no buffering adult to help the child cope. Chronic stress is linked to a lot of long-term health conditions like auto immune disorders, cardiovascular issues as well as depression, anxiety and addictions.

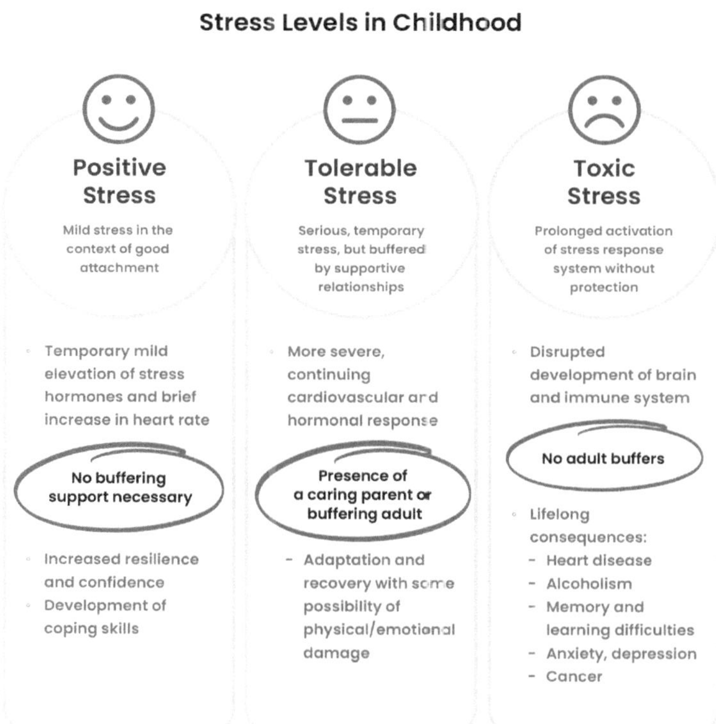

Figure 7: The Stress Spectrum and Its Impact

Cost of Toxic Stress: How Childhood Trauma Shaped Vidya's Life

Vidya, twenty-eight, grew up with an alcoholic father. Whenever he drank too much, he came home in a fit of rage and beat up the mother. The marital stress and abuse led to negligence from the parents, and they did not realize that their house help sexually molested their daughter from the age of five to fourteen. The client, as a child, did not feel safe enough to bring it up with her parents.

The mother suffered from anxiety, and she would take out all her frustration on the kids. She would criticize and shame them, especially about their studies. She would also insist that her daughter excel in her studies so she could be an independent woman and not have to suffer as she did. The mother frequently also threatened to commit suicide. She shamed them through reminders that she had to protect them from their father. Vidya said she felt like she was walking on eggshells throughout her childhood—always expecting the worst to happen any time, every time.

Vidya always topped her class from grade 1 to grade 10, and because she was the teachers' favourite, her classmates did not like her. She was bullied for her dark skin and spectacles, isolated and body shamed by her classmates. Her only respite was her studies and her grades. In order to cope with the toxic environment, she directed all her energies into her studies and always strived to be the class topper. This further added to her stress and anxiety. She started having migraines in the tenth grade, because of which she stood fifth in her class for the first time. She ended up self-harming from ages sixteen to eighteen, and by the time she was in college, she was experiencing suicidal thoughts.

She married a man who turned out to be physically abusive. Vidya came to us with extreme anxiety, severe depression and marital issues. She also beat up her children frequently, even though she knew she should not do it. She suffered sexual dysfunction, which caused further problems in her marriage. In this case, for no fault of hers, and entirely due to the family environment and other adults, the client went through chronic, toxic stress as a child, which continued to haunt her adult life and relationships too.

The Stress Trap: Impact of Multiple ACEs on Parents and Children

When children endure multiple ACEs, they experience chronic stress, which releases higher-than-normal levels of cortisol and stress hormones into the bloodstream. This can cause permanent changes to specific brain centres. It also dysregulates the hypothalamic-pituitary-adrenal (HPA) axis and leads to hormonal and immune system imbalances.[1] Moreover, it may also affect cortisol, serotonin and oxytocin secretions.

Thus, a system that is meant to go into fight–flight occasionally remains in a hypervigilant state all the time. This can be due to the child being abused, feeling unsafe in a violent family environment or even feeling fearful due to threats. All of this can keep the child in a stress mode for long periods and subsequently, affect digestion, sleep and hormonal balance. Over time, the entire system becomes dysregulated, affecting the entire body as well as emotions.

Such children frequently fall ill, have difficulty staying calm, have problems with digestion or absorption of food and sleep issues. They may have ADHD later on, be prone to impulsive or violent behaviour, be socially awkward or have learning and memory difficulties. When a child freezes, they may appear 'insensitive', 'hardened', 'zombie-like' and may not have many past memories. Such children do not learn from past mistakes and are prone to taking irrational decisions as adults.

When parents are in a state of chronic stress, they may be anxious, angry, impulsive and reactive or completely shut down. This affects their ability to parent the child positively or to be responsive to the child's emotional and physical needs. Parents, who are violent and abusive, are usually going through stress and hence, they are highly dysregulated. Work stress, marital stress or financial stress cause many parents to become either emotionally distant or violent and aggressive towards their children. Upon later reflection, they realize that it is not the child who is causing the stress. To manage stress and stay regulated as a parent is to take the first step towards positive parenting.

The last chapter covers self-regulation techniques. When the nervous system is regulated, parents are able to manage their responses better and choose their behaviour as opposed to becoming victims of their triggers and stress responses.

By speaking of these experiences in such detail, we do not mean to imply that all children, who have been exposed to ACEs, will experience trauma. Criticizing your child once or occasionally spanking them might not scar them forever. However, repeated ACEs over prolonged periods without any buffering support from an adult, does have damaging effects.

Having said this, we understand that trauma is subjective and cannot be measured. The same action by a parent can be highly traumatic for one of their children but not so much for another. A lot depends on the child's emotional and physical resilience, coping structures and other environmental factors, such as buffering adults or external support systems. Their familiarity with stress shapes their emotional and physical resilience. All children will face stressful situations in their lifetime. No parent can protect them completely, but it helps to work on building emotional resilience in the child (discussed in the parenting guidelines chapter).

The Brain Under Siege: How Trauma Rewires the Brain

Now that we know what stress is and how it impacts children and adults alike, let us also understand how chronic stress and trauma affect the developing brain of a child. We know that a child's brain grows in size and complexity in the early years of their life, changing in size, structure and neural pathways during the developing years. During this high-growth period, the child's environment and experiences have a huge impact on how the brain develops and, subsequently, how it can affect adult life, health and behaviours.

Robust studies in neuroscience suggest that prolonged or repeated exposure to stress and trauma can result in structural and functional changes in brain development, which increases the risk of psychiatric disorders such as PTSD and depression (Figure 8).[2]

Over-Activated Fear Centre

One such change occurs in the fear centre, or the amygdala, which is responsible for impulsive and reactive behaviours. It is the centre of our fight-flight response and governs the basic survival instincts and bodily functions. It is generally overdeveloped

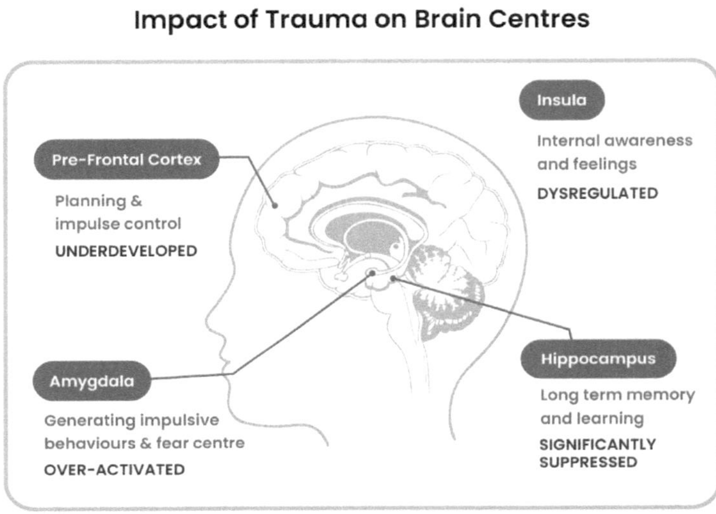

Figure 8: Brain Under Siege: Impact of Trauma and Chronic Stress on a Child's Brain

among children growing up in stressful environments. Due to this, they tend to be hypervigilant and overactive, and have difficulty resting or staying calm. They can be easily triggered and have impulsive, violent behaviour towards self and others.

Underdeveloped Planning and Thinking Centre

On the other hand, chronic stress causes the prefrontal cortex to remain underdeveloped. This part of the brain controls executive functions, such as impulse control, attention control, planning and emotional regulation as well as rational thinking. Children with an impaired prefrontal cortex tend to react with aggression or heightened emotions. They are unable to think through the long-term consequences of their actions and often take impulsive or rash decisions. They are also not able to think of the long-term consequences of their actions or decisions.

Underdeveloped Memory Centre

Similarly, stress hormones impact the hippocampus, leading to atrophy in this region (reduced size of hippocampus),[3] which can cause difficulty in learning, memory retention and learning from one's own experiences. The insula is a brain centre used to introspect and is responsible for a person's self-awareness. When it is affected, people struggle to connect with their own bodies and experiences and can either be hyper reactive in situations or freeze up. Research has also shown that, in case of PTSD or trauma, the right side of the brain is more developed and both sides of the brain are not integrated either.

Physically, these changes in the brain centres can manifest as headaches, stomach issues, chronic inflammation, fibromyalgia and even autoimmune disorders, such as lupus. In the long run, it can lead to hormonal imbalance, cardiovascular disease and compromised nervous and immune systems. Mentally, it can result in poor social skills in children, which may persist into adulthood, along with academic and professional underachievement, eating disorders, high anxiety, hypervigilance and aggression.

Many Indian parents still believe that beating, punishing and threatening children are required to make them strong and resilient enough to face life's challenges. They argue that since they went through a lot of abuse as children and turned out just fine, their children would also be all right. This approach is flawed because not all children are equally resilient, and we cannot compare the previous generation and its challenges with the current generation.

As the times and the environment change, the approaches must also change. Most children give up or give in to the abuse and become dysfunctional as adults. Those who seem to have survived often do so by numbing themselves. This affects their ability to develop deep connections with their family and peers. Many others survive trauma by resorting to addictions—work, alcohol, drugs or porn.[4]

When these children grow up and become parents, they approach parenting with a dysregulated nervous system and a

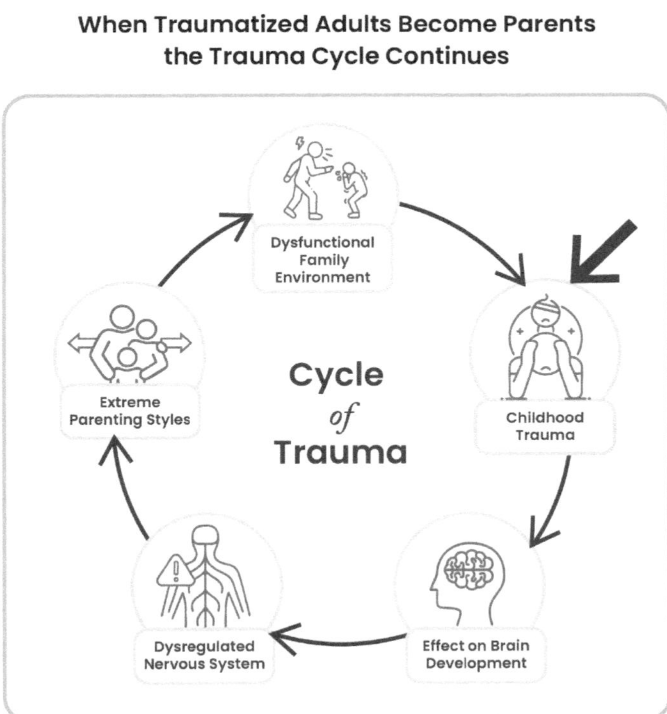

Figure 9: How the Cycle of Trauma Continues

brain that is trauma-loaded and bottom-heavy. They carry the baggage of their trauma by being highly triggered, reactive and impulsive or completely shut down and distant. Let us now understand how childhood trauma affects parenting experiences and parenting approaches. (See Figure 9)

Parenting With Past Wounds: How and Why Our Childhood Impacts Our Parenting

Trauma simply DOES NOT heal over time.
'How can something that happened to me thirty years ago be relevant to my life as a parent?'
'How is this connected to my present problem? I don't even remember things that happened twenty years ago.'
'I have a phobia of water, and so I could never swim or go on beach holidays. I don't want my child to also experience the same, and so I keep pushing him to learn swimming. But he is also scared—are phobias hereditary?'

These are the questions we hear from parents who come to Wellness Space for their mental health issues or seek counselling on their parenting journeys. Our answer is usually rooted in the idea about how we deal with memory.

Implicit and Explicit Memory

Humans tend to store long-term memories in two ways: explicit memories, which contain details about specific instances, such as where you were on a specific day, with whom and what you did, and implicit memories, which are somatic, non-verbal memories of how you felt in a situation. (See Figure 10)

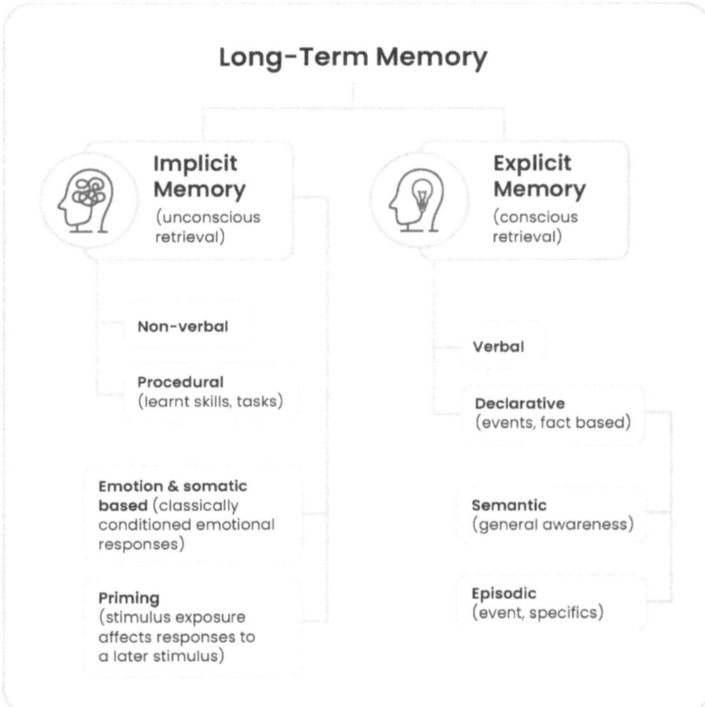

Figure 10: Implicit and Explicit Memory

Let's understand this with an example. If we ask you, 'How did you learn to drive a car?', you would describe how old you were when you learnt driving, who taught you to drive, what the colour of the car was, where you learnt to drive etc. This is conscious retrieval of the memory with details such as 'who, what, when, where, how'. This is known as explicit memory.

However, if you get into the car and start driving, you're accessing your implicit or body memory of knowing how to drive. There is no conscious retrieval or detailed explanation required.

Your body will access the long-term memory. Research shows that explicit memories may change over time. For example, the way you remember your fifth birthday party, and in how much detail, will change as you age. However, memories of trauma, which are stored as implicit memory, do not change over time, unless you consciously retrieve those experiences and deal with the associated emotions.

When Logic Fails

Vamika would drive to work every day, but one day while taking her car out of the car park she ran into two Activa riders and injured them. It's been ten years, she hasn't been able to drive a car since that incident. Each time she sits at the wheel, her hands freeze and she starts trembling. The images of the injured men float in front of her eyes each time she tries to drive.

Rishi would get depressed only between 5 and 7 p.m. It had started a few months ago at age of thirty-six. He was a successful businessman and the father of a four-year-old daughter. There was no apparent reason why he would feel depressed only in evenings. He was unable to feel happy or play with his daughter or engage in any positive way during this time. Upon probing the ACEs we found out that as a single child of working parents he would be picked up from school by his father, brought home and locked inside. His father would go back to work and Rishi would spend the evening standing at the window looking at all kids playing freely outside while he was stuck inside. At 6 p.m. his tuition teacher who had the key would come in and spend one hour teaching but—but not without threatening and hitting him almost daily. For Rishi, throughout his childhood, evenings were associated with helplessness, sadness, fear and dread. At night his parents would frequently fight with each other and also beat him up if he woke up to intervene. This is how for his body, evenings were associated with trauma. These memories were buried deep inside as implicit memories and at some point in his life evenings started triggering these memories. Logically he never connected his evening depression with these events that had happened years ago. But once we worked on those during therapy, his evening depression vanished, and he was back to being present with his child and business.

Both, Rishi and Vamika know that what happened in the past is not going to happen any more and their present reality is different, but their memories of past trauma hijacks their body response and their logic.

This is why, unless you deal with your traumas, they will have an impact on how you react in a triggering situation. Parents often feel overwhelmed when their child is not co-operating, throwing a tantrum or simply requiring some attention and care. This can bring up implicit memories and, without realizing it, they act in ways they regret, such as scolding, spanking or criticizing the child. This is the internal struggle parents refer to when they say that they didn't want to react badly, but they felt like they couldn't control their emotions.

The implicit memory loaded with an emotional trauma response often hijacks the rational, logical mind, and its ability to respond to situations that are triggering. Hence, the most logical and intelligent parents, who have read many books on parenting and know exactly what they should or should not do in difficult situations with children, end up not being able to follow that. When their trauma response is triggered, all logic and rationale fly out of the window! Soon afterwards, they are filled with guilt and remorse for the outburst and they may end up overcompensating by bribing the child or giving in to their demands!

The Trauma Triggers

Dr Shital, thirty-one, a mother of two children, narrated how the behaviour of her older child triggers her all the time. When the nine-year-old clings to her, forgets things or insists that she put her to sleep or give her a bath, she loses her cool. Though she's trying her best to not be violent or abusive when her child shows signs of being messy or less than perfect, she starts to shout and even hit her. Later, she regrets it and wonders why she doesn't do that with the younger one. She hates being such an abusive parent.

Eventually, through therapy, she realized that, as a child, she was exactly like her older daughter. She was slow, suffering from an inferiority complex, not good at studies, careless and overweight. She was bullied about her appearance. At some point, she decided to completely change and work hard to be a high-achiever, a go-getter. She hated herself in her childhood. She had rejected traits of herself that had caused her to feel ashamed. Now, her daughter reminded her of her own self, whom she had rejected and hated. Her own childhood experience was driving the reaction with her older daughter. Eventually, in her therapy sessions, she worked to acknowledge, accept and heal that inner child within her, who was feeling hurt, ashamed and rejected. Through this journey, she was able to connect with her daughter more deeply, accept her fully without being triggered, and reduce her violence towards her.

Similarly, Nitya, a successful entrepreneur and mother of two kids was unknowingly triggered by an incident with her four-year-old son due to an implicit memory. She had stopped beating her children for almost eight months after attending workshops on positive parenting and doing some self-work. However, one day, her son ran after her with a slipper. That completely unnerved her, and she reacted violently. She beat him for it, only to realize that he was only four years old. This was not something that warranted such an extreme reaction. In her therapy session, she realized that she had grown up seeing her father beat up her mother with a slipper quite frequently. The slipper triggered her childhood memories of witnessing domestic violence and feeling angry and helpless about it. That drove her reaction. Now, being aware of this trigger enables her to pause and use self-regulation techniques to calm herself down when she is faced with such situations. We have discussed self-regulation techniques in detail in the last chapter of the book.

Thus, we can see how implicit memories can become the source of many triggered responses in parents. Because these reactions, as parents, come from childhood memories and are deeply implicit, they show up at the most unexpected times and situations, making the parent feel helpless in the face of their own automatic impulsive behaviours towards their children. Recognizing these patterns and working at consolidating them have shown to reduce these behaviours in parents. Self-regulation techniques, coupled with therapy sessions, using evidence-based modalities that work on trauma memories (inner child integration therapy, Reconsolidation of Traumatic Memories (RTM)), have shown to be very effective in such cases.

Wounded Parenting

Parents who have repeatedly experienced four or more ACEs in their childhood tend to be volatile and easily triggered.

Alternatively, they can feel numb and shut down, thereby, unable to emotionally connect with the child or read the child's emotional cues. Someone who has witnessed physical and verbal abuse while growing up is prone to either be controlling and violent or extremely permissive because their trauma response takes over. For example, this is what one of our clients said about his childhood:

> *I grew up with parents who were highly controlling and very abusive. I was never allowed any freedom, and I was regularly beaten and punished—sometimes with a belt, a cane, a slipper or whatever my parents could get their hands on. Today, I have made sure my child has all the freedom he wants. We are like friends. I don't care if he doesn't study or doesn't want to do anything. I have told him he doesn't need to feel pressured by me. he can do what he wants, and I will always be his friend. He doesn't even need to work hard to make a career of his own. He can join my business and live a comfortable life.*

While the parent believes they are changing the pattern with their own child, by being too permissive, they are probably not instilling enough discipline or giving their child enough opportunities to experience good stress and develop emotional resilience.

This shows that even when parents willingly want to adopt a healthy parenting style, they are unable to do so until they deal with their own trauma. The qualitative research Riri has conducted with over 1,000 clients, as part of her PhD, has also shown that parents who often experienced ACEs may be emotionally unavailable, negligent or unable to give their child the right care because they are dealing with their own physical and mental health issues and chronic stress.

We saw this happen with another client, who told us:

> *I grew up being sexually molested by my uncle for eight years. Today, when my little girl is around any adult male, I get anxious. Even though I know, logically, that she is not in danger, my body experiences extreme anxiety, I am worried I will be passing on my fears to her unconsciously.*

The mother is unknowingly passing on her mistrust and anxiety around men to her daughter. In a lot of cases, this need not even be intentional or spoken, as children can pick up on parents' body language, mood and habits because they're so closely bound to them.

We often see clients who want to redeem and redefine their own experiences through their children. They talk about how they used to get bad grades in school, which led to low self-worth, bullying and isolation by classmates. They focus so hard on ensuring their child does not go through the same thing that they constantly nag them about everything—from homework, school grades to skin care. Of course, the intention is to protect their child from the suffering they went through as children, but, unknowingly, they end up causing the child distress and anxiety due to constant pressure.

On the other hand, there are parents who believe that spanking a child, threatening and punishing them will make them well-mannered and successful. They claim that because they were raised in this manner by their parents, it is an acceptable way of parenting. However, none of the facts about abuse and trauma that we have laid out for you corroborate this theory.

So parents may either unconsciously imitate their parents parenting styles or follow a completely opposite style!

Sometimes, parents also look to prove their self-worth through their children's achievements. This is typically seen in mothers who give up their careers to care for their child and put extreme stress on the child to be an overachiever. This can make the relationship toxic and even lead to abuse. To us, these are prime examples of when parents start out with the right intention but act disproportionate to the situation because their own fears and traumas bring up implicit memories. These memories then trigger poor, unregulated behaviour.

Mothers who have grown up with highly critical parents, emotional abuse and/or neglect tend to be emotionally neglectful towards their own children because that's how their parents treated them. They may find themselves taking care of all the physical needs of the child and pushing the child to perfection in all areas but are unable to connect with the child deeply or meet their emotional needs. Children feel distant from such parents and, as they grow older, only tend to have a relationship of respect or responsibility with the parent.

We hope these examples serve as effective reminders as to why it is so essential to parent your inner child before becoming a parent yourself. Until our traumas are healed, those implicit memories will keep hijacking our parenting responses. Before you proceed to the next chapter, we request you read the following questions and spend some time reflecting on the answers. The more honest you are with yourself, the more you will be able to gain from this book. It may also shape how you answer questions about your own parenting style.

Self-Reflection for Parents

1. What methods did your parents use to discipline you? How did you feel about those as a child?
2. Which of your parental approaches are similar to those of your parents?
3. Which of your parental approaches are the opposite to those of your parents?
4. What are your own unfulfilled needs as a child that you may be overcompensating with your child?
5. What are your own fears that you may be projecting on your child?

3

The Parenting Compass

'Fire can warm or consume,
water can quench or drown,
wind can caress or cut.

And so it is with human relationships:
we can both create and destroy,
nurture and terrorize,
traumatize and heal each other.'

—Bruce D. Perry, MD, PhD
American child psychiatrist and co-author of
The Boy Who Was Raised as a Dog

Now that you understand how past experiences can impact a person's parenting journey, it's important to apply this information to yourself. In this chapter, we will share the parenting approaches that guide parents' behaviour with their children and how they influence the child's psychology. Usually, parenting is based on the parents' own experiences—either subconsciously imitating them or rejecting them.

The Science of Parenting: Four Styles that Shape Childhood

Parenting styles are like a compass—they tell you which direction you've been going in and guide you on where to go next in your parenting journey. Psychologist Diana Baumrind, who conducted seminal research on parenting styles in the 1960s and 1970s, outlined two factors crucial to parenting—control and warmth. Control or demand encompasses the amount of authority parents choose to exercise over their child's activities and their expectation of how their child will behave. On the other hand, responsiveness or warmth indicates how well the parent can connect with the child. It gauges how well they understand the child's emotions and engage positively with them. It's easy to understand why this research is valid even today. Control and responsiveness are common to all parenting styles, but the range of both factors varies significantly. The research identifies four types of parenting styles, by plotting demand or control on one axis and warmth or responsiveness on the other. Subsequent studies in India, though very few, also validate that these parenting styles are relevant across cultures.[1]

The four parenting styles are authoritarian, permissive, uninvolved and balanced/authoritative. The graph below (Figure 11) makes it easy to understand the four styles and compare how each relates to control and responsiveness.

My Way or the Highway (Authoritarian Parenting)

As you can tell from Figure 11, an authoritarian style of parenting is high on control but low on responsiveness. Often seen in helicopter parenting, it is characterized by one-way

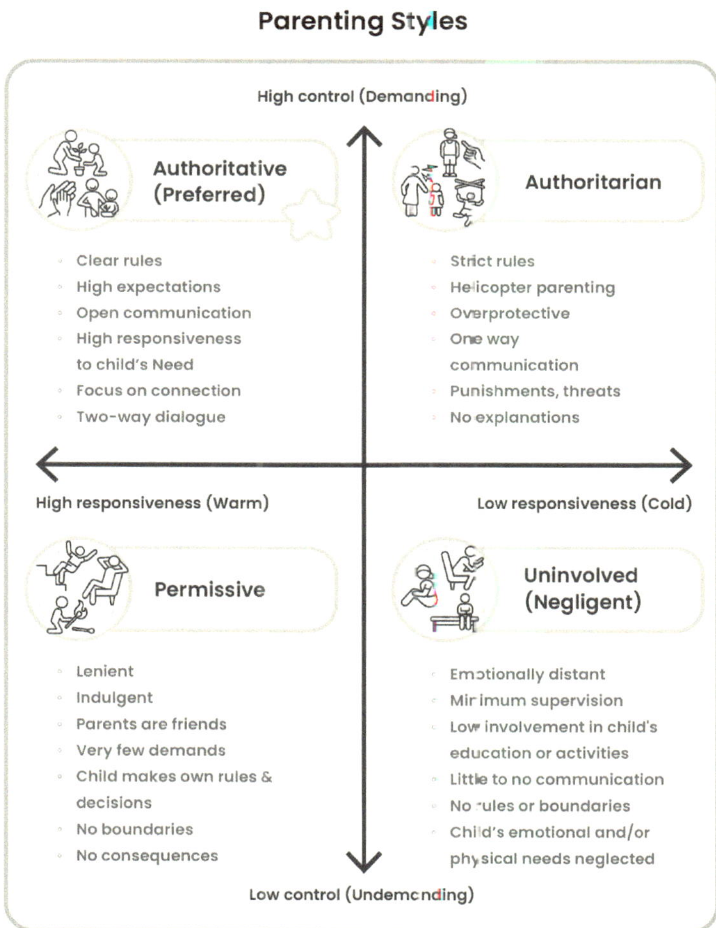

Figure 11: Four Types of Parenting Styles (Based on Published Research)

communication, with not much scope for the child to express their point of view. These parents tend to take a 'my way or the highway' approach. If their child tries to challenge their point of view, they shut down the conversation and may even threaten the child with punishment.

Authoritarian parents often keep nagging and correcting their children because they believe they are the final authority on what is good for their children. This is especially so with parents who like to be perfectionists.

Unfortunately, this can produce severe anxiety in the child or a tendency to rebel, be aggressive or bully their peers. Children exposed to this style of parenting can struggle to form their own identity and may experience depression and loneliness later in life. Research shows this parenting style is associated with eating disorders, addictions, panic disorders and social phobia.[2] Most people, who come to Wellness Space to seek help because they have self-harming or suicidal thoughts, have at least one authoritarian parent. Let's consider the example of one of our clients.

Anita grew up with very controlling and authoritative parents. She was not allowed to go out with friends or play with them after school. She had to come back home and study or help with household chores. She was not allowed to wear short skirts or sleeveless clothes. Once she was a teenager, she was not allowed to talk to boys. Her mother was always nagging and critical of her appearance and her behaviour. Anita was always told she was 'like a tomboy' and unnecessarily friendly and talkative.

Her father was physically abusive, and she was even scared to speak in his presence. Her mother forced her to attend spiritual discourses as a teenager by threatening and guilt-tripping her. She grew up in such a controlling environment that it made her extremely angry and rebellious by the time she was sixteen.

She would argue with her mother or completely disregard her comments.

She would confront her father when he raised his hands on her or her mother. She got into multiple relationships with boys older than herself, only to prove to her parents that she could do it. She also started smoking and drinking in college, knowing very well that it was something her family abhorred. As an adult, she admits that she did all that only to get back at her parents' controlling behaviour and to punish them in a way she knew best—by hurting their sentiments and challenging the values they held very deeply.

This is an example of how children react to authoritarian parenting. Those who don't rebel may grow up with irrational fears, phobias, anxiety or toxic shame. Some even continue the same behaviour with their own children even though they may not wish to.

Love without Limits: Permissive Parenting

The exact opposite of an authoritarian parent is the permissive parent. They are present for all of the child's emotional needs but do not show the kind of authority a parent must convey. They tend to give in to *all* of their child's demands and be more like a friend to them. They are high on responsiveness and warmth but low on control and demand. This means there aren't many boundaries in the relationship, and there aren't many demands on the child.

This makes the child believe that everything revolves around them, and they don't learn to take responsibility early on. They tend to become entitled, demanding and inconsiderate. In these households, children assert themselves in larger familial decisions, such as where to go on a holiday, what should be cooked for dinner, which car to buy etc. Because children with permissive parents are so used to getting their way at home, they find it hard to deal with failure when they are refused something or they have to take on responsibility.[3] Research shows such children are at high risk of developing poor mental health, linked to a lack of impulse control, high-risk behaviours, aggression, poor adjustment skills and academic entitlement.[4] They also tend to blame others for their failures and cannot handle setbacks easily.

One of our clients, Rasesh, grew up with an abusive father, terrified of the latter's anger. As an adult, he joked about how his father hit him regularly with a belt to discipline him. His friends went through the same thing at their homes and got older joking about it. Rasesh grew up watching his father's financial struggles and losses in business. He wanted to be a businessperson, but his father forced him to study engineering and take up a job, which he absolutely hated.

Eventually, he set up his own business and did very well for himself. He is now a father to an eight-year-old boy. He says, '*My son will never have the childhood I had. He is like a friend to me. I have told him he can do whatever he wants in his life. Whatever he asks for—any toy, however expensive, he gets it. He should never feel like we cannot afford something. I told him, he can study if he wants to or not study at all. My business can take care of him and his needs. If his teachers say anything about him, I scold the teachers. My son has all the freedom in the world to do whatever he wants.*'

Here, we see how parents tend to overcompensate for what they have missed in their life. What they have missed as children, they want to give it all to their child—not realizing that their child's needs may be different and it might not be beneficial to the child in the end! Such parenting approaches may not help the child develop emotional resilience or problem-solving skills.

Parents become permissive due to their own fear of not being able to see the child sad or angry and hence they tend to give in to all the demands of the child. They believe that by not letting the child experience sadness, rejection or defeat, they are helping the child. Alternatively, they may be doing it out of their own fears and insecurities. Either way, it doesn't help the child build resilience.

Rashi grew up with both parents who were working doctors. They didn't have any time for her emotional needs and were hardly around. She was highly independent as a child and did everything for herself from an early age—a quality her parents always appreciated and praised. But the deep-rooted neglect she experienced as a child was something she carried with her and when she became a parent to Kiana she became an over-involved, helicopter parent. She spent every minute with her child and got involved in every little aspect of her life way into her teens. Kiana saw her as an anxious control freak and as she became a teenager, she resented her mom's over interference. She was also very dependent on her mother for everything who planned and managed all aspects of her life including academics, friendships, hobby classes etc. The intention was of course, to not let her daughter experience the neglect that she did!

Uninvolved and Absent: Negligent Parenting

At the other end of the control spectrum is the negligent parenting style. Here, parents fail to meet their child's needs—physical (food, clothes, medical aid, safe environment, etc.), emotional (love, belonging, warmth) or otherwise (educational needs, social needs etc.). In such cases, parents are often unaware of their child's interests and schedules. The lack of interest also means they are usually unable to connect with their child emotionally. This style emerges when the parents are dealing with their own stress and trauma or if the parents have their own mental and physical health issues to grapple with which keep them preoccupied and they become unavailable for the child's daily physical and emotional needs. Parents, who are in freeze mode or are highly dissociated and numb due to their own past traumas, can also end up becoming negligent parents.

The child seems to grow up on their own, without being able to turn to their parent for guidance and affection. This can cause feelings of loneliness and depression for the child, who may become prone to eating disorders and struggle to mingle with other people. Later in life, this can show up as poor social skills, sometimes leading to social anxiety, poor academic performance, low self-esteem, suicidal thoughts and addictions. Pre-teen or teenage girls who have body image issues and grow up with negligent parents, especially negligent fathers, are more likely to struggle with eating disorders, such as anorexia and bulimia.

A client of ours, Swati, grew up outside India. Her father is a wealthy businessperson and her mother a socialite. She grew up in luxury, surrounded by nannies. She was overweight as a child and was always compared to her sisters, who were petite. Her father was mostly absent but was always highly critical and had very high expectations from her each time he interacted with her. Swati always wanted to please him and craved his love and attention. The only way she could do this was to do well in her studies and other activities. Thus, she learnt from her father that love and self-worth only came with achievements. Her mother, who had depression and anger issues, due to her own marital problems, was overly critical about her weight. She would constantly fat-shame Swati till she was sixteen years old. Her mother was always busy, with either social commitments or spiritual pursuits, resulting in Swati feeling emotionally neglected all the time.

Thus, from the time Swati turned sixteen, she started experiencing panic attacks due to the extreme stress and pressure to do well academically. She started suffering from anorexia and, by the time she was seventeen, she also had bulimia. However, the mother never noticed any of this, and the girl grew up in an environment of toxic shame, emotional abuse, neglect and great anxiety because the love of her father was associated with her achievements. Swati is a textbook case of negligent and authoritarian parenting.

Parallely, Sudhir grew up with an older brother who was the golden boy of the family. His parents never paid any attention to Sudhir but always compared him with his brother. As a child, Sudhir tried to get attention by being naughty and always getting into trouble. He was called dumb and black sheep of the family. Even when Sudhir was injured or hurt, his parents ignored him completely and never bothered to take him to a doctor. He has extremely low self-worth and always doubts his abilities. He is always looking for love and validation from his multiple romantic relationships. As an adult, he hates his older brother and has distant formal relationship with his parents.

Parents may deliberately neglect a child due to their own triggers from the child or might do so unconsciously due to their own mental health challenges, marital stress or financial constraints. Sometimes, in large joint families, the child feels neglected as parents are too caught up in the family dynamics and mothers are busy taking care of the extended family. Nobody knows how and when the child grew up!

The Power of Balance (Authoritative or Balanced Parenting)

The most desirable parenting style is balanced, or responsive, and firm (authoritative but not authoritarian). Here, the parents display control over their child's life and decisions but are also sensitive to their emotions and concerns. There is a healthy balance of control and responsiveness, of demand and warmth. They set rules and guidelines that require the child's obedience, but also allow space for the child to express their discomfort or displeasure. This can enable effective communication. It is good for children to feel that they have a sense of control over their life.

We have consistently seen that parents who have a low ACE score, have better and balanced parenting styles. Parents with high trauma scores do not usually have balanced styles. Parents who have done self-work, healed their own traumas and worked on their mental health challenges are more likely to adopt a balanced parenting style.

To achieve a balanced style of parenting, it's important to focus on connecting with the child while also teaching discipline. This ensures that the child is not always stressed in their environment but understands the importance of shouldering responsibility. It creates the right conditions for cultivating resilience and high self-esteem. Research shows that children with exposure to balanced parenting are less susceptible to addictions, are able to cultivate better self-esteem and achieve better academic success. This style is best for bringing up emotionally resilient children.

Authoritative (balanced) parenting style can be learnt by applying the guidelines stated in Chapter 4. The guidelines, coupled with age-specific solutions, will help parents learn the

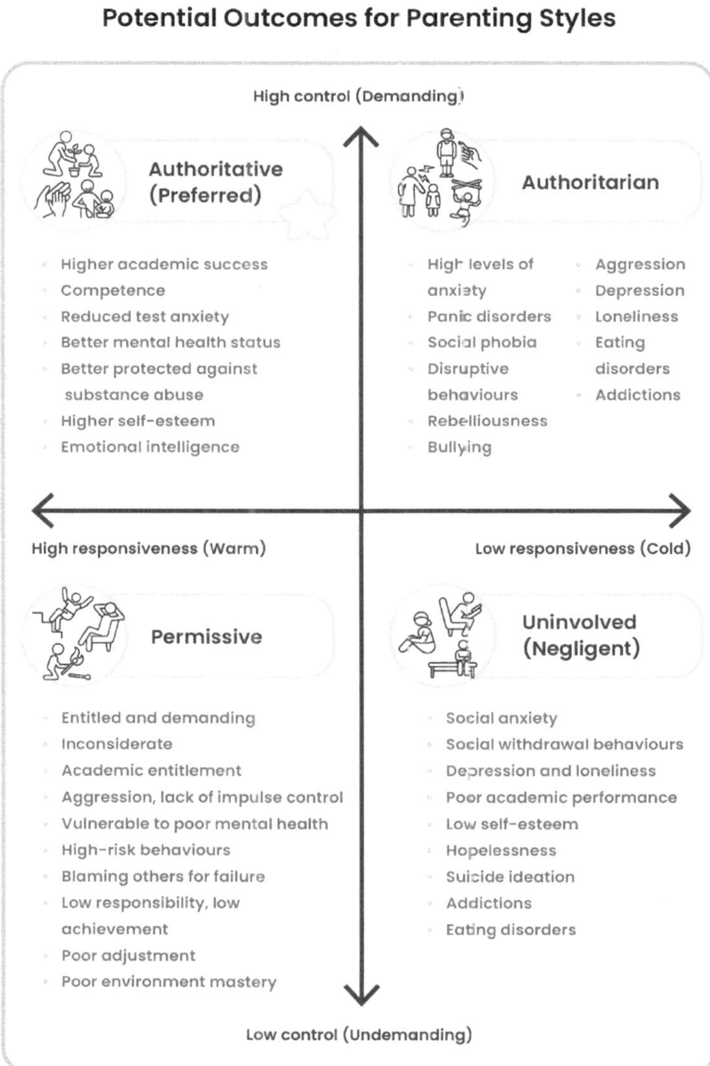

Figure 12: Potential Outcomes of Parenting Styles Based on Existing Research

most balanced approaches to handling parenting challenges at every stage of the child's growing years. They will serve as a compass to the parents in achieving a more balanced and authoritative parenting style that is proven to result in better outcomes among children. (Figure 12)

Parenting Styles Can Aso Cause Marital Conflict!

Both parents may have very different parenting styles, and children may grow up scared and disconnected from one parent, with the other becoming a buffer against the authoritarian or strict parent. This happened to our client, Rashi, who came to us for counselling, with her husband. She complained that her husband was verbally abusive towards the children. He was not close to them and thought she was too lenient towards them.

Her husband, Ayush, had grown up with physical and emotional abuse as well as neglect. He was severely bullied in school, had a high trauma score and was on anxiety medication. His father was highly authoritarian, and he grew up learning that discipline had to be implemented at any cost. Even on Sundays, Ayush would expect his young kids to wake up early and have a routine for everything. Even the time he spent bonding with the children had to be followed like clockwork—at a fixed time after dinner. This also made the kids and his wife very anxious about sticking to his 'bonding time' at any cost! Anything out of routine would upset Ayush, who would get anxious and start shouting at his children. His history of bullying made him anxious at work, as he was involved in the family business with his father and cousins. His only way to cope was to follow a strict, disciplined lifestyle. Because of all this, the kids were naturally closer to their mother.

Rashi, on the other hand, grew up in a relatively permissive household, and her trauma score was very low. She was a confident child and had learnt to speak her mind. She would always step in to rescue the children each time Ayush lost his cool. She kept correcting him in front of the kids. She had an authoritative (balanced) parenting style, while Ayush's parenting style was authoritarian.

This had also become a cause of marital conflict. Ayush felt Rashi was taking the kids away from him. Only when we addressed his own childhood traumas and recognized the patterns from his childhood was he able to find a middle path and tone down his anger and anxiety. Therapy not only helped him become a better parent but also made him more confident at work. He could speak up in front of his parents and cousins and share his point of view. Rashi was also made to understand the reason behind her husband's behaviours and coached to support him in his transformation journey. We had to ask her to allow Ayush to build his unique relationship with his children, without her interference, and to resist her constant need to correct him.

We Constantly Change and Grow as Parents!

Riri was a more permissive-negligent parent with her first child because her husband was more authoritarian in his approach. She was too caught up with her own emotional challenges during that phase. However, with their second child, Riri had undergone self-work and therapy, thus becoming a more balanced parent with a touch of permissiveness. Her husband, too, had become less authoritarian than before.

'We must remember that we, as parents, grow with our children! Hence, we will not be the same with all our children and our

parenting approaches will change with our changing life experiences. This is normal! My daughter complains that her dad is not as strict with her younger brother as he was with her. My son complains I am firmer with him than I was with my daughter. ☺'—Riri

We hope this chapter has given you a fair understanding of each style and how your own approach measures up. Very few people fall neatly into one of the four quadrants. In our workshops, we advise parents to evaluate exactly where they think they, and their partners, fall on each axis. It can be an effective way to understand how they've been interacting with their children so far and how much they need to change. Understanding the other styles also works as a compass as to which direction to avoid. Parents have to find a balance and not swing to extremes on either axis.

To go beyond self-evaluation and understand your parenting style in more detail, scan the QR code provided in Chapter 8 and fill out the questionnaire that appears on the website.

The next chapter lays down several guidelines for positive parenting to help you become a more balance and authoritative parent.

Self-Reflection for Parents

1. What is your predominant parenting style?
2. Is your parenting approach same with all of your kids or different for each child?
3. How is your spouse's parenting style the same or different? What kind of situation is that creating within your marriage and with the children?
4. What was the parenting style that you were brought up with and how has it affected you?
5. What do you need to do to become more authoritative?

4

Guiding Principles of Parenting

'Children do not need us to shape them. They need us to respond to who they are.'

—Naomi Aldort, author of *Raising Our Children, Raising Ourselves*

This chapter contains guidelines on adopting a positive parenting approach to all the situations and challenges you may face with your children, regardless of their age. We will go into such things as how to deal with them when they are angry, how to correct them gently, what kind of things to share with them and lots more.

Each section in this chapter is dedicated to one guideline, complete with examples from our own experiences. If you can adopt these behaviour patterns in your parenting style, you will naturally raise emotionally resilient children, ready to handle any situations—however stressful—they will face in their lives.

Emotionally resilient children are confident, good at problem-solving and can cope with challenges and failures. They can navigate through situations and thrive when they have age-appropriate independence and good social skills to support them. These guidelines will teach you how to ensure your children can adopt these traits.

Remember that these guidelines will help you regulate your behaviour and not your child's, but the impact will be evident for both. These are simple, fundamental principles that you must always keep in mind. For all parents, especially those dealing

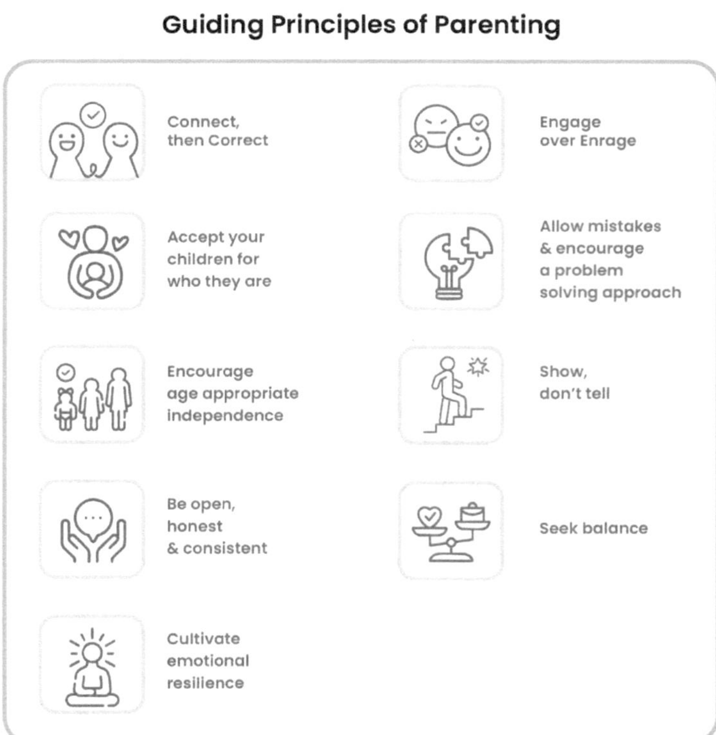

Figure 13: Guidelines for Positive Parenting

with their own trauma, it takes time to inculcate these into your day-to-day interactions with your child. As you see the results and the simple logic of these guidelines over time, you will find it easier to adopt them.

Connect, then Correct

Correcting your child is an integral part of parenting, and it comes easily to most parents. Sometimes, too easily. As adults, we are quickly able to spot where our children are making a mistake, and we instinctively tell them what to do and what not to do. The intention of correcting is good, but how you go about it is very important.

Imagine this—your child is learning a new skill. Depending on their age, it could be learning to draw, sing, play an instrument or something similar. This is their first foray into something completely new, and what they need is encouragement, not correction. If all they hear from you is how they can be better at this or that, they will start thinking that they are not good enough or that you don't accept them the way they are. When correction becomes too frequent, it can border on criticism and nagging for a child. The child stops trying out things, develops a fear of trying anything new and stops being creative at work or play. You don't want them to grow up thinking that the parents' way is the only way to do anything. We're not saying you should never correct them, but be intentional about what, how and when you correct them.

Avoid Shaming or Humiliating

Correction that is loaded with blame, or shame, and humiliation can be toxic. Make sure you completely avoid statements such as

'You never get it right', 'You are so slow', 'You are so sloppy', 'You are a bad boy.' 'You are a crybaby', 'How could you do this?' or *'I am ashamed of you'* are frequently used phrases in the correction process that make the child feel flawed. Instead of focusing on the mistake or the lesson to be learnt, the child starts feeling as if they are flawed. Correction must happen in a healthy way—where the child can be made aware of their mistakes, learn what they did wrong, and learn how to correct it. This can be done without assassinating the child's character.

Share Your Observations

Do not expect your child to feel motivated after hearing negative labels such as slow, sloppy, bad, crybaby etc. Instead, share your observations about the child's behaviour and your expectations in a non-judgemental way. '*I see that you have been doing this activity for the past thirty minutes. What is keeping you from finishing it faster? Do you need help? I am tired and I have to go to bed early today.*' If the child has spilled food on the table, instead of saying, *'You are always so sloppy',* simply say, *'Let's clean up.'* Show them how to clean up. Once the child helps, say *'Thanks for helping. This table looks so clean now.'* If the child has not developed fine motor skills to eat properly, lower your expectations. Expect some mess. Serve smaller portions in a bigger bowl or a plate with edges. Try to think of what can be done the next time to eliminate the problem in the first place, rather than blaming the child.

Ask Open-Ended Questions

Before correcting, connect with your child by acknowledging the situation and their feelings. Ask them how they feel, if they are facing any problems or if they think there is a better way of doing the task. Remember to ask open-ended questions rather than leading ones: '*What happened? What are you feeling right now? What is it you could have done instead? What do you think of this (situation/person/behaviour/reaction/idea)? Do you have any other ways of doing it? What do you think he/she (other person/friend/cousin) felt? Why do you think so? What else can you do? What else can you say?* These are all open-ended questions that will make your child think, reflect and train their brain to not impulsively react. They will engage the upper brain (more on upper brain and lower brain in the upcoming chapters).

No matter how much you may want your child's opinions and way of working to match your own or preferred style, it would be best if you let them decide for themselves. They must feel like they have the space to feel and process their emotions. Understanding their emotional landscape and motivators will help you build a deeper relationship over time and make it easier to have these conversations.

Work Together for Solutions

After you've been able to discuss the situation, come up with solutions together. At this point, some parents find it very easy to summarize the problem and quickly give their child a solution. For example, if your child stopped talking to their friend because the friend hogs all the toys during play dates, avoid telling them that not speaking to the friend will solve anything. Don't just order them to make up with the friend. First, you must understand what has happened and how your child is feeling about the situation.

So, ask questions, listen and empathize with your child's feelings. If they cannot articulate how they are feeling, ask if they could be feeling angry, sad or disappointed. Small kids may not have the right vocabulary to articulate their feelings—we can help them with it! Once the child feels understood, they will be more receptive to what you have to say. Gradually guide them to a sensible solution: you can ask if they miss their friend or if they feel comfortable gently telling the friend to share the toys. Sometimes, you may want to wait for some time before offering suggestions.

If you are prone to constantly imparting advice or giving orders using threats or punishments, your child will probably feel scared, rebellious or angry and may even freeze. Moreover, this kind of correction stops working over time. Children may eventually shut down and reject everything their parents tell them. Sometimes they might want to do exactly opposite of what the parent is expecting—just to rebel or establish their independence. Sometimes children who grow up with too much criticism and correction may grow up with lot of self-doubt and low confidence as they have not been encouraged to think independently as children.

Constantly correcting the child is also characteristic of overprotective and helicopter parenting which is not a balanced style of parenting according to research, as explained in the previous chapter.

Power of Prioritization: The 80/20 Rule in Parenting

As parents, we usually have a list of things we want our child to learn and do/not do. Daily, we keep going through that list and correcting, nagging or advising our child. After a point, nothing works. Here, it is essential to understand and apply the Pareto Principle, which says you should use eighty per cent of your energy and resources on the twenty per cent that is most critical and spend only twenty per cent on the remaining eighty per cent. This makes the use of resources most effective and applies to almost every area in life, especially relationships and while dealing with children.

Be firm about the two or three things you wish to teach your child (based on your own values, family culture and what you feel is an absolute must) and let go of the nagging and reminding for the remaining eight small things you worry about. The chances of your child following those two or three things is much higher when you are flexible eighty per cent of the time. That way, your child will take your words seriously and not become selectively deaf or rebellious. This also works very well for teens. They learn to prioritize, and you avoid toxic arguments and heated discussions in this way.

This principle also applies to the amount of time spent on correction vs connection. That means, whenever your child needs guidance, make it a point to spend only twenty per cent of the time correcting them, and eighty per cent of the time connecting with them.

If you need to correct, do it after you have connected with them, and not vice versa. If at any point, they are upset or shouting, instead of asking them what's wrong, acknowledge their feelings. Just say, 'you seem upset', with a kind and concerned tone and expression. The child will recognize that you are willing to understand how they feel and be more open to sharing what happened. On the other hand, if you ask, 'What's wrong?', they might become defensive and shut down, give one-word answers, like 'nothing', or get even more upset.

Once you become used to employing this technique, children too are better able to understand other people's emotions. This is because you make them reason out logically, understand and introspect about their actions in each situation. This is the key to helping them feel safe and trust you.

The Perfection Trap

Our advice to parents is not to rush to correct and make your child perfect. Perfection is merely a concept. Children are individuals, who need to make their own path. Spend a lot of time connecting with them when they are younger. They are less resistant at a young age, and it becomes harder to rebuild bonds later. While correction is quick, it won't serve you well later on. Children who are corrected may often grow up to be tough-to-handle teenagers, where they are fearful and suspicious of you, rebellious or angry. Connecting, rather than correcting, may seem very simple, but it will need time and patience.

Overly focused correction can either result in power struggles with the child or blind obedience on the child's part, depending on their temperament. A strong-willed child will learn to argue endlessly, become selectively deaf and ignore the parent's voice. The child will feel controlled and instead of being cooperative, they might become rebellious. This will only increase the gap and widen the gulf between the parent and the growing child, which will later become more difficult as the child becomes a teen. Overcorrection builds emotional disconnect. Some children may blindly obey their parents just to avoid conflict and may never develop the confidence to think for themselves or trust their own feelings. They might also become perfectionists who are highly critical of themselves and others. The parents' critical voice becomes their own, and this voice makes them procrastinators, indecisive or highly anxious adults.

Connection with a parent makes a child feel emotionally secure, leading to calmness and reduced anxiety. Feeling loved and understood makes a child more receptive to guidance and better choices. Encouraging safe emotional expression promotes cooperation, listening, and acceptance of parental perspectives. Being heard and respected also improves a child's communication skills with peers. Calm, effective connection builds collaboration, and when calmly encouraged to consider consequences, children are more likely to learn valuable life lessons.

Engage over Enrage

As parents, we have all been and will be in situations when our children seem hell-bent on doing something that isn't right for them. The hard but necessary task of telling them 'no' falls on us. Depending on the age of your child, the tantrum could range from not wanting to eat the nutritious lunch you painstakingly prepared for them to insisting on eating a third piece of chocolate, not wanting to go to school, repeatedly asking for a mobile phone they're not yet ready to have—the list goes on. The situation always starts calmly, but soon enough, there is crying, yelling, anger and a refusal to listen—sometimes from the child, but sometimes from the parent as well.

Most, parents who come to us, share that it is hard enough to just meet all of their child's needs. So, when they have a tantrum, it becomes too much, and they lose their temper. While they feel guilty about this, they just don't know how to break out of the pattern. This chapter will show you exactly what you can do—how and why.

It's crucial to realize that when your child is overwhelmed and having a tantrum, they are in an emotionally unregulated state. This means they aren't thinking clearly. In such a situation, when parents try to rationalize the situation, explain things logically to the child or teach them something, it doesn't work. It is necessary that you don't add more triggers. Therefore, you must avoid yelling, displaying anger, issuing threats, isolating or taunting them or using any form of coercion or physical aggression at this point.

Children's brains aren't fully developed, especially the prefrontal cortex, which continues to develop till their late twenties. It controls impulses and manages self-regulation, logic and reasoning. So, expecting them to listen, understand, rationalize or self-regulate and control themselves is unrealistic. However, when parents use their upper logical brain, stay regulated and model behaviours that are rational and regulated, their children slowly learn how to do the same thing.

These skills have to be taught through practice and correct methods. Sometimes, parents expect their small children to see and understand the situation with the logic they have developed over thirty or forty years. Thus, parents need to recognize when their lower brains have hijacked their upper brains due to the child's triggering behaviours and learn to immediately switch to more upper brain responses like asking questions, staying calm, being firm yet compassionate and trying to understand the child's perspective.

Upper Brain and Lower Brain Approach

Daniel J. Siegel and Tina Payne Bryson's groundbreaking research in *The Whole-Brain Child* tells us that when children have a tantrum, they think with the lower brain.[1] The upper brain is responsible for logical reasoning and self-regulation, while the lower brain is responsible for fight-or-flight responses. During a tantrum, the child is stressed and, in fight-or-flight mode—operating from impulsive, reactive survival-based programmes. So, if you also react by being triggered and becoming impulsive, aggressive or violent, it becomes a clash of two people only engaging their lower brains. (Figure 14) will help you visualize the parts of the brain mentioned and the functions associated with each of them.

Child's Brain Simplified

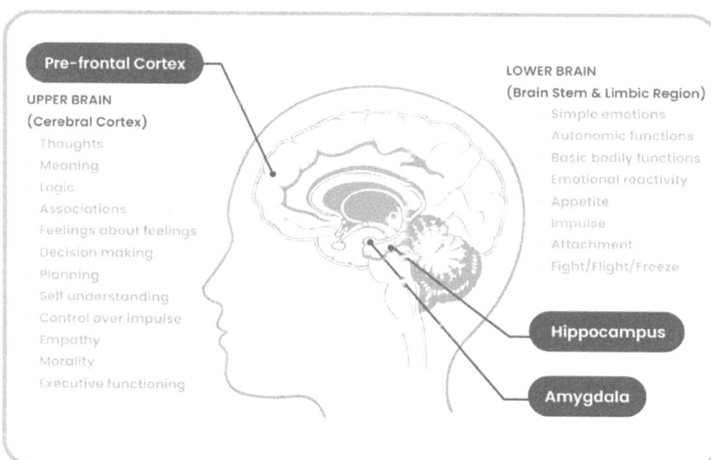

Figure 14: Upper Brain and Lower Brain Function Simplified

Instead, what you need to do is to engage the child. You need to bring a pause to the situation, help them calm down first. You can do this by acknowledging their feelings. You could say, '*I know you really want to eat more chocolate. I understand that you're angry with me for not letting you have that third piece of chocolate.*' Let them know that you are still saying no, but also opening up space for them to express themselves and reason it out logically. It would sound a little like this, *'I'm sorry, but I can't let you have more chocolate. It's almost dinner time. Do you think you'll be able to eat your dinner if you have more chocolate now?'*

This approach forces them to come back to the present and employ the upper brain to think about the situation rather than merely feeling denied. In most cases, the child will eventually calm down and move on from the situation. You will stay firm but loving and will experience relief and pride that you did not lose your cool.

Sometimes, just being there and taking deep breaths or doing coherent breathing really helps because the child picks up the calm coherent patterns in your energy and calms down. Standing in front of the child or over the child vs sitting down at the child's level or sitting beside the child and calmly breathing or talking can help the child feel supported as opposed to confrontational. This also helps with teens—instead of taking a confrontational stand against them, if the conversation is carried out by sitting or standing next to them, it can be more engaging.

Yelling, blaming or taunting the child will only make them feel threatened, fearful and rebellious. After all, when the adult is triggered and unable to self-regulate, how can we expect the child to do so? If parents, while growing up, were prone to flying into a rage, they will find it hard, in the beginning, to respond calmly. However, over time, it will get easier. It may also take a few attempts to get it right with your child, but eventually, they will learn to appreciate that you have created a safe space for them and that the right way is to calm down.

Whatever pattern you follow is what they will get used to. For example, if you begin to argue with your child, then that will become their habit and you will find yourself in an argument in every situation. Each situation will escalate into a

Step by Step Guide:

What to do when you are getting angry at a tantrum or argument with your child?

1 

Acknowledging the child's feelings: 'I see you are upset', 'I understand you are angry because I didn't let you go out to play right now', or 'I see you are sad because your friend didn't invite you to his party'.

2 

Active listening: Give 100 per cent attention to what the child is saying, feeling, and communicating through nonverbal cues.

3 

Offering choices: Allow the child to choose from various options given by you or suggested by the child. This should be done within the given boundaries. 'Would you like to go and play now for thirty mins or go later for an hour after you have completed the homework?' or 'Do you want to go and play with the other friends who are also not going to the party?'

4 

Physical touch: Young kids love a hug, or their parents holding their hand, rubbing their back, or just holding them calmly when they are distressed. Physical touch can soothe the dysregulated nervous system of the child. Along with slow calm breathing, it is all it might take for your child to feel the same energy and quickly calm down. For this, the parent needs to learn to do slow deep breathing and stay regulated and calm so they can mirror this to the child.

Figure 15: How to Handle Triggers and Tantrums

power struggle, which won't be good for either side. Enraging the child will only lead you down the path where the child is neither able to form a connection with you nor do they learn to self-regulate. They become less accustomed to turning to you in challenging situations, which is a hard habit to break.

Engaging the Upper Brain

As children are still developing, it is the parent's responsibility to engage the upper brain so that the child can learn to moderate their emotions. (See Figure 16) The benefits of engaging and not enraging are manifold. It improves compliance to agreements, the ability to solve problems and the learning

Ways to Engage the Upper Brain of Your Child

1. **Practice slow, deep breathing** so the child can unconsciously follow and imitate you.
2. **Ask the child** to name their emotions or narrate what happened.
3. **Ask open-ended questions** like "What happened?", "What are you feeling right now?", "Where are you feeling all that in your body?" or "What can I do for you to help you with this?"
4. **Offer choices** such as "Do you want to eat right now or after one round of this game?" or "Do you want to finish your homework now or after dinner?"
5. **Encourage physical activity** such as jumping, jogging, dancing or shaking the body as this can release the pent-up energy of unexpressed and unprocessed emotion.
6. **Explain** that it is **normal to have different emotions** as they are like clouds—they come and go but they do not define who they are.
7. **Normalize conversations about emotions** and talk about your own emotions and how you deal with them (but do remember to have an age-appropriate conversation).

Figure 16: Ways to Engage the Upper Brain

of new approaches to tough situations. Moreover, it helps avoid stressful situations when you feel guilty about losing your temper. Most importantly, it helps you develop a deeper connection with your children.

For more information on how to engage your child's upper brain, please see *The Whole-Brain Child* by Daniel Seigel.[2]

Remember: authoritarian parents enrage; authoritative ones engage.

Accept Your Children for Who They Are

In our experience, many Indian and Asian parents tend to have very high and often unrealistic expectations from their children. They want their child to do well at school but also excel at extracurricular activities, follow their religious and cultural practices and also be socially active. All of this while being the epitome of humility, politeness, punctuality and respect. 'Good children' are depicted in Indian epics and folk-tales—the role models parents compare their children to—as eternally obedient. Children can, of course, sometimes be all-rounders, but putting pressure on them to excel at everything is harmful and unrealistic.

It is hard for parents to accept that their child is average at some or many of the activities they try their hand at. Not everyone can be bringing up the next Gukesh or Niraj Chopra. Instead of feeling disappointed that your child is not a prodigy, it is important to make them feel confident about themselves because this is a quality that will hold them in good stead all their lives. It'll be especially hard for parents who look to fulfil their dreams through their children or rely on them to bolster their own self-worth. But remember, if the parent is full of self-doubt and unable to accept their child, how do you expect the child to accept themselves?

Most children don't know what they like or what they are good at. They need to be given the freedom to explore and discover this on their own. We observe that, sometimes, parents can be overbearing if a child expresses even a little bit of initial interest in a hobby. For example, if your child enjoyed a few tennis classes, feel free to enrol them for more, but don't rush to dream up a future for them in the sport. Don't start looking for a professional coach already, don't fill their entire schedule with tennis and don't show them only books and posters of tennis players. Give them space and see if they want to pursue the sport. It is also not compulsory to achieve mastery in a hobby. It is completely fine to keep exploring different things and learn a range of skills.

Riri's son used to love art since he was in kindergarten. Behind every school worksheet, she would find elaborate drawings of aeroplanes and submarines. When he was about ten, she decided to enrol him in art classes so he could get better at his passion. However, in just two sessions, he lost interest and refused to go any more, she accepted this and promptly cancelled the classes. However, he kept exploring art in his own way over the next few years at his own pace.

Eventually, he chose a career in design after graduating from high school. His creativity blossomed at its own pace, and Riri believes that the structure of an art class at that early age was stifling his love and curiosity for art. By listening to him and making space for him to give it up early on, his parents made sure that he did not lose interest in the long term. When he was seventeen and had to prepare for an entrance exam for a design course, he chose to enrol in a class to help him prepare. By that time, his creativity was intact, and he needed structure and the right guidance. This focus helped him clear the exam a few months later.

In the early years, when children are most creative, they do not need structure in their creative pursuits—unless, of course, they tell you that they wish to develop it into a career or use the skill competitively. Parents can introduce structure and enrol them in classes if they are still interested in that field when they grow up. If done too early, without the child's interest and agreement, more often than not, the child loses interest completely. Note that this may not apply to children who wish to become professional athletes or compete at the national level for art or other pursuits. In that case, a completely different approach is required.

Riri's daughter, on the other hand, willingly went to classes for everything she showed interest in—Kathak, sitar, Indian classical vocal music, art, Gita chanting, swimming, tennis and football. She agreed to learn everything because her parents wanted her to, and she thought she would be good at those things. She also didn't know what she really wanted to do (many children do not know what they are good at or what they like and that is perfectly fine), so she tried everything. She attended classes for all these things, ranging from a few months to years, but did not pursue anything to its highest level. It just goes to show that no two children, even within the same family, will be the same. You shouldn't expect them to be so, either! Today, she feels, due to so much over exposure, she just doesn't know what she really likes! There is never a right way to do it! (sigh)

Hobbies: Fun or Forced?

Parents need to remember that the process of their child choosing hobbies is not about them. It's about the child having fun, growing and making great memories. When parents forget this and force their child, there is a risk of them becoming extremely critical, and resorting to nagging, pushy behaviour. In some cases, it even turns into verbal abuse. One of the worst things you can do in an attempt to motivate your child is to compare them with other kids or siblings. It sends the signal that you can't accept them as they are. Do not worry if your child does not hit milestones as quickly as their peers do. All children have different growth paths. They will be better at different things. You just need to watch out for the signs. '*Your sisters are doing so much in their summer holidays, why can't you do anything?*' can actually demotivate a child to not do anything at all!

When Anagha's daughter was four years old, she enrolled her in an after-school ballet class. She thought her daughter would love wearing the tutu and enjoy the dance. Once, when Anagha went to her class to observe, she saw that, while some girls were completely engrossed in following their teacher's instructions and movements, her daughter was busy observing them rather than doing the steps herself. She could tell her heart was not in it. After the class, Anagha asked her about it, and she said she found it boring because the same tune was played repeatedly in every class. It wasn't that she didn't want to go, but she was clearly more interested in the music than ballet. The following year, the tutu found a new owner, and Anagha's daughter a new activity—piano lessons.

Trap of Overpraising

Remember not to fall into the trap of overpraising. Sometimes, children get so addicted to the praise that they keep doing an activity just to get attention and praise from their parents and not because they enjoy doing it. Instead, observe and ask your children what they like and how a hobby makes them feel. It is crucial that the child feels good about their own effort and progress. You don't want them to become people pleasers when they grow up, because this will set them up for disappointment and stop them from focusing on their own happiness.

Celebrating the Silent Child

Please don't force your children to seek the spotlight. Focus on encouraging them and making sure they enjoy themselves. Today, even kindergarten schools train all kids to go up on stage and perform. All parents want to see their child dancing, singing and speaking to an audience with confidence. Most parents cannot accept that their child is happy to be the audience, clap and listen to others. Not all children love attention and not all children are extroverted. That should not make them feel they are less or incapable. Listening is an art. Observing, reflecting and appreciating others is as important as answering and making a point. Not every child can be outgoing, extroverted and great at public speaking—skills many parents seem to insist on. Instead, notice who they are. Introverted kids may be really observant or thoughtful, creative and empathetic, and those are wonderful skills to have. You don't want your child to grow up thinking they aren't accepted or that they need to do something to be loved by you.

If your child is quiet and introverted, you can still help your child be confident and self-assured. Confidence is not about speaking on stage or being the centre of attention at a party – it can be about being sure of who we are, what we can do well and how we think. Many creative children are introverted and it's okay! Being extroverted is not required for confidence and self-worth though most people associate one with the other. In a world where extroversion is glorified, we need introverts to keep the balance!

Embrace Mistakes to Grow

If accepting your child is one side of the coin, the other side is allowing them to make mistakes. Same as accepting, it doesn't come naturally to parents, and they find it hard not to be upset when the child makes a mistake. It can even bring out their own insecurities, as they may see their own failure in a child playing a prank at school or getting a simple question wrong in class. Some parents can also become overprotective, never letting their child get close to a mistake. Many parents lay out all the possibilities to the child beforehand, preparing them so that they can avoid mistakes or failure. They think they're helping the child, but it also does not encourage the child to think on their toes.

How Do You Handle Failures?

Parents need to be prepared to see their children fail. This is inevitable. Failing at something is never the end of the world. If this is something you fear, ask yourself 'why'. Is it because you might be looking to your child's achievements to bolster your self-worth? If you feel anxious at this thought, it might have to do with your own history with failure and how you were taught to deal with it as a child. Just ask yourself, '*What is the worst that will happen if my child fails at something?*' You'll realize that ninety-nine per cent of the situations you are worrying about are reversible or can be fixed.

It is good to allow your children to make certain mistakes and encourage them to reflect upon the experience. This helps them learn from it and avoid making the same mistake again. How the parent deals with the situation determines how the child remembers the mistake. If the parent blames, shames or humiliates the child and makes the child feel he/she is flawed due to the mistake, the child may experience toxic shame (feelings such as '*I am useless*', '*I am worthless*', '*I can't do anything right*', '*I am underserving of love*' etc.). If the parent treats the mistake as a learning opportunity for the child or a chance to learn something new, and does not make the child feel fundamentally flawed due to the mistake, then the child develops healthy shame (which is required for the child to recognize that they were wrong and try to learn from it).

Healthy Shame and Toxic Shame

It is important for parents to recognize the difference between healthy shame and toxic shame. Healthy shame is a natural emotion that helps us recognize when we've made mistakes or hurt others. It is a valuable tool for personal growth and development. By fostering healthy shame, parents can help their children develop a strong sense of self-worth and empathy. Toxic shame is a deep-seated feeling of inadequacy or worthlessness that can have a significantly negative impact on a child's self-esteem and development. It often stems from hurtful or judgemental comments made by parents.

Children usually feel toxic shame when the parent blames or shames them for the mistakes. It may be accompanied by statements such as '*You are always sloppy*', '*You are so stupid*', '*See, you did it again, why can't you ever get it right?*', '*You always embarrass me in front of people because of the way you talk*' (*Tumne humari naak katva di, apna muh bandh kyu nahi rakh sakti?*) or

'Why can't you be like your sister?' etc. Parents who taunt the child in front of others, or use sarcasm, or poke fun at the child in front of friends or relatives also cause damage to the child's self-respect and worth. When the child feels humiliated, ashamed and embarrassed, they begin to feel worthless and undeserving of love. The child learns to accept that he/she is flawed. *'I am dumb', 'I am slow', 'I can't learn as well as my sister'* become their reality. Some children end up becoming apathetic and stop caring or bothering to change this image, while others foster a lot of anger and resentment towards adults and their own selves.

Children who experience toxic shame often suffer from low self-confidence and are afraid to try out new things, which hampers their creativity. They may suffer from self-doubt and self-loathing, and become highly self-critical. Such children may also grow up with the fear of judgement, fear of failure, procrastination and a constant need for perfection.

Children who are prone to feelings of toxic shame in childhood are more likely to put themselves in risky situations when they grow up. This could be due to shame-prone children having less developed interpersonal problem-solving skills. The painful feeling of shame can lead to withdrawal and depression, but it can also provoke defensive externalization and irrational anger. Shame-prone children are more likely to have unprotected sex and use illegal drugs in young adulthood.

The next time your child makes a mistake, make an effort to acknowledge the issue calmly. For example: *'I see that the milk has spilt again. Let's clean it up first and then figure out what we can do so it doesn't happen again.' 'That was not appropriate for you to say in front of people, but let's talk about how we can express that next time in a better way.' 'Everyone makes mistakes, let's see what we can learn from it.' 'I'm disappointed you didn't clean your room, but I know you can do it now.' 'It's not okay to lie, honesty is important.'*

Turning Blame to Bridges

Adopting a problem-solving approach can work very well with young kids. Instead of blaming your child, such as *'You always watch so much TV'* or *'This is why you aren't doing well at school'*, try to make your child also realize that there is an issue that both of you can work together to fix. *'I see that you are watching a lot of TV, and I feel it is affecting your studies. What do you think?'* If the child agrees with you, then you can find a way to solve it. You can try asking, *'What can we do so that you can reduce your TV usage?'* or *'What can we do to make sure you study better?'* Once you change your language and present it as a problem to work on together, you engage the child, build trust and avoid blaming, shaming and criticizing. The problem-solving approach enables you to make them feel that you are there to help and support them in the problem. If there has already been a history of abusive or violent parenting, this approach might not work immediately, and it will take time for your child to work with the new approach. Try it out and see if this reduces the toxicity and abuse in your relationship.

During Riri's son's school years, she faced a rather serious situation, which she confronted by using a unique problem-solving approach. In Riri's words:

> *When my son was in grade nine, I got a call from school asking us to come immediately—my son had been caught cheating! Apparently, he had had scored one out of twenty on a class test for which he had not studied. Scared to show us his results, he*

changed the one to eleven by overwriting it in his mark sheet. His teacher caught him, and the principal called us to school. We had always taught our children to be truthful, and we prided ourselves on being very honest and upright as far as values were concerned. So, the idea of my child having done something like this was very shocking and hurtful. Internally, I was also angry and very upset, but I kept my cool. We never punished him for scoring low marks, so the question kept coming to my mind: 'Why did he have to do this?' Once we got to school, the principal obviously scolded him soundly while we listened.

On the way home, I was quiet at first. He was probably petrified of the drive and how we would react once we were alone with him. I knew that my reaction would affect how he remembered this experience. Rather than expressing the irritation, shame and anger I was feeling, I asked him how he felt about all this. He sobbed silently and looked upset—he told me that he was ashamed of himself and should have never done it. This was all that I wanted to hear. I also asked why he had to do it when we never punished or scolded him for scoring low marks. He had no answer to that, but I suspect he also wanted to see if something like what he did would actually work! Since he had already realized his mistake and felt ashamed about it, saying anything more or humiliating him would have made him feel toxic shame, and that feeling would hijack any self-reflection or learning that he was capable of.

Looking back, I think I realized that this situation was about him and not me—it was about what he had to learn and reflect upon. In such situations, parents often make it all about themselves 'How could YOU do this? How could MY son ever cheat? I am so ashamed of you!' would have been the most common reaction, but I was mindful, and it helped! My son also learnt that he could be honest with his parents about his mistakes.

Together, we learnt to embrace difficult situations and confront each other with respect. Today, we laugh about it because we both know he was going through a phase of trying everything that was not allowed!

No Two Children Will Be the Same!

Interestingly, Riri and her husband were never summoned to the school for their daughter, except when she won a prize or came first. She was outgoing, had leadership qualities and usually topped the merit list. She was known to all teachers and was the 'ideal student'. However, for her son, they had to keep going to school frequently, as he would keep doing creative things that put him in a spot with the teachers throughout his high school years. He was caught stealing lemons from the school tree and taking a camera to class (which was confiscated, and he had to do without it for the rest of the year). Unlike his sister, he was introverted and rarely participated in any school events. But Riri ensured that she shared her pain with him, heard his side of the story, taught him to reflect on his behaviour and let him face the consequences of his actions, but never disrespected, humiliated or shamed him for it. Today, they share a very close bond because of how they handled his behaviour during those years. It should be noted that while Riri's son was an average student in school, when he found his passion—design—he got into a top design school with a 50 per cent scholarship. He continues to maintain those grades and the scholarship. Once he found his passion and calling, there was no looking back! Once he found his space he also got elected to the students council, much to the surprise of Riri and her husband!

Don't be quick to jump to conclusions and label your children based on their childhood experiences. They change at every stage. Every child comes of age and matures at different times in their life. Do not assume that the challenges will also remain the same.

Similarly, Riri was always the favourite student of her teachers, getting good scores and being the 'good girl' throughout her school and college years. Her younger sister was completely opposite—she would fail in a few subjects every year and was sadly always compared to Riri. She was always made to feel dumb and slow by everyone to the point where she also started believing she could never do anything! But today she has done her Post Doctoral research and is a professor in a college, while Riri is still struggling with her PhD!

Celebrating Differences

This brings us to the next point: avoid comparing your children—it does not motivate them!

No two children will be same, and many parents unconsciously compare one child to the other, either for studies or behaviour or a hobby. One child may be very obedient and follow all rules, being a diligent student and ideal child, and make the parenting journey a cakewalk, while the other one may be completely different, rebelling or triggering you or simply remaining average in studies. Not all kids are talented, and not all kids have hobbies. Not all kids can be class toppers. Most importantly, respect what they wish to do and who they wish to become in life. What is most important is that the child needs to feel confident and happy with who he/she is and feel reasonably motivated to do their best. Comparison not only kills the child's sense of self-worth but also builds animosity among siblings that can last a lifetime!

Overprotected and Underprepared

A child who has never failed at something may have been protected from that pain and embarrassment. However, crucially, they also haven't developed the skills to overcome that failure. We have noticed that children who are not allowed to fail have less emotional resilience as adults. For example, if your child is being stubborn about not doing their homework, don't let it escalate into an argument, where both of you emerge upset. Don't force them to finish the homework. Even worse would be finishing it for them. Let them face the consequences at school. One missed submission will not ruin their life, but facing the teacher's questions the next day will teach them some responsibility. Children who haven't made mistakes can grow up with fear and anxiety, be risk-averse and struggle with problem-solving. Or they may overcorrect as adults and make reckless decisions.

This happens when parents instil the fear of failure in the child from a young age: *'if you run so fast, you will fall down and hurt yourself' 'you can't do it, don't even try' 'it's not worth trying, it's too complicated'* or micromanage all their decisions with undertones of fear and descriptions of worst-case scenarios, telling them exactly what will happen at each step. As a result, they don't have very good judgement of their own and act rashly. Or they will keep turning to their parent for guidance and support in small things, long after they have become adults!

They aren't wired to think through decisions because they grow up following only their parents' guidelines. So, when they get some freedom, such as going to college, away from home, they want to try things that may not be safe or may get into trouble more frequently, due to lack of judgement. Helicopter parenting will also result in the child not being able to take responsibility and blaming others or circumstances when things go wrong. This trait should definitely not be encouraged. Learning from failure builds resilience and makes the child confident as an adult—they can take big decisions or handle risks knowing very well that they have the ability to bounce back from failures.

So, when your child makes a mistake the next time, don't nag them, shame them or say, '*I told you so*'. Remember that they're most likely feeling embarrassed, hurt and possibly even angry. Challenge the problem that caused the failure. Encourage them to engage the upper brain and come up with a solution. They will be more likely to follow an idea that is theirs rather than one forced upon them by you. Close on a positive note, and appreciate the effort they put in. Most importantly, for yourself, learn to move on.

Foster Age-Appropriate Independence

To be a parent is to take many decisions for your child daily—what to feed them, what clothes to pick out for them, what activities to schedule—the list goes on. Parents get so used to making these decisions that when their child is older and wants to have a say in these choices, it doesn't come naturally to the parents to give up control. They assume that their child will not be able to choose wisely about what to eat, what to wear and when to play, and almost become scared of giving their children independence and autonomy. In India, this pattern of being unable to relinquish control generally continues well into teenage years and sometimes even beyond, which is a lot longer than in other cultures.

Parents don't realize that what they fear is actually the loss of control over their child's life rather than them making a bad decision. As parents, we've been there too, but we've learnt through personal experience and helping our clients that giving your child agency does not mean they will forget about you. They will still come back to you for advice, for help and of course, hugs, at the end of the day. They will still need your guidance to learn or your advice when they are confused and scared while making decisions. Because children look to their parents for their cues on how to handle something, your relationship with failure will shape how they handle it too. You don't want your impatience or fear of failure to hold your child back.

Let's consider something as basic as using cutlery. Little children don't have the fine motor skills of adults, and it takes time for them to learn how to eat off a plate, not to spill and how to use cutlery. So, when they eat by themselves, they are bound to make a mess, smearing food, mixing it and being untidy. However, all this is extremely natural. It is a crucial part of the child learning about texture and taste, and how to use a spoon. But some parents struggle to accept this messy way of eating and, instead, prefer to feed the child themselves.

Spoon Fed to Self-sufficient

It is common to find parents and nannies chasing even five-year-olds with a plate at every meal. This is more common among Indian parents than those in the West, where children are encouraged to feed themselves, even at school. It is so much better for your child if you put a plate down in front of them, encourage them to pick up their own food and gently guide them on how to use cutlery. It builds their confidence and makes them more independent. They also pay more attention to what they're eating.

Right from when we're born, our brain gives us signals of when to eat and how much to eat. Little children are much attuned to this instinct. Parents who like to implement a strict schedule and are particular about how much their child eats every day will often force-feed the child even when they keep rejecting the food. Alternatively, they turn to distracting their child with videos on the TV or phone. We have seen many parents using threats and fear-inducing statements to ensure that the child eats at mealtimes. *'If you don't eat, the ghost will come and eat you.' 'The policeman will take you away.'* They talk about punishments like *'If you don't finish what is on your plate, I will lock you up in a dark room.'* These threats make your child eat their meal out of fear and not willingness.

When using this method becomes a pattern, the child develops an unhealthy association with food, which may later contribute to eating disorders. The child also grows up to associate food or mealtimes with fear or stress, which is not healthy. Moreover, some children, not all, end up with a lifelong fear of ghosts, darkness, police officers etc., due to such childhood experiences.

When a child is stressed, they may be in a state of fight or flight. The body automatically deprioritizes digestion and inhibits the secretion of digestive juices because it focuses on the secretion of adrenalin, cortisol and other stress hormones. So, force-feeding a child when they are afraid, stressed or crying is not a good idea at all because the body will not be in the right state to absorb nutrition. Instead, even if the child eats less, but in a relaxed or happy state, the digestion and absorption will be much better.

Here are some tested approaches you can use to make mealtimes calm:

- Do not let your child get used to eating snacks throughout the day, especially just before mealtime.
- Let the child eat food of different textures and colours. Make the food more attractive and let it be a creative activity rather than a task. You could teach them different colours and make different sounds to help them identify textures. This way, they are engaged while eating and not distracted by toys or gadgets.
- Involve the child in making the meals, giving them small tasks appropriate to their age. It could be washing, cleaning, peeling or organizing. This helps build an association with the food, and they will be more interested in eating what they have helped to make.
- Do not insist that the child eat everything that is served at all mealtimes. Let the child eat one or two things that they can eat properly. It is completely fine if they eat only 2–3 healthy options you put on their plate. This way, the child feels they have a choice and feel happy about what they are eating.
- Have relaxed and positive conversations during mealtimes. Make sure the tone of your voice does not convey irritation, anger or too much excitement.

- Let children eat the food in their own way. Initially, they will find it tough to eat Indian food by themselves. Give them easier dishes like dal and rice initially, which they can eat with a spoon. Teach them to eat chapatti with sabzi and dal when their motor skills have developed further.
- Do not use phones or TV to engage the child's attention while feeding. Many busy parents do this to make mealtimes easier. Unfortunately, it can soon become a habit and, as they grow older, they are unable to eat without looking at a screen. The body's ability to modulate hunger and satiation gets impaired when the child's attention is on the phone or TV. As adults, they will not know when to stop and how much to eat. Most adults, with binge-eating issues, mention that their mealtimes are stressful or that they regularly watch TV while eating.
- Physical activity helps the child develop a healthy metabolism. You can encourage your child to play or be active before a meal where you are going to introduce something new. There is a higher chance of new food being accepted when the child is hungry.
- Do not bribe the child to eat by promising them sweets, extra TV time or gifts in return. They get used to it and mostly focus on the reward at the end.
- A child's food choices and palate change every few years. Do not stress if your child is suddenly not eating a particular type of food (eggs, fruits, yoghurt, milk, pulses, rice etc.) at a particular age. As they grow up, visit their friends' homes, go to school and try other kids' lunchboxes, their palette and taste change. The reluctance to eat a particular food will not last for a lifetime, and they are unlikely to develop deficiencies if their diet is balanced.

Very few kids, who have health issues or extreme stress at birth, may have issues eating regularly on their own. Only if their health is affected should you resort to being more forceful at mealtimes. It should be the last option, not the first one.

Parents will see positive changes if they adopt this attitude for other parts of their children's life as well. There are many small lessons and skills to be picked up from everyday tasks, such as putting away toys, helping in the kitchen and learning to get dressed independently. So, start introducing them to these slowly. Gradually, you will have to modify your approach of automatically doing everything for them. First, let them help with certain steps. As they gain in confidence, you can give them more control and freedom.

The Messy Path to Mastery

At first, it will feel daunting to give children responsibility. It will also be a little tough to stop yourself from reaching out and taking over. However, remember that you are doing it for their benefit. Being afraid to let your child create a mess, deviate from their schedule or try their hand at new tasks can stop them from gaining confidence and crucial skills by the time they are ready to go to school. They will be able to adjust far more easily to classes and a school schedule if they gain confidence with tasks such as packing their bag, doing their homework, eating on their own and putting away their toys. This is a precursor to the responsibilities they will take on as adults.

If your child is reluctant or upset about learning, the onus is on you to guide them slowly and gently. Forcing a child is never the right way to get them to do something. Instead, if you connect with them and understand their fear or displeasure, you will have far more insight into how you can help them. If you need some help on where to begin, here are Montessori-inspired tips on teaching self-care and other household activities to your children:

- Follow your child's interest when they want to help.
- Take time to teach. Be patient.
- Show how to do the activity with slow deliberate movements and minimal words.
- Break down a bigger task into smaller ones.
- Build on skills already learnt.
- Be specific. Your child's understanding of a 'clean room' and your expectation may be very different. It would help to show them photos of a clean room/tidy desk/tidy shelf/made bed.
- Make tidying up easy by using colour-coded baskets/bins. Give specific and clear instructions. For example:
    i. Blocks in the red basket/bin, other toys in the blue basket/bin
    ii. Dirty clothes in the hamper/bucket
    iii. Books stacked on the shelf
- Foster independence by making things easily accessible to small children. Keep things they need on lower shelves. Get a step stool so that they can use the kitchen sink easily.
    i. Don't expect perfection. Compliment the effort.
    ii. Give the child opportunities to practice.

Homes with a House Help

It is common in Indian households to have help around the house, who usually do household chores, especially when both parents are working. They also usually insist on doing everything for the child in order to be in the family's good books. However, it is important to communicate to your help that they should let the child do the allotted chores (such as cleaning the table or putting back their toys), as you are trying to teach them. The same applies to grandparents who are staying with the children. They also usually end up doing many things for the child as a way of showing their love. Please make them aware how such small things will help the child when they grow up.

Do It to Make Them Do It!

It is common that when parents themselves do not do any work around the house, the children do not either. They learn from what they observe. Occasionally, we need to do the things that we want our children to learn as adults so they can be independent in life. Cooking, cleaning, making their own bed and managing to wash and iron their own clothes are basic life skills that all children should know, irrespective of their gender and economic status. It helps them stay confident when they have to move out of home for further studies – whether in another city or country.

Here is a table of appropriate tasks that you can give your child. Start out small and build up to the next level when you think your child is ready.

Independence Chart

Age group: 1-2 years

Care of self	Contributing to the family
• Attempt to brush teeth • Wash hands with water and soap • Feed themselves using a spoon • Drink from a cup • Fetch diapers/wipes • Take off socks • Brush hair • Get dressed with assistance • Fetch shoes	• Put a few toys away in a box

Age group: 2-3 years:

Care of self	Contributing to the family
• Attempt to brush teeth • Wash hands with water and soap • Feed themselves using a spoon • Drink from a cup • Fetch diapers/wipes • Take off socks • Brush hair • Get dressed with assistance • Fetch shoes	• Put toys away • Put clothes in a laundry hamper

Age group: 3-6 years

Care of self	Contributing to the family
• Get dressed without assistance (4+) • Undress themselves (with some help) • Wear socks and shoes • Brush teeth with supervision • Brush hair without help (5+ years– depends on type/length of hair) • Wash body and hair (independently 6+) • Use toilet independently (3–4+) • Flush toilet • Polish shoes (4+) **School related:** • Fill water bottle • Carry water bottle and school bag • Pack school bag with assistance (3+) • Polish shoes (4+)	• Fold hand towels (3+) • Fold clothes (4+) • Match socks (3+) • Help mop spills • Dust with feather duster • Sweep with small broom/ dustpan • Help shop for groceries • Help put away groceries **Food preparation/Dining:** • Wash and peel vegetables • Help knead dough • Crack eggs into a bowl • Chop vegetables/fruit with supervision (4+) • Prepare simple snacks (6+) • Measure and mix ingredients for cooking • Rinse plate/cutlery

Age group: 7-11 years

<table>
<tr><th>Care of self</th><th>Contributing to the family</th></tr>
<tr><td>

- Brush teeth
- Iron clothes (8+)
- Cut nails (9+)
- Wipe dining table (10+)
- Wipe kitchen counter (10+)
- Sweep/mop kitchen floor (10+)
- Make bed

School-related:

- Pack a bag for school without assistance (HW/books/notebooks/sports/musical instruments etc.) as per timetable (7+)
- Iron uniform (8+)

</td><td>

- Use washing machine
- Hang clothes for drying/use dryer
- Fold clothes
- Mop floors
- Clean bathroom sink
- Clean toilets

Food preparation/Dining:

- Prepare simple meals (9+)
- Help make meal plan
- Buy some items from a neighbourhood shop/pharmacy

</td></tr>
</table>

Age group:12+

<table>
<tr><th>Care of self</th><th>Contributing to the family</th></tr>
<tr><td>

- Clean screens: phone/tablet/PC
- Travel using public transport (where it is safe)
- Manage their own schoolwork and homework entirely on their own
- Complete school projects
- Vacuum the house
- Do complete laundry
- Clean dishes and organize kitchen
- Pack their own snack or lunch box

</td><td>

- Supervise younger children
- Help younger siblings with homework
- Run errands for grandparents/elderly neighbours
- Teach grandparents how to use a mobile phone/computer
- Help plan holidays
- Buy groceries/medicines
- Deposit cheques
- Pay bills online
- Help fix things around the house (change lightbulb etc.)

</td></tr>
</table>

We, too, have learnt how to give our children more independence as they have grown up. It was only through specific instances that we gained confidence and learnt to pass that on to our children as well.

Riri used to live in Japan with her family when her children were very young. When her daughter turned five years old, she asked her parents if she could go to school by herself on her cycle. In Japan, this was common as the roads were very safe and parents did not always have flexibility in their work schedules to be able to drop kids off to school. At first, Riri and her husband were a bit sceptical as none of her daughter's friends were going to school by themselves. They were scared, thinking of all the things that could go wrong. Then they decided to trust her and give her a chance to prove her independence.

The first time she bicycled away, Riri followed her, keeping some distance without her knowledge. Her daughter managed well and was happy and proud when Riri went to pick her up in the afternoon. From the next day, she started going to school by herself with other children (not her friends!) who joined in on the way. It gave her immense confidence, as she was the first one in her age group of Indian kids to do so. Eventually, her younger brother started going with her at an even younger age of four years.

This one habit lay the foundation of many such travels that she did alone. She built on the confidence that was inculcated. At age nine, she travelled with her five-year-old brother, alone, from Singapore to Ahmedabad (with airline assistance, of course), and this also continued to build her confidence. They had no mobile or smartphones on them to keep in touch during the journey. Of course, as parents, Riri and her husband were worried each time they let her go. They had to manage their anxiety and fear while they thought of all the things that could go wrong. But it was a small price to pay for empowering their kids to become self-reliant and confident.

These are aspects you can't teach in textbooks, which is why Riri exposed her children to opportunities where they could learn, make mistakes and find their own way. Again, we want to emphasize that, as parents, we have to prepare ourselves first and not frighten the child. You may know all the worst-case scenarios, but you do not have to scare your children. Instead, educate the child and tell them what they need to be alert about, what to avoid and what to do. Only when we work on our own fears will we be able to let our kids thrive. Being practical and teaching them to be safe is important.

Show, Don't Tell

For the first few years of their life, children are constantly learning—to walk, talk, eat and how to behave in all sorts of situations. So many of these lessons are survival instincts that they pick up from the moment they are born. They are most attuned to the behaviour, mannerisms and emotions of their primary caregiver (usually, their mother) and then the secondary caregiver (most often, their father) till they are young. This is why all the parenting advice you will find in this book will encourage *you* to model the behaviour you want to see in your child. You are your child's first source of learning and being aware of this will change how you approach each situation.

The brain tends to normalize and emulate the behaviour it experiences, which means that volatile parents should not magically expect their children to be calm and well-adjusted. If you expose the child to arguments, anxiety and stress, it is likely they will adopt the same behaviour. This is because so much of the stimuli and the situations they are in are brand new to them. Subconsciously, they pick up the signal that the way you behave is the appropriate way to behave. For example, if your child throws a tantrum, and your response is to get angry and scold them, the child will think that anger is the correct response in a stressful situation. If the pattern continues, they will react with anger to tantrums by their younger siblings and cousins, and later with their own children. If the questionnaire at the beginning of this book indicated that your style of parenting is authoritarian, We want you to think back to your childhood. How did your parents react to your outbursts and rebellions?

Your behaviour patterns will also influence the soft skills you want your children to learn, whether it be how to have a conversation or how to treat their peers. If you talk down to your child, telling them '*Oh you never understand, you're so slow,*' they learn that it is okay to speak like this and that they don't need to respect others. Children learn compassion when they are treated with kindness. This is especially helpful to remember when you are irritated and exhausted.

A woman called Manisha wrote to us in the comment section of Riri's Instagram video about not beating children while disciplining them. She said: '*My child is hitting everyone in his school, and even though I keep telling him not to, he doesn't listen. So, when nothing works, I gave him two tight slaps so that he learns his lesson to not hit others.*' This seems to be a very common situation, right? However, from a child's point of view, what they are learning is that if nothing works, slapping or hitting is okay—because their own parent is doing the same thing! Here, the parent is contradicting her own behaviour with what she is trying to teach the child! How can we teach children not to be violent and hit others when we use that method ourselves? How is our hitting our child different from the child hitting others? Children do not understand logic; they just see what they see and imitate! When parents send out mixed messages (such as shouting loudly at the child while saying 'Don't shout!'), the child gets confused and continues to do what the parent is doing.

The same applies to children who are picky eaters—more often than not they have a parent who has a habit of complaining about the food at mealtimes. *'Iss mein namak kam hai, daal bahut patli hai, roti bahut moti hai, mirchi thodi zyada hai.'* Even the ways of expressing anger and frustration are often learnt from parents or elder siblings, grandparents or teachers, with whom the child interacts most frequently.

These guidelines extend to your behaviour with other people as well. Avoid fighting with your partner, complaining about them or disrespecting them, in any way, in front of your children. Not only will this colour their opinion of the other parent or caregiver, but it'll also give them signals on how to treat the people close to them.

At times, you will slip up, and that is okay. No one can be perfect. Children do trouble and exhaust parents, and you should not feel guilty about using a harsh word occasionally. Children learn by patterns and repeated behaviour, so, unless scolding is a pattern, do not feel guilty about occasionally losing your patience.

This is also important in terms of understanding how you can change their habits. The younger they are, the sooner you'll see them adapt to your changes. Neural networks take time to be created, and younger children adapt quicker. Teenage behaviour, particularly, is a reflection of the child's early years. You can still get through to them, but it will take longer, and you will have to monitor your behaviour consistently to see a change in theirs.

It can be scary to think that you, as a parent, will mould many of their behaviour patterns, from how much they use their phone to how mindfully they eat, how they take care of themselves and their sleep habits. However, you must remember that this is a great way to teach them habits that will help them throughout their lives. Perhaps, it can be a starting point for you to adopt better habits too.

Stepping Away Helps

Parents don't realize that their reactions are also triggered by their child's behaviour. Children may unknowingly push your buttons with their behaviour, but it is for you to recognize this. If you've felt guilty about often losing your temper with your child, remember that you can change that, starting today. When it gets too much and you get close to shouting at them, choose to step away so you can cool down. Let your child know you can't speak now and need some time. Your child will learn that it is okay to step away when agitated. In our experience, giving your child your undivided attention, especially at a younger age, will help them a lot. It'll show them that you are present in the moment and make it easier to open up to you. So, the next time they come running to you, put away your phone or an unimportant task and give them all your attention.

How you respond to your child and how you treat your child in the most emotionally charged situations also teaches the child how to behave with others in similar situations— subconsciously!

Be Open, Honest and Consistent

Being vulnerable with others and accepting your mistakes is hard in every situation. As a parent, it may seem more so because you are in a position of authority and responsibility. But, it's very important for your child to recognize that you, too, are human. This is one of the most effective ways to draw closer in your relationship. If you yell at them and feel guilty about it, admit to it. You can't change what happened, but you can change how your child remembers the fight. It'll also normalize the idea of having conversations about feelings and encourage them to share their own feelings. Openness also extends to admitting when you don't know something. You do not have to be all-knowing, and it is okay to take time before you come back to your child with an answer. For example, children in India receive increasingly complex holiday homework as they progress in school. You may not remember every concept from school or may have never learnt it in the first place. Instead of hiding the fact that you may not know how to approach a project, make it an opportunity to spend time with them and learn together.

Filter the Flow: Avoid Oversharing

Being open does not require you to share everything with your child. Sometimes, it can be detrimental to share your emotions and experiences that are not age-appropriate. For example, telling your eight-year-old about a fight with your spouse or your financial stress is not something they may be ready to grapple with, and it can traumatize them further. Similarly, don't share your teenage mistakes with your ten-year-old or criticize your in-laws in front of your toddler. We admit that it is a fine line between oversharing and hiding too much, and you will have to decide this based on your unique situation. Fights with your spouse and in-laws should definitely be kept out of conversations. Observe how your child reacts to the things you tell them. We have also seen, from personal experience, that it is easier to be open and honest with your children if you are honest with yourself about your triggers.

The Weight of Family Secrets

We believe that families should not encourage being overly secretive. Indian parents will often tell their child *'don't let the neighbours find out about the arguments at home'* or *'don't tell your friends that things at home are not okay.'* Not only does this deny them an outlet for feelings, but they may grow up keeping secrets of their own, especially from you. When people continue to be secretive throughout their lives, it can feel like a burden to carry. Because they never choose to confide in people or be honest about their situation, they often don't have enough support from friends and other members of the family to deal with hard situations. Children who grow up with family secrets also end up having a lot of fear of judgement that impairs their ability to make social connections. They are always worried about what others will say, which causes anxiety and stress.

Another way of being open and honest is to apologize when we have lost our cool as a parent. In Riri's words:

> *Whenever I got triggered or dysregulated and said or did something I should not have, I would always make it a point to go to my kids and sincerely apologize to them and say, 'I lost my cool' or 'I said this and I shouldn't have'. Do not add 'but' to your apology—do not make conditional apologies. Avoid making it sound like you lost your cool and you are sorry, but the child misbehaved too! Then, the entire point of the apology is*

lost. Keep it honest. Children learn to accept their mistakes and apologize to others when they see parents doing the same.

Fine Line between Being Consistent and Becoming Rigid

As we've discussed earlier, all these guidelines will only be effective when backed with consistent action on your part. Consistency is what helps your child find comfort and balance at home. It is a way to teach them about values and discipline. As parents ourselves, we've also had instances when we've mixed up rigidity with consistency. If you ever feel stuck about this, ask yourself, '*Am I responding to my child's needs? Am I responding appropriately to the situation?*'

Consistency is spoken about a lot in modern parenting guides, but mostly in terms of maintaining a schedule for the child. It is said to be a crucial part of developing good habits. More and more, we see children being brought up with fixed nap times, mealtimes and organized play dates. Following this in your home might be easier, but our advice is to not be too caught up about adhering to the schedule on holidays or outside of your home, for example, while visiting grandparents, aunts and uncles. Personally, visiting our grandparents during the summer holidays are some of our best memories. It was a time filled with so much love and indulgence. We knew we could get away with things that our parents would not let us, like eating ice cream every day, snacking before mealtimes or avoiding a meal altogether. We're sure you too have some such fond memories from your childhood. Wouldn't you want your child to have them, too?

Trying to make your child stick to the exact same diet and same routine in another household will be stressful not just for you and the child, but also your relative. Allow some freedom and space for different experiences. It'll help them explore and learn. You can institute a strict schedule when you get back, and your child will learn to fall back into that pattern. Treat the visit away from home like a holiday. Riri remembers when her children would visit their grandparents (her in-laws) every year in summer holidays, a wholesale box of chocobar ice-cream carton would be waiting for them at home—the same parents who had been very strict with her husband in childhood were now pampering the grandchildren like there is no tomorrow! In fact, they would occasionally have only ice cream for dinner!! The children fondly remember these special times spent with their grandparents and how they were pampered. Those moments of fun, freedom and unconditional love by grandparents is something that every child deserves. It can become their anchor in adult life and guide them through low periods. So best to avoid creating issues with grandparents over such matters as they love indulging the grandchildren – something they could not do with their own children in the past. For many of our clients, their grandparents and memories of their unconditional love and pampering stays with them as the only childhood anchors of joy and freedom amidst all the disciplining that happens around with parents and teachers.

Be Parents, Not Pals!

Many parents believe that being modern or using positive parenting tools means being friends with the child. Such parents end up treating their child like a confidante and expect the child to do the same. The parent thinks they are being honest with the child, but this does more damage than good because the child is not emotionally mature enough to handle the issues being discussed. Instead, the child also starts sharing the burden of the problems, adding to their anxiety.

We had a client who was sixteen and suffering from severe anxiety, OCD and panic attacks. It all started from the age of eight, when her mother started sharing all her marital problems with the girl. The mother thought she was being friends with her daughter. The girl shared the mother's anger and lack of trust for the father. However, because she could not provide any solutions, she felt anxious about the situation. She also grew up hating her father and carrying a lot of anger for him—which was not hers to carry! As far as she was concerned, he had been a very good father. She was only able to mend her relationships with him when she recognized the damage done by her mother's oversharing with her.

We must understand that friends have a distinct role in a child's life and so do parents. Parents provide comfort, nurturing, support and stability, and create and maintain boundaries. Friends cannot provide this. Children benefit from having friends in their own age group. Parents should definitely seek to be friendly, but they must not replace parenting with the role of a friend. Nurturing them and instilling discipline becomes hard when you approach the situation as a friend or peer.

Being a friendly parent is more about participating wholeheartedly in the activities your child enjoys and putting yourself in their shoes to understand their behaviour. Practically, you can do this by connecting with your child through games and hobbies.

Parents as Guides and Mentors

To learn more about their mindset, communicate in a way and language that is easy for you to understand. They need to feel safe to share anything and everything for which they may seek help. However, you also need to be firm when required. Your rules and principles should be consistent, your role as a parent and guide should be clear. To be friendly, you need to be permissive or indulgent. Children need to see parents as adults from whom they can learn. You should be the role model from whom they can learn self-regulated, adult-like behaviour. If the parent becomes a friend, boundaries are breached. The child may not feel safe to share their issues out of concern for the parents' well-being. It is possible to be a friendly parent, but you should not give up the position as a parent and become only a friend to the child.

All these guidelines are important to remember, especially when your child becomes a teen. The friendliest child might also not share everything at this age. Teenagers need space, independence and some boundaries. So, even if parent tries to be a friend, the teenager may push back or pretend to share everything. It's best to stick to being a parent who can guide and mentor as opposed to being one who asks for their phone or social media password. Instead, make sure that you set reasonable ground rules that you discuss with your child.

Once your child is an adult you can start sharing some things that the adult can handle or help you manage. Till then its best to remain a friendly parent and not a friend!

Seek Balance

We hope all the guidelines we've explored have helped you so far. Our aim is to give you tools to make your relationship with your children fulfilling and manageable, rather than be an aspect that causes you constant stress. A theme you'll find reiterated throughout this book is the idea that parents need to parent themselves first. If you haven't yet unpacked your childhood experiences, you will find yourself being triggered by your child's behaviour quite often. For example, if your child throws a tantrum and calls you 'the worst mother in the world', it will hurt you deeply if you struggle with insecurity. However, if you can recognize it as an outburst and deal with it calmly, in the beginning, and with gentle guidance later, it will be better for you and your child.

You may struggle with the idea of revisiting your past or discovering that your parents may not always have been supportive. This is normal as, in India, children are taught to unconditionally accept parental guidance and never question it. However, you are a parent now, and you owe it to yourself and your child to feel at peace with yourself. This helps you show up more mindfully in your relationship with your child, too.

Parenting becomes easier when you are not swinging between extreme moods and behaviour patterns. For example, if you have severe anxiety, depression or anger, it is almost inevitable that this will show up in your parenting style. To avoid this and the downsides of extreme behaviour, it is crucial to be in balance with your childhood self. If you had issues with one or both of your parents, it is likely that your relationship with your child will be coloured by it, and your behaviour in certain circumstances will not be measured.

For example, we had a client who had extremely overprotective parents. When she became a mother, she insisted that her daughter be independent. However, this meant that she was sometimes pushing her away and forcing her to fend for herself when she actually needed help. Inadvertently, she wasn't always paying attention to her daughter's needs.

Riri has herself faced this because of her childhood experiences. Her parents made her sleep alone from the time she was three months old and celebrated it alone she was so independent. It gave her confidence as a child and later as an adult. So she decided her daughter would also sleep alone as a toddler. She, however, needed more time and cried when Riri made her sleep in another room. Riri continued to enforce it with her daughter to the point of traumatizing her and later saw the downside of it. It resulted in her experiencing anxiety, some insecurity, clinginess and feeling of being unloved for a long time, into her teenage years. After her own journey of dealing with her childhood, Riri realized that she had been wrong to force her daughter. She repeated her parents' approach with her own child, thinking that that was the best way to make a child independent. However, much later, she realized that what her parents glorified as 'independent behaviour' had made her isolated, insecure and uncomfortable with physical touch as an adult and a parent. So, she changed her approach with her younger child. She and her husband were gentler with him and let him have a greater say in the decision on where he wanted to sleep and until which age. She weaned him into gradually sleeping by himself alone—starting with a few hours and then entire night.

This was not the only time Riri's childhood experiences shaped her parenting. In another situation, she polarized her parenting style with her parents, and she overcompensated her children with what she missed in her childhood! In Riri's words:

> *When I was a child, my mom was never at home when I came home from school, as she was a practising Chartered Accountant running her own firm. From the age of five, I*

> *would open our locked house, eat by myself, read a book and keep myself busy until mom came home from her office at 7.30 p.m. As a child, I felt neglected, compared to my friends, whose moms would be waiting at home with hot snacks every single day. When I became a mother, I had a compulsive need to be home when my kids returned from school. I would schedule everything around this, and I would ensure they got hot snacks every day! I avoided doing full time job during those years only to be there when they go home from school. I overcompensated for what I had missed as a child! Once my children were pre-teens, I realized that it was more my need than theirs. When I asked them, to my surprise, they said they didn't really need me to be home for them every day when they came back from school. They were absolutely fine if I was not there to greet them or serve hot snacks!*

A balanced or authoritative parenting style is achieved when we become aware of our own childhood programming and how it is affecting us. We need to find a balance between warmth and expectation, firmness and compassion, expectation and responsiveness. When we are able to raise children with a balanced parenting style, we have children who are emotionally resilient and more likely to have better academic or non-academic achievements, better relationships and less self-sabotaging behaviour.

These examples are to remind you that if you believe you have experienced childhood trauma or your early experiences are influencing how you parent, please seek out the self-regulation techniques outlined in detail later in this book. If you feel you need more help, you can always turn to therapy as well. We've provided detailed resources at the end to guide you.

Cultivate Emotional Resilience

> 'The most beautiful people I've known are those who have known suffering, known struggle, known loss, and have found their way out of the depths.'
>
> —Elisabeth Kübler-Ross

Emotional resilience is the ability to adapt to and recover from stressful situations. It's like a mental and emotional springboard that allows you to bounce back without getting overwhelmed. The term 'resilience' has been defined in many ways. Masten, Best and Garmezy (1990) define resilience as 'the process of, capacity for, or outcome of successful adaptation despite challenging or threatening circumstances.' As parents, we cannot protect our children from the environmental stressors that children will face while growing up and as an adult. Helping children build emotional resilience is an important pillar of parenting and can be done by using positive parenting strategies.

Emotionally resilient children tend to have some common traits and here is what parents can do to help:

i. **They are confident:** Children are confident when they have a safe, secure and loving environment at home. This encourages them to explore, learn, make mistakes and overcomes challenges without shame, guilt or fear. Remember, a child who is growing up in toxic fear or toxic shame will have low self-worth and confidence. Whether your child is an introvert, naughty or curious, love them and make them feel safe. The most important thing, as a parent, is to give your child a nurturing loving environment. The child needs to feel that they are loved in spite and despite of who they are: *'I could be an introvert, I could be a naughty child, I could be curious, I could be doing a whole bunch of things in this curiosity but in spite of that my parents love me, and I am safe around them.'* If the child is assured of this, then they most likely would become extremely confident. Even if they are not outgoing, introverted, children can also be very confident about who they are. Work on building your child's confidence.

ii. **They are good at solving problems:** As we learnt in the guidelines section, do not jump in to solve your child's problems. It could be problems at school, in the playground, with their teachers or friends. Keep asking your child questions that will help them find solutions or different perspectives. Let your child make mistakes, face those age-appropriate problems that all children face and come up with their own solutions. Sometimes, a solution that the child has come up with may not work. That is okay. You can still ask questions and encourage the child to do something different because making mistakes is also a great learning experience for a child. Remember, in all your interactions with your children, please focus on helping them develop problem-solving skills as opposed to being scared of problems or running away from problems. Do not jump in to solve your child's problem yourself.

Work on healthy fear and do not use toxic fear to protect your child. Building a strong, nurturing relationship with the child, where they feel valued, supported and understood, can help them become more confident. Fear seldom helps with confidence; in fact, it erodes self-worth and curiosity. This does not mean we do not correct or discipline them—it only means we help them navigate life's challenges while making them feel supported and loved no matter what! That way, the child has the confidence to try new things (some good, some bad), learn from those experiences without fear and become confident!

iii. **They bounce back in the face of challenges:** Resilient children are the ones who have survived and thrived in spite and despite the challenges they have faced within and around them. When you are faced with a difficult situation as a parent, how do you cope? Do you run from the problem or face it head-on and learn from it?

Encourage your child to learn from challenges. Sit and discuss with people, take help and resolve those challenges. Make sure you do not discourage your child or instil fear about the possible challenges. Let your child face challenges with the mindset that challenges will come but there is always a solution for it and a lesson to be learnt.

Sometimes, parents unconsciously pass on the fear of failure or fear of judgement to the child. This makes the child scared to try out new things or new experiences, and if there is a problem, the child feels helpless. Parents must focus on helping the child understand the situation, find alternative perspectives and look for possible solutions. This is possible when parents ask the right questions with the right frame of mind!

So, as parents, when your children come to you with a problem or when they come feeling absolutely scared or overwhelmed with whatever they are facing, it is important to make them understand that life will throw challenges at them. However, there is always a different perspective to look at, a different way to deal with it and there are multiple ways to solve the problem and learn from it. This can be done through many indirect ways, something you can't teach your children through lecturing.

The child can learn it in the everyday interactions that you have with them. Assume you have asked the child to do something and the child did not do it, or made a mistake, or did it incorrectly. That is the moment when you teach the child how he/she can do it differently as opposed to shaming, blaming, threatening or punishing the child.

The ability to bounce back from failures is a sign of an emotionally resilient child—as parents, we cannot teach this through lectures but allow them to learn by observing and imitating us! They need to be handled accordingly when they have failed or are faced with a problem. Parents must be self-regulated and mindful in order to bring this approach into their interactions with the child.

iv. **They are independent and autonomous:** Children must be allowed slow, gradual age-appropriate independence for building their confidence and coping with life's challenges. They need to be independent enough to make their own decisions and to live with the consequences of the decisions. Many parents find it hard to give this autonomy to their children due to their own fears, insecurities or childhood traumas. It is important for children to have their own life experiences so that they can build neural pathways to rise after a fall, to sense caution and become emotionally resilient. Independence also helps children express individuality and creativity. The only way that parents can help children become independent is by stepping back and watching the child make mistakes and learning from them.

Remember, as parents, we do not have control over what the child is going to face when he/she goes out into the world as an adult. Allowing the child to be independent enough to make their own decisions and to live with the consequences of those decisions is a very important trait that we need to instil in children early on. It could start with something as small as independence in deciding whether they want to eat or go hungry or deciding what they wish to do with their life and career—if it does not work out, they should also have the independence to learn from those mistakes and to correct their actions.

Age-appropriate autonomy and independence are very important but very difficult for many parents to give to their children due to their own fears, insecurities or childhood traumas. A parent, who was sexually abused, will be overprotective about his/her child, and a parent who was betrayed will always want to protect the child from such experiences! This is a normal parental reaction, but it is equally important for the child to have his/her own life experiences and lessons. A sense of independence helps build confidence. Independent children are street smart and usually have good survival skills, which are missing in children who have not been given autonomy or the freedom to make mistakes.

v. **They have healthy coping skills:** One way to help children develop this is by allowing them to talk about emotions and teaching them certain techniques to process emotions. Remember, emotional resilience does not come by suppressing your feelings. You do this by teaching them self-care and an emotional vocabulary. When they can understand, recognize and process emotions, they are also able to be supportive friends and supportive partners.

It is also essential to teach your children the importance of self-care and how to understand others' emotions. An emotional vocabulary is also important in bringing up emotionally resilient children for when they grow up and have adult relationships. This is how you help them build their emotional resilience. You can learn self-care techniques yourself and when your children watch you doing all of that, they learn it from you.

vi. **Good social connections**: Another trait of emotionally resilient children is that they have good social connections. This is something you can start developing when the child is much younger. Allow the child to be exposed to different individuals—children, teenagers, adults, relatives, friends. Allow the child to go to different social events and gatherings and let them participate in team sports. In this way, they can learn how to interact and work their way around people from different age groups. Thus, building social interactions is a very important skill to teach your child to be emotionally resilient, and it starts at home. Let your child interact with the different people who visit your home, while ensuring the child is safe from potential abuse. At the same time, do not instil a fear of social interactions in your child. An introverted and shy child can be encouraged to have their close friends who may be supportive. Children do not have to be extroverted to have good social connections—even one good friend is enough to feel supported! Many clients who come to us with social anxiety have had childhood where parents restricted them from meeting friends, going for social gathering or family events. They are not comfortable in groups of people or around unknown people long after becoming adults—this affects their work and career choices also.

Finally, there is no denying that teaching your child healthy coping structures to face physical, mental or emotional challenges is important. This doesn't require special classes as they learn by observing you. Having a well-developed emotional vocabulary, coupled with the tools to process and manage difficult emotions, is something we all need in order to have healthy and functional adult relationships.

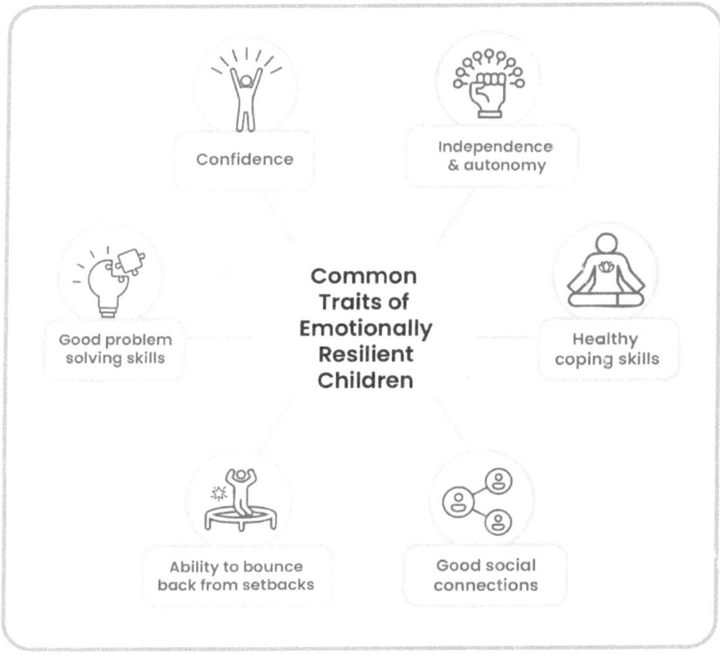

Figure 17: Common Traits of Emotionally Resilient Children

Figure 17 summarizes the traits commonly seen in emotionally resilient children (and adults!). As parents, we need to understand and internalize that we cannot spend our lifetime protecting our children from the environmental challenges, but we can focus on building their strength and resilience! The guidelines we have gone through will help you build that for your child.

If these parenting guidelines are followed, you will help your child become resilient, which will not only help them face challenges confidently but considerably reduce your own stress of parenting once they have grown up!

Navigating the Stages

In this chapter, we shared important guidelines that may help you develop a balanced parenting style. These principles offer a strong foundation. However, we know that putting them into action isn't always easy. Children act differently at different ages, and what works for a toddler won't work for an older child. The problems you face will change as your child grows, and so will the solutions!

In the next three chapters, we have answered many of the common questions parents have asked us in our workshops and one-on-one consultations, using a simple Q&A format. You might have other questions and be looking for quick solutions. While we can't provide a single answer that fits every situation for every child and parent, we do offer information about how children develop at different stages (from birth to age 6, ages 7 to 12 and the teenage years). We explain what your child needs physically, mentally, socially and and emotionally at each of these stages. This will help you understand what your child might be going through and why they might be acting in a certain way. To deal with your unique situation, use the guidelines from this chapter as the compass, keeping in mind both your child's needs and your own.

Your child's development can be divided into three key stages:

Stage 1. Birth to 6 years:	Infancy, toddlerhood and early childhood
Stage 2. 7 to 12 years:	Middle childhood
Stage 3. 13 to 18 years:	Adolescence or teenage

Stage 1 is a foundational stage when children need to form strong attachments with caregivers and build basic skills in language, motor development and emotional regulation.

Stage 2 sets the groundwork for academic and social success. Children learn to think more logically and manage relationships outside their immediate family, helping them navigate social environments.

Lastly, in Stage 3, identity formation becomes central. Adolescents strive for independence and focus on forming deeper relationships, often relying more on peers for social support. This is also a time when risk-taking behaviour may emerge as teens test their boundaries.

Each stage represents distinct milestones and challenges. In the day-to-day challenges of parenting, we may forget that children are growing and changing rapidly. To you, these changes might seem natural. For them, they are experiencing so many things for the first time. For toddlers, this can be taking their first step, while for teenagers, this could be about being in a relationship for the first time. Putting yourself in your child's shoes is perhaps the first step to realizing how you should approach the situation.

Once you develop empathy and understand your child's developmental needs, you will be in a clearer frame of mind to recall and apply the guidelines. You can choose to focus on the part that corresponds to your child's age, but we recommend that you read all the stages. These will help you unpack past experiences and prepare you for such instances in the future.

5

The Early Years: Birth to 6

'A child's world is fresh and new and beautiful, full of wonder and excitement.'

—Rachel Carson,
American marine biologist and writer

Specific Traits of Infants, Toddlers and Kindergarteners

The period from birth to 6 years is divided into three distinct stages:

1. Infancy (Birth to 1 year)
2. Toddlerhood (1–3 years)
3. Early Childhood (3–6 years)

Each of these three stages marks a unique phase of your child's development, where they have distinct needs and milestones. Infants, toddlers and kindergartners grow at very different rates, whether it's in terms of mobility, speech, social interactions or emotional development. By breaking these early years into smaller stages, you'll be able to better understand what your child needs at each step and give them the right kind of stimulation, learning opportunities and care. This will help your child move smoothly from one phase to the next.

Developmental Traits and Challenges with Babies (Birth to 1 year)

Infancy, spanning from birth to one year, is a period of rapid growth and development. This is when your baby transforms from a tiny, helpless newborn into a curious, mobile and increasingly interactive little person. Understanding the developmental traits and challenges of this stage can help you navigate these precious early months with confidence and joy.

Power of Early Connection

From the moment they are born, babies have a fundamental need to develop a secure bond with at least one caring, loving and responsive adult. Beyond physical needs like nutritious food, sufficient sleep, clean clothes, exercise and a safe and hygienic environment, babies need to feel safe and loved. This essential emotional connection is beautifully illustrated by the Still Face Experiment developed by Dr Edward Tronick in the 1970s.[1,2]

In this well-known experiment, a mother interacts with her baby by talking, smiling and mirroring the baby's reactions. The baby is fully engaged, relaxed and happy. Then, the mother stops interacting and keeps her face expressionless for two minutes. The baby tries everything to re-engage her mother, including moving her arms, pointing, screeching in frustration and eventually crying. When the mother goes back to engaging, the baby is visibly relieved and calms down quickly. This experiment highlights how crucial it is for parents or primary caregivers to respond to a baby's need for connection. Through each interaction, the baby learns how to best respond and interact with the world to get their needs met. If a secure bond is not formed in infancy, it can have lifelong implications on the baby's ability to form healthy relationships with others in childhood and later in adulthood.

Anagha remembers that she and her husband had help from both their families during the first six months with their newborn twins. The support made it much easier for them to not just take care of their two babies but also develop an emotional connection without being burned out. It gave them a little more time to rest and recover, which allowed them to show up with more love, patience and energy with the babies.

Ask for Help: It's Okay!

Her own positive experience reminds Anagha to always ask her clients if they're getting enough help. She makes sure they understand the importance of getting sufficient rest and the need to reach out to family or friends in times of need. Whenever they hesitate to ask for help, she reminds them that it is for the benefit of their baby. To be able to connect with their children, parents themselves need to be in a good emotional and physical state. Moreover, in India, it is often easier to find support, as people tend to live close to their parents or in joint families.

If you are staying away from family, recognize that it will be hard to look after the baby if you are trying to do everything on your own. See how you and your partner can work together to take care of the baby. Having a close-knit circle of friends even before the baby is born would certainly help. Invest time and effort in creating a support system. Hire some help to take care of daily household chores such as cooking, washing dishes, laundry etc. so that you can get some rest and have enough energy to take care of the baby. Consider taking additional time off work or reducing work hours. If this is not possible, find a reliable crèche or a nanny with excellent rating. Ask other parents in your community about their experience using those services. Hire a nanny or start sending your child to a crèche at least a month before rejoining work so that both you and your baby get used to a new routine. Consider joining an online support group of new parents so you don't feel lonely and isolated.

It's Not 'Just the Blues': Postpartum Depression

Some of our clients who have gone through postpartum depression found it harder to connect with their babies. However, at the time, neither the family members nor the clients themselves completely understood what they were going through. The lack of support and medical attention made it very hard for these mothers to take care of their babies and form a secure bond.

Two to three days after childbirth, some new mothers may begin to feel depressed, anxious or angry with the new baby or other family members. They may cry for no reason, or have trouble sleeping or eating. They may also question their ability to care for a baby. These feelings are often called 'baby blues', which may subside within a few days or a couple of weeks without any treatment.

Postpartum depression (PPD) is different from baby blues. The symptoms of PPD include intense and persistent sadness, a sense of hopelessness, severe mood swings, changes in eating and sleeping patterns and an overwhelming feeling of exhaustion. Some mothers may have difficulty bonding with their baby or even have thoughts of harming the baby. Riri had gone through almost a year of these symptoms after her second delivery. Being alone with no help in a foreign country made it worse. And in those days (twenty years ago) there was no awareness of PPD. She thought there was something wrong with her that she couldn't feel all that love and affection for her children that mothers are expected to feel and instead she was mostly angry, sad, depressed, tired and exhausted! Today thankfully there is a lot of awareness and discussion around this and hence mothers can get help. Hence, instead of feeling guilty or inadequate for not being able to care for the baby properly, seek support from family members and consult your obstetrician-gynaecologist to receive guidance on how to treat this mental health condition and if required, take therapy or counselling.

From Tummy-Time to Toddlerhood: The Physical Leap

From the moment they are born, infants are on a rapid physical development journey. In the first few months, babies develop control over their body. At 3–4 months, the baby starts lifting their head during tummy time, a crucial exercise that strengthens their neck and shoulder muscles. Whenever you help your baby do tummy time, keep a mirror on the wall next to the baby's mat so that when they roll over, they can see themselves in the mirror. As they grow stronger, they'll start to roll over, sit up and eventually crawl. Put them on a mat on the floor rather than leaving them on the bed when they are learning to crawl so that they have a stable surface. Keep a couple of small toys on the mat that they can grasp with their fingers. By their first birthday, many babies start to pull themselves up to stand, and some might even be taking their first wobbly steps.

Brain Builders: Infant Cognition

Infants' thinking skills develop as they start interacting with the people and environment around them. They are born scientists, constantly observing, experimenting and making discoveries. They start to figure out how things work by interacting with the world around them. Provide nurturing experiences to support their brain growth. Talk to them and sing to them while holding them in your arms, face-to-face, so that they can observe your lip movement. Infants absorb language when they interact with a real person, not through videos on a screen. While changing their diaper or giving them a bath, talk to them about what you are doing. Anagha used to read stories from children's books to her twins when they were just a month old. Board books (with thick sturdy pages) can make reading an interactive experience for babies since the pages can be turned without being torn.

You can play simple games, such as peek-a-boo, patty-cake or little piggies, with your baby that do not require any equipment. From recognizing familiar faces to exploring the concept of object permanence (the understanding that objects continue to exist even when they can't be seen), your baby's brain is working overtime when they are just a few months old. When you play peek-a-boo, at first, your baby might seem perplexed when you hide your face, but as they approach the one-year mark, they'll start to anticipate your return with giggles and excitement. This is a clear sign that they're starting to grasp object permanence.

Hang a colourful mobile above the baby's crib. You can tie a ribbon loosely to your baby's ankle to connect it to the mobile. As the baby kicks, the mobile will move. The baby will soon figure out that the kicking is causing the mobile to move. They will learn to control their movements and kick faster to make the mobile move more.

Infants also experience rapid changes in their sensory perceptions. They're learning to see, hear, touch, taste and smell the world. Providing a stimulating environment with different textures, sounds and sights can aid their sensory development. Give your baby objects with different textures to touch and hold, for example, a soft blanket, rattles or small balls. The hospital where Anagha's twins were born had soothing music playing in the background while they slept. She continued this practice when they came home. If she played the same songs when they were awake, they would move and respond to show that they recognized the familiar tunes.

Instead of keeping babies at home the whole day, make sure to take them for a stroll outside in their pram. Let them feel the breeze, listen to the rustling leaves, look at the swaying trees and flying birds.

Decoding Baby Emotions

Emotionally, infants are learning to express and manage their feelings. In the first few months, crying is their primary way of communicating needs and discomforts, whether they're hungry, tired or in need of a diaper change. However, hearing your baby cry can be stressful. In such times, remember that they are trying to communicate a specific need to you.

Sometimes, babies cry for reasons that aren't immediately clear, leading to frustration for the parents. By paying attention, and with practice, you will surely learn to differentiate between different kinds of cries—hungry, wet, sleepy, tired, overstimulated, bored or sick. Learning to read your baby's cues and understanding that, sometimes, they might just want to be held and comforted can make these moments much more manageable. However, this is easier said than done. Whenever you are feeling overwhelmed, don't hesitate to ask for help from other household members. If no help is available, take a small break and do self-regulation exercises before addressing the baby's need.

As they grow, you'll notice more varied expressions of emotion. One of the sweetest milestones is when your baby starts to recognize and respond to you with a big, toothless grin. This social smile, which usually appears around two months, is their way of engaging with you and other caregivers, building the foundation for future positive social interactions.

Bonding and Beyond

Infants begin to form strong attachments to their caregivers, which is crucial for their social development. They find comfort in your presence, voice and touch. This attachment is evident when your baby quietens down upon hearing your voice or snuggles into your arms when held.

Separation anxiety, which often peaks around 9–12 months, is another hallmark of social development. While it can be challenging to leave your baby with someone else, this anxiety is a normal sign that they've formed a healthy bond with you. With time and reassurance, they learn that even when you leave, you always come back.

Working Parents

If you are planning to leave your baby with a nanny or in a crèche when your baby is still just a few months old, do your research. Talk to previous employers or parents whose babies are in the same crèche. At least a month prior to resuming work, hire the nanny or start sending your baby to the day care for a few hours every day so that the baby gets used to other caregivers. You can also see for yourself whether you are satisfied with the service. At eleven months, Anagha's twins started going to a day care for a few hours a day. After about a month, they started going full time, when she went back to work after a year of maternity leave. Having a month of transition helped them settle into the new environment. Some parents choose to work flexitime or part time during this time which can help balance both—parenting and career without taking a complete break!

Help from Grandparents

If you are planning to leave the baby at home with grandparents, ensure that grandparents are physically and mentally in good health, and up to the task of looking after the baby. For example, if they are too weak, they may lose their balance while holding the baby or may not be mobile enough to take the baby outside for a stroll. In such cases, they may prefer to keep the baby in one place (in their lap/highchair etc.) all the time, which may hinder the baby's physical development.

Caring for the baby should not become a burden for them. If they are stressed or anxious, the baby will sense this energy and may feel anxious.

Also, recognize that their approach to raising children may be different from yours. Do not be too prescriptive about how they should take care of your child. As long as you trust them to provide safe, secure and responsive care, do not worry about their occasional indulgent and permissive behaviour. Different parenting styles can be a huge point of difference between grandparents and parents, and can cause a lot of stress around the child. It is best to have open and honest conversation, share your views and reasons behind those, understand grandparents' intentions and find a middle ground. It's not ok to expect them to completely change their approach and follow your parenting style.

The Challenges

Crying, Crawling and Chaos: Trials of Early Parenthood

One of the biggest challenges you will face as a new parent is managing sleep—for both your baby and yourself. Newborns sleep a lot, but their sleep patterns can be unpredictable, which can leave you feeling exhausted. It's common for babies to wake every 2–3 hours during the first 3–6 months, as frequent wake-ups are a normal part of their developmental process. While it's essential to be patient, it's also crucial for you to take care of yourself. Whenever possible, try to nap when the baby naps or ask for help so you can catch up on sleep. Sleep deprivation can make it harder for you to care for your baby, so prioritize your own when you can. In Japan, Riri realized she was getting angry, frustrated and very stressed out, managing two kids aged four years and two months old while adjusting to a new environment, having no help and a husband who used to travel a lot for work. Eventually, she started calling a nanny just for two hours in the afternoon to take care of her son so she could catch up on her sleep or take out some time for herself. Looking back, she feels it was the wisest decision for her at that point of time.

Around four months of age, you may consider sleep training to help your baby sleep longer stretches through the night. Sleep training methods range from the more traditional 'Cry It Out' (CIO) approach to gentler techniques like 'Camping Out' and 'Controlled Comforting.' The CIO method involves letting your baby cry without immediate intervention, based on the idea that they will eventually learn to self-soothe. However, crying is your baby's primary form of communication, signalling needs like hunger, discomfort or the need for comfort. Ignoring your baby's cries may lead to stress, insecurity and anxiety for both you and your baby. On the other hand, gentler methods like 'Camping Out', which are commonly practised in cultures, such as in India, offer a more responsive approach. In this method, your baby's cot is placed in the same room as you, allowing easy access to comfort. The Indian Academy of Paediatrics recommends this method for babies under six months, as well as holding and soothing babies to sleep. After six months, 'Controlled Comforting' encourages you to respond to crying after brief intervals, providing reassurance without picking your baby up.[3]

In addition to choosing a sleep-training method, establishing a consistent night-time routine is key to helping your baby develop healthy sleep habits. Dim the lights, close the curtains and eliminate any distractions. Instead of playing with your baby, engage in calming activities such as a gentle massage, singing a lullaby or playing soft background music. After feeding, place your baby in the crib when drowsy but awake, and offer gentle reassurance if needed. Avoid rocking your baby to sleep, as it may create a dependency that makes independent sleep more challenging.

Some babies may take longer to adjust to independent sleep, and sleep training may not work if there are underlying medical issues, such as acid reflux or allergies. If you suspect a medical issue, it's always a good idea to consult your paediatrician to address any concerns.

Feeding is another area that can present challenges. Whether you are breastfeeding, formula-feeding or both, there will be times when feeding schedules, growth spurts or teething disrupt your routine. Being flexible and responsive to your baby's needs is key during these times.

Developmental Traits and Challenges of Toddlers (Aged 1–3)

New parents often feel that infancy is the most challenging period of parenthood—until they bring up a toddler. As your little one learns to navigate the world, they encounter a variety of developmental milestones and challenges.

Toddler on the Loose: Childproofing for Safety

Physically, toddlers are on the move, mastering everything from walking to climbing. Their curiosity knows no bounds as they explore their surroundings with newfound mobility, often keeping you on your toes to ensure their safety.

You have to put in some work to make your home child-friendly. This includes not having small objects lying around and putting away heavy decorative items that can fall, such as crystal and glass vases. Otherwise, parents often find themselves telling their child 'don't touch this' or 'don't go there'.

Riri remembers, when her son was little, he would put everything in his mouth, including slippers. They had a carpet in the house where tiny things would collect, which he would find while crawling and put them in his mouth. It became stressful to monitor him all the time, and they eventually removed the carpet entirely. They also put all shoes out of reach in a closed cupboard as he loved chewing on slippers and shoes. They made sure to childproof kitchen drawers, cabinets and houseplants. They ensured the home did not have anything accessible to him that he could break or harm himself with.

Beyond Babble: Navigating Toddler Language

Cognitively, toddlers are like sponges, absorbing information at an astonishing rate. Language development is a highlight of toddlerhood. They're beginning to grasp language, although their verbal skills may not yet match their understanding. They may still struggle to communicate effectively, leading to frustration and, occasionally, aggressive behaviour.

Anagha's twins attended a day care since they were eleven months old. After about a year and a half, her two-and-a-half-year-old son suddenly started complaining about going to day care. It was hard for his parents to understand what had changed. When they asked him, he said that no one at the day care spoke Marathi, the language they spoke at home. Even though he had been going there for more than a year, he could not speak the local language as well as Marathi. He was a very communicative child, so he felt constrained when he could not express himself fully.

The Power of Mother Tongue

Riri believes that starting by speaking the native language or mother tongue is good. Both her kids, though raised in Japan and Singapore speak fluent Gujarati. It also helped them bond with their grandparents and relatives when they visited India. We would also record our little kids telling stories in Gujarati—something we cherish listening to, even after twenty years! Sometimes, parents have different mother tongues, in which case it is okay for the child to be listening to both. Children's brains are capable of picking up multiple languages. Initially, when they are exposed to many languages, they might take time to start speaking, and parents often panic—but eventually, these children do end up learning both languages! English is something they usually learn in school anyway, so we believe speaking one's native language at home becomes very important, especially for Indians living outside India. Language roots the child in the native food, culture and values. It also becomes a good way to start native language stories at bedtime.

The Emotional Roller Coaster

Emotionally, toddlers are a roller coaster of feelings. Not knowing how to regulate emotions leads to tantrums. When Anagha's son was two years old, he loved one particular white T-shirt because it was extremely soft. He would want to wear it every day. Putting it in the wash had become difficult. He would wake up happy but as soon as he realized he was wearing a different T-shirt, he would start crying and demand to wear his white shirt. He was too small to understand logical explanations about why it was important to wash his T-shirt. The only strategy that worked was to distract him with his favourite activity like going out to play or playing with building blocks. In a couple of months, his obsession with the T-shirt went away. He started holding any piece of clothing while sleeping, as long as it was super soft.

First Friendships: Navigating Toddler Relationships

Socially, toddlers are dipping their toes into the world of relationships. They are starting to show preferences for certain playmates and engage in parallel play, though sharing is still a foreign concept. Witnessing two toddlers fight over the same toy can quickly turn a playdate into a chaotic affair.

Despite their budding independence, toddlers still crave a secure connection with their caregivers. This need for a loving and responsive adult forms the cornerstone of their emotional and social development. Responding to their needs and offering comfort help them feel safe and loved, even during their most challenging moments.

The Challenges

Taming the Toddler Tornado: The Reasons for Misbehaviour

Sometimes, you may feel that your toddler is misbehaving but it is nothing but age-appropriate behaviour, reflecting their stage of development and unique needs.

Here's why they misbehave:

- **Need to Explore with All the Five Senses:** Toddlers are naturally curious and eager to explore the world around them. For example, they might grab objects off shelves in a store or try to taste unfamiliar items they find. When they are stopped, they may get angry or annoyed.
- **Need for Independence:** Toddlers want to assert themselves and make their own choices. For instance, they might insist on picking out their own clothes or refuse to hold your hand while walking, wanting to explore on their own. Taking away this agency may agitate them.
- **Lack of Impulse Control:** Toddlers may act on instinct, without considering the consequences. For example, they might impulsively snatch a toy from another child or throw a tantrum when it's time to leave the playground.
- **Limited Understanding of Logic:** Toddlers may engage in behaviour that seems illogical to adults. For instance, they might pour water onto the floor just to see what happens, without understanding the mess it creates. Be patient and remember that they don't do it to annoy you.
- **Difficulty Understanding 'NO':** Toddlers may not interpret the word 'no' in the same way as adults. For example, they might want to touch a hot iron despite being told not to, out of curiosity, and because they don't fully grasp the danger. It is best to keep dangerous objects away and supervise your toddler instead of saying 'no' repeatedly, expecting a different outcome.
- **Short Memory/Attention Span:** Toddlers have short attention spans and may quickly forget instructions or rules. For example, they might repeatedly climb onto furniture

even after being told not to, simply because they forget or get distracted.

- **Limited Verbal Communication:** Toddlers may resort to misbehaviour as a means of communication when they can't express themselves verbally. For instance, they might throw a tantrum because they're hungry but can't tell you that they need food.
- **Lack of Motor Skills:** Toddlers may not realize that some tasks are beyond their current motor abilities. For example, they might become frustrated when they can't fit a puzzle piece into its place or struggle to put on their shoes independently.

Try to notice such behaviour and understand if there is a good reason behind it. It helps if you respond with empathy and patience and also address the underlying needs of your child.

Developmental Traits and Challenges of Children Aged 3–6 (Kindergartners)

Preschoolers, aged 3–6 years, are in an exciting and dynamic phase of growth. They are constantly developing their independence, social skills and emotional regulation. They build on everything they have learnt as toddlers and hit new milestones.

The 'I Do It Myself' Stage

Preschoolers are eager to assert their independence. They want to do everything by themselves, from dressing to eating and choosing activities. Your child may insist on wearing their own clothes, only to get frustrated when they cannot put their arms through the sleeves. This desire to be self-sufficient often leads to meltdowns when their abilities don't quite match their ambitions. Take the time to teach them how to dress themselves, tie laces or button their shirts.

In Montessori[4] classrooms, children are given a lot of freedom to move around and choose activities, as per their interest, to foster independence. Every activity is carefully designed to help children develop skills progressively. For instance, to foster fine motor skills, a toddler might start with a bead stringing activity that uses large beads, a thick string and a blunt wooden needle. If the child shows interest in the activity, they may repeat it daily, gradually mastering the skill. Once they feel confident, they can move on to a more challenging task, such as stringing smaller beads. As a Montessori teacher, Anagha consistently observed how aligning with a child's interest accelerated their learning through repetition and encouraged the mindset of 'I can do it!'.

Preschool Cognition

While preschoolers are curious and eager to learn, their understanding of abstract concepts like time, cause and effect and sequential order, is still limited. This can make following multi-step instructions difficult. Give them clear, simple instructions and break down tasks into manageable steps to help them succeed and build their confidence. You might have to repeat the instructions since the brain's processing time is slower than in adults.

Feelings and Frustrations

Emotionally, preschoolers are beginning to identify and express their feelings more clearly, but their emotional regulation is still a work in progress. Limited verbal skills often result in physical expressions of frustration, like hitting or biting, and frequent tantrums.

Preschoolers' brains are more developed in areas responsible for immediate responses like freeze/flight/fight, while the frontal lobes, which handle impulse control and regulation, are still developing. This imbalance often leads to impulsive and, sometimes, aggressive behaviour. Balancing their need for exploration with safety is a constant challenge, as they rapidly develop their motor skills and test their physical limits.

Learning to Share

Socially, kids in this age group are learning how to interact with peers, form friendships and understand social norms. They are starting to grasp the concept of empathy and the importance of co-operation. However, sharing and taking turns can be particularly challenging. It's common to see a preschooler clutching a toy and refusing to let anyone else play with it. Conflicts with peers are frequent, and resolving these disputes often requires adult intervention.

When Anagha's three-year-old twins frequently clashed over toys, purchasing duplicates seemed a simple solution. However, she chose to intervene selectively, only when physical fights broke out. She would separate them, guide them towards calming down, and encourage them to take turns or find different activities. These skills were also reinforced in their preschool. Gradually, they learned to compromise and play collaboratively. Their growing individual interests also reduced the frequency of conflicts over toys.

The Challenges

Focus and Attention

Preschoolers have short attention spans and their reasoning skills are still maturing. They can easily get distracted and may have trouble following complex instructions, requiring simple and clear guidance. Think of trying to get them to clean up their toys; unless you break it down into specific steps, they might just wander off mid-task.

Children of this age can also become deeply engrossed in a single activity, making it challenging to transition to a different task. Expect resistance or a tantrum if you ask them to clean up when they are in the middle of playing with blocks. When Anagha used to teach in a Montessori classroom, she did not force children to come for circle time if they were engaged in some other activity of their choice. Children would join as soon as they finished what they were doing. Riri recollects her son playing with Lego and train tracks for hours together with complete attention and focus to the point of not even hearing the sound of the doorbell or someone calling! If he was disturbed or asked to stop in between he would get really upset. Allowing him to do that really helped him as an adult to focus on his work well (of course, it needs to be of interest, otherwise there would be only distraction!).

Socially, preschoolers are still learning how to navigate interactions and relationships. They may struggle with sharing, taking turns and resolving conflicts peacefully. As an early childhood teacher, Anagha had to be vigilant, especially when the children would be on the playground. Pushing others to get on the slide or swing first or grabbing someone's toy could happen any time. Knowing each child's temperament and anticipating such incidents was key to prevention.

Transition Troubles

Preschoolers can find it challenging to move from one activity or environment to another. When Anagha's twins were three years old, she would take them to a wooden toy store, which had a children's play area, after school, almost every day. Initially, her son would cry every time they had to go home. Once it became a ritual, he understood that he would get to play there again and he stopped crying.

Routine and predictability are crucial for preschoolers. They thrive on routine, and any changes in their schedule or transitions between activities can be upsetting, leading to resistance and anxiety. When Anagha's twins were preschoolers, they established a routine. Since she would go to work early in the morning, she would ask her kids to choose what they wanted to wear the night before. They could open and close their clothes drawer by themselves and choose their clothes.

Having picked out the clothes in advance would help her husband get them ready without any hassles. He would drop them to school, while their part-time helper would pick them up. Anagha had prepared a menu of snacks they liked, so they could tell the helper what they wanted to eat after school. By the time they finished their snack and had taken a nap, Anagha would be home. The evening routine was also set: playtime, wash hands, help set the table, dinner, followed by the bedtime routine of brushing teeth, bath, massage with a moisturizing lotion, story time and sleep.

Preschoolers may also develop new fears related to unfamiliar experiences, like starting school or going to swimming lessons. Remember to introduce new activities gradually. For example, prior to starting school, visit the school a few times and let the child meet the teacher. Involve your child in preparing for school, such as buying a school bag of their choice. Talk positively about school when you interact with them to get them excited about the experience.

Preschool Tales: Truth and Fiction

Preschoolers may be dishonest for various reasons. They might lie about breaking a toy to avoid getting in trouble or embellish a story to make it more exciting. Young children often blur the lines between reality and imagination. Anagha's three-year-old would tell tall tales about how he climbed a tree to see a nest. He claimed he had found beautiful blue eggs of a robin. He was fascinated by a story they were reading about robins, and this had made its way into his own story. For such stories, a gentle nudge back to reality can suffice. Try saying, 'Wow, that sounds like a great adventure story! This will make a great book. Tell me more!' in a playful tone.

They might also lie to manipulate a situation or test boundaries to see how adults will react.

For example, after eating two biscuits, they may ask for one more saying that they had only one. Instead of saying, 'Why are you lying? I just saw you eat two biscuits', say, 'I know you really want another biscuit because it's yummy. You have already eaten two. You can have two more tomorrow.'

Recognizing their need for independence, social interaction, emotional expression and routine stability will guide you in providing the right support and encouragement during this critical stage of development.

Bedtime Stories

Riri remembers her husband would spend every night telling stories to their three-year-old son and soon enough, their son, too, started making up and telling stories to us. They recorded those and, today, when they are much older, they listen to those, feel good and laugh. Bedtime stories are a great way to develop the child's imagination and creativity, and if done in the native language or the language spoken at home by parents, it can be very effective. Moreover, the words and images that form in the child's mind just before bedtime find their way into the subconscious mind and create new programmes. Therefore, this is the perfect age and time to inculcate values and good habits using stories and imagination. Bedtime stories are a great way to build a routine and bond with the child. Riri would read bedtime stories from the book so that her kids would listen, get bored and eventually sleep! It was a well-planned strategy to get them to sleep on time. But her husband would actually make up funny, incredibly crazy stories accompanied by funny sounds and gestures which would make the kids laugh and giggle and eventually tire out and sleep. Both approaches helped them build a bedtime routine with the children but in completely different styles.

Montessori-Inspired Activities for Cognitive Development:

'What the hand does, the mind remembers.'

—Maria Montessori

More than a hundred years ago, Dr Maria Montessori discovered the role of the child's hand in brain development just by observing children. Many neurological studies now validate her observation in developing intelligence.

Children do not learn by just watching; they learn by doing. Instead of buying iPads and showing them educational videos, give them tangible objects to play with. With everyday objects, you can design activities for young children at home.

Use objects made of natural materials such as metal, wood, ceramic. Keep each activity in a tray on a low shelf, which your child can access easily, without your help. At a time, keep only three to four trays on the shelf. Once the child masters the activity or loses interest, introduce new activities. Keep rotating the activities every few weeks so that children can repeat the activities and master the skill.

Choose an activity that matches the child's interest and skill level. Sit in a quiet place without clutter and no other distractions. Demonstrate how to do an activity with deliberate, slow movements. Then, allow your child to do the activity on his own. Unless the behaviour is unsafe, do not correct or intervene. Allow your child to practise without any interruptions.

Activities for 1.5–3-year-olds:	Activities for 3–6-year-olds:
• Pouring lentils/rice from one cup to another • Pouring water from one cup to another • Scooping stones with two hands • Scooping beans from with one hand and transferring to another bowl • Spooning big beans from large bowl to small bowls • Opening/closing containers: empty clean cream jars, small bottles, small purses with zipper/buttons etc. • Lock and key • Cutting paper strips with scissors • Stringing large beads/ wooden shapes • Tearing old paper into small pieces and gluing them on to a colourful paper • Collecting leaves and gluing them on paper • Gluing colourful paper shapes using a brush and liquid glue • Boxes full of fabrics with different textures • Sorting socks by colour/size/ pattern	• Spooning rice into a bowl through a funnel • Scooping stones out of water using strainer • Pouring water from a small pitcher into small cups • Pouring water from a small kettle into small cups • Transferring water from one bowl to another using a sponge • Picking up cotton balls using small tongs and transferring to another bowl • Transferring coloured water using a dropper • Transferring beans using a tweezer • Whisking liquid soap to make bubbles • Mixing different coloured water with a small whisk • Screwing nuts onto bolts • Stringing small beads • Sewing a button (large/small) • Sorting beans/buttons/shells/ leaves/flowers/blocks by colour/size/pattern • Smelling different fruits/ flowers/spices Note: For water activities, add some food colour to make the activity more appealing.

Parenting Tips for Handling Specific Challenges for Children of 2–6 Years

1. My toddler says 'NO' to everything! How should I handle this defiance and stubbornness?

Do Not Take It Personally!

Your toddler is not being defiant and stubborn just to make your life harder. Do not take his 'no' as a personal challenge to your authority. He is at a developmental stage where he wants to do everything by himself. He wants to be in control. However, he lacks the skills, so he gets easily frustrated. He might be hearing 'no' a lot from you and might just be repeating it back to you. He is not doing it on purpose. Stay calm and patient as reacting with frustration or anger can exacerbate the situation.

Model the Behaviour You Want and Make It Fun

Children learn by observing their parents. So, show them how to handle frustration and make good choices through calm and respectful communication. Redirect your child's attention if they are fixated on saying 'no'. For example, if they're refusing to wear certain clothes, divert their attention to the occasion. Whether you are getting them dressed for school, a party or just to go to the park, speak about what they will do once you get there. Get them to focus on the enjoyment they will get from the activity. Once they are calmer and not just focused on saying 'no', you will find it easier to reason with them. Another way to redirect attention is to say, 'Let's play a game while we put on your shoes. Can you count to ten with me?'

Acknowledge the Child's Feeling and Then Offer Choices

One of the best ways to defuse the situation is to acknowledge your child's feelings. For example, if your toddler refuses to wear shoes, acknowledge their wish and calmly state what needs to happen next: '*I know that sometimes your feet don't want shoes, but we need to wear shoes to go to the park.*' Then, offer choices in a non-threatening tone, '*Do you want to wear your blue shoes or your red shoes?*' This way, you can engage her mentally and redirect her focus away from her objection.

Use Positive Reinforcement

Next, use positive reinforcement, '*Yesterday, you put on your shoes all by yourself! Can you show me how you did it?*' You can even engage them by asking for help: '*I want to go to the park. Can you show me the way? As soon as your feet are ready, we will go.*' If they still refuse, calmly say, '*We need to wear shoes to go outside. Let me know when you're ready,*' and then wait patiently. Remember to avoid power struggles.

Be patient if you don't see results immediately. Sticking with it will help your child develop good habits for life, while also making routine tasks more pleasant for both of you. A daily routine and a stable environment also provide predictability, reducing the chances of defiant behaviour.

Creating a chart with photos of your child doing routine activities can help gain their cooperation. Take photos of your children doing various activities and print them. Photos become proof that they can do those activities on their own. Engage them in creating a chart. Discuss the sequence of activities and let them paste the photos in the correct order. Making a chart with their own photos gives them a sense of ownership. Instead of telling them what to do, you can just ask them what the chart says. They can see what's next on their chart and follow the sequence. This reduces power struggles since they feel they are in control, instead of being told what to do.

When you know a big change is going to affect them, inform them and explain what to expect in advance.

Engage the Upper Brain

Refer to the second guideline in Chapter 4 and try using methods that engage the upper brain. A child throwing a tantrum is a child enraged. He/she is operating from the impulsive lower brain. A soothing touch, asking a few open-ended questions and helping the child describe his/her feelings is a great way to engage the upper brain and calm down the child.

2. How do I handle tantrums and meltdowns?

Toddlers often struggle with controlling their impulses as well as managing their feelings. So, they might have sudden emotional outbursts that can test even the most patient parent. Tantrums usually happen when toddlers don't get what they want, or are frustrated because they are not able to do something due to lack of skills. Meltdowns happen when they are completely overwhelmed by intense emotions, overstimulation, or tiredness.

When facing such emotional outbursts, it's essential for you to remain calm and composed. Reacting with anger or frustration can escalate the situation and prolong the episode. Instead, take deep breaths and focus on soothing your child, offering reassurance and comfort amidst their distress. Riri recollects her four-year-old daughter rolling on the floor in a department store demanding a barbie doll. All she did was quietly tell her that she cannot have it. When the crying and rolling continued much to the amusement of all shoppers, Riri, who was embarrassed about creating a scene, calmly pretended to walk away from here. Her daughter realized her tantrum is not getting her anywhere, so she stopped howling and quietly followed Riri. Later on, she had to be explained how this was not the way to get things. It never happened again. *'Thank god I didn't scream, shout, hit her or drag her out physically—which was what many anxious and embarrassed moms would do. Looking back, however, I wish I had given her a hug or calmed her down which is a more positive way of dealing with it vs just walking away. But then, I didn't know any better as a young first-time mother!'*

Create a Quiet Space

Create a safe space for your child to calm down. Whether it's a quiet corner at home or a bench in a bustling market, provide a refuge where they do not have a lot of external stimuli and can be comforted. Validate their feelings by acknowledging their emotions without judgement, letting them know that it's okay to feel upset or angry.

Use Distraction

Distraction can be a powerful tool in defusing tantrums. Redirect your child's attention to something else, whether it's a favourite toy, a comforting hug or a change of scenery.

Recognize Repetitive Triggers of the Child

Identifying triggers is another crucial step in managing meltdowns. Pay attention to the circumstances leading up to the outburst, whether it's hunger, fatigue, overstimulation or frustration. By recognizing these triggers, you can intervene the next time, before the meltdown occurs, or better understand how to support your child through it.

Recognizing Own Triggers

When a child throws a tantrum in public, more often than not, the parent is more triggered due to the embarrassment and shame they experience. Fear of being judged as a bad parent or an out-of-control parent or a parent who has not raised the child well are all reasons for parents using threats and force to control the situation. It is important to understand that such situations are common with all toddlers and parents; hence, it is nothing to be ashamed of. Working on your own triggers and building confidence to handle the 'drama' calmly and patiently is something every parent needs to work on! Chapter 8 on self-regulation will help.

While toddler meltdowns can be challenging, they are also a normal part of development. By remaining calm, identifying triggers and offering support and validation, you can help your child manage these turbulent episodes.

3. My child is a picky eater. How can I make mealtimes less stressful?

In Indian households, mealtimes can be quite stressful for parents. Many mothers feel guilty if their child doesn't eat well and are often blamed by other family members for their child's picky eating habits, which can increase their anxiety. If this sounds familiar, try to manage your own anxiety first. Your stress can turn mealtimes into power struggles with your child. Kids can sense your anxiety, and when their fight-or-flight response is triggered, it directs blood flow away from the digestive tract to the limbs, literally causing them to lose their appetite. (See Figures 5 and 6 in Chapter 2) This only compounds the problem.

Riri says, *'My son was a picky eater, and that comes from the fact that he loves his food in a certain way. When he was small I never force-fed him. If he wasn't hungry, he wouldn't eat and that was fine with me. I knew that when he recognized hunger, he would eat. And for that, he must experience hunger! As he grew up, went to school, camping etc. he had to eat whatever was given and eventually he learnt to eat everything anyway! Fussing over a child's food on a daily basis can be very stressful. I remember being constantly told I was not a good mother because I was not insisting that he should eat two chapattis or I was not trying hard enough to feed him dinner. I had pressure to force feed him or cajole him into eating his meals regularly but I didn't give in and let him be. He has developed the most healthy eating habits at twenty-one among all of us! In contrast, I had force fed my daughter (first child). Her nanny would cajole her, sing songs and take her down to the garden—all in order to feed her! She never got to decide how much she wanted to eat—we all made sure we fed her based on what we felt was right. Today, as an adult, she believes she cannot recognize hunger or satiation and tends to over eat or not eat enough. She is now mindful about her food choices, thanks to information and the Internet! Life and experiences teach everything, and as parents, we don't have to get it all right!'*

Avoid Negative Associations around Food or Mealtimes

If a child is forced to eat or is constantly nagged about food, they may develop an aversion to it. This can become a hard-to-break pattern, turning every meal into a struggle. Many of our clients struggle to have healthy relationships with food because of negative experiences during their childhood. Some feel anxious around food, while others tend to overeat and then feel guilty. Some mimic the behaviour they saw in their parents, such as constantly criticizing food, throwing food or berating their mother about what was cooked, and regretting it later. All of this can be avoided by making mealtimes positive and stress-free.

If your child doesn't always eat what is given to them, refrain from labelling them as a 'picky' or 'fussy' eater. Treat your child with the same respect you'd give an adult who is particular about their eating habits.

Use Creativity and Include the Child in the Preparations

Encourage exploration of new foods without coercion by involving your child in food preparation activities, such as washing vegetables or setting the table. Introduce unfamiliar food gradually, understanding that your child may be hesitant due to the texture, smell or appearance. Offer small portions, alongside familiar favourites. If you are patient, you may see their tastes evolve. Keep mealtimes fun by being creative with food presentation, such as cutting sandwiches into fun shapes or arranging veggies into a rainbow. Anagha's twins still remember the 'sun' their grandmother used to make out of rice, corn and carrot sticks. In Indian families usually kids don't get to help the mother because of grandparents, extended family members or house help being present. But if this is done, it can help the child develop healthy curiosity around food and food preparations.

Avoid Frequent Snacking and Bribing

When you set clear expectations around eating habits by trusting your child's hunger cues and sticking to a consistent meal schedule, it really makes life simpler for you. Limit grazing between meals to ensure they're hungry when it's time to eat and encourage them to try at least one bite of new foods. Avoid giving sweets to children as bribes. For example, it is not good to make such promises, 'If you eat your lunch, you will get an ice cream.' Treat sweets as any other food, instead of a reward or a special treat.

You can also influence them with your own behaviour. Model healthy eating habits by enjoying a variety of food. Show appreciation for meals by complimenting the cook and expressing gratitude for the food prepared.

Encourage Eating by Themselves and Be Okay with the Mess!

Promote independence by allowing your child to practise using utensils from a young age and give them a comfortable place to sit, such as a booster seat or high chair. This will also involve them in family meals. Use cutlery that is child friendly and let them make a mess. It might seem a lot of effort to clean up later, but this teaches them the much required independence around food. Very soon they will learn to eat without the mess.

Avoid Using Gadgets and Have Positive Conversations

Make it a point to sit together, turn off the TV and put away distractions such as phones. This creates an enjoyable atmosphere that your child will look forward to. Start with bite-sized portions and keep the focus of the meal on pleasant conversations rather than solely on the food.

Avoid Power Struggles and Provide Choices!

Respect your child's preferences by avoiding power struggles since it distracts from food and brings in blame, complaints and negativity. If they dislike certain foods, like eggplant or okra, offer alternatives that they enjoy, to keep mealtimes stress-free. Indian meals and their diversity are often difficult for children to adapt to easily and eating some foods is a challenge for small kids. The gravies can be all mixed up, making them look messy. Many kids don't like it. Additionally, honour their preferences regarding how food is served. If they don't like different things on the plate mixing or touching, use bowls or plates with compartments. It is ok for them to eat chapatti separately and sabzi separately or have plain rice and then daal later on. Eventually as they grow older, they always learn how to eat it the right way!

4. My child hates going to preschool. What can I do?

Transitioning to preschool can be a challenging time for both you and your child, especially if they express reluctance or anxiety about attending. It is natural for children to feel anxious about leaving the comfort of their home and familiar faces. However, also check your own feelings about sending your child to school. Your child will pick up on your energy and body language, so approach the topic with enthusiasm and positivity.

Understand Their Perspective

Before trying to convince your child how fun school can be or comparing their feelings to those of other children, take the time to understand why they are reluctant. They may be anxious about leaving you, overwhelmed by the rules and routines of preschool, or disconnected due to a recent lack of quality time together.

While choosing the preschool, check in your social circle and ask them about their experience. Preschoolers do not require fancy facilities such as expensive furniture or supplies, libraries, swimming pools etc. The most important factors in choosing a school should be the teacher and a stimulating and safe (physically and emotionally) learning environment.

Build Familiarity

Visit the preschool together before their first day to familiarize your child with the environment, teachers and classmates. Engage your child in playful conversations about school, using stuffed animals or role-play, to make the experience more familiar and less intimidating before they actually start attending school.

Is Your Child Ready for Preschool?

Most children are ready for preschool between the age of 2.5 and 3.5.
To decide whether your child is ready for preschool, use the checklist below:

- [ ] My child can separate from a parent or caregiver without excessive distress.
- [ ] My child is potty-trained.
- [ ] My child can wash their hands independently.
- [ ] My child can manage basic clothing (e.g., putting on and taking off shoes).
- [ ] My child can hold and use a pencil or crayon.
- [ ] My child shows interest in playing with other children.
- [ ] My child can follow simple instructions (e.g., 'Put the toy away').
- [ ] My child can ask for help if needed.
- [ ] My child does not need afternoon naps. (Not all preschools have nap times.)

Figure 18: Preschool Readiness Checklist

Independence

Encourage independence by practising simple tasks, such as getting dressed and packing their backpack. Establishing a consistent routine at home can also provide a sense of security and predictability for your child.

Once they are used to the idea of going to preschool, talk about all the fun activities, new friends and interesting learning

☑ Important Considerations for Choosing a Preschool

	YES	NO
Is the preschool licensed?	☐	☐
Does it have safe and clean surroundings?	☐	☐
How far is the school from your home? Are you comfortable with the commute?		
Is transportation provided?	☐	☐
What is the school policy if the child gets sick at school? Will you be able to pick the child up easily?	☐	☐
Is the building/campus secure? (Compound wall, security guards, pick-up/drop off policies)	☐	☐
Are the teachers trained and qualified?	☐	☐
What are the teaching methods?		
What is the daily routine?		
Is there an outdoor play area?	☐	☐
How many children will be there in your child's class? How many adults will be in the class in addition to the teacher? (e.g. assistant teacher or helper)		

Request to observe a class:

	YES	NO
Is the teacher interacting with the students with kindness, respect and understanding?	☐	☐
Are children engaged in purposeful activities?	☐	☐
What kind of learning materials are provided?		
How are meltdowns being handled?		

Figure 19: Considerations for Choosing a Preschool

opportunities. Avoid pressuring or comparing your child to others; instead, focus on their individual interests and needs.

If you can, stay connected with your child's teacher and be informed about their progress and concerns. Reassure your child that you're always there for them, ready to listen, support and provide comfort whenever they need it.

If your child continues to struggle with preschool attendance, consider the following additional tips:

- Ensure you have chosen the right school that aligns with your values and child's needs, where children are encouraged to play freely and have space for physical activity and naptime.
- When dropping off your child at preschool, do so quickly and confidently, avoiding prolonged goodbyes that may increase their anxiety.
- Connect with other parents and arrange playdates with classmates to provide your child with familiar faces and support in the school environment.
- If permitted, keep a family photo in the classroom to provide your child with a sense of connection and comfort during their time at preschool.

Harnessing the Power of Subconscious Mind

You can even use this method of guided imagery and autosuggestions that we recommend to our clients. Many have benefitted from this method:

While the child is half-asleep, whisper a few positive sentences in their ears about going to school, such as, 'Aarya loves going to school', 'Aarya goes to school happily' or 'Aarya gets ready for school on time'. Just pick one sentence for one problem you are trying to address and repeat it softly, ten to fifteen times, in the child's ears before she goes into deep sleep. Repeat them once again in the morning, just before the child fully wakes up. Keep doing this for a few weeks, and you may find your child's behaviour changing! This has worked for our children and for many others in activities such as bathing, going to school and brushing their teeth. For more information on this technique and its applications please see Chapter 8.

Riri has personally used it for her son to help him get to bathe every day without fuss and her sister used it to help her child go to kindergarten without crying. It can also be used to help children memorize their poems or tables—just record it in their voice, let them listen to it playing all night in the background and let them read it once again in morning after waking up.

5. My child does not sleep through the night. What should I do?

Night-time can present its own challenges. Preschoolers have active imaginations. They may refuse to go to bed because of a fear of the dark or imagined scary things. A dim night light can help quell those fears. They might be overstimulated and not yet ready to go to bed. It would be best to avoid high-energy activities before bed. Sometimes, if the child is not getting sufficient physical activity during the day, he may not feel tired. Ensure that the child gets enough exercise. Establish a calming bedtime routine involving a bath, story time and calming music.

Establish a bedtime routine. Consistency is key. Create a calming routine before bedtime to signal to your toddler that it's time to wind down and prepare for sleep. This could include activities such as reading a book, taking a warm bath or listening to calming music. Until Anagha's twins were six years old, they followed a predictable bedtime routine: brushing their teeth, taking a warm bath, listening to calming music while getting

Strategies for Addressing Nighttime Woes

1. **Create a conducive sleep environment:** Ensure that the bedroom your child is sleeping in is comfortable, quiet, and dark. Consider using blackout curtains to block out any light that might be disturbing their sleep, such as street lights or car headlights.

2. **Set a fixed sleep time:** Try to establish a consistent bedtime and wake-up time for your toddler, even on weekends. This helps regulate their internal clock and can improve overall sleep quality.

3. **Limit screen time:** Avoid exposing your toddler to screens (TV, tablets, smartphones) close to bedtime, as the blue light emitted can interfere with their ability to fall asleep.

4. **Encourage physical activity during the day:** Make sure your child is getting plenty of opportunities to burn off energy. Whether it's a trip to the park, or dancing to their favourite songs indoors, keeping them active during the day will tire them out to sleep better at night.

5. **Encourage independent sleep skills:** Teach your toddler to fall asleep on their own without relying on you to soothe them. This might involve gradually reducing your presence at bedtime. If your child needs reassurance when they wake up in the night, provide them with a comforting object to help them feel safe. This could be a special blanket, a favourite stuffed animal or your scarf or T-shirt.

6 **Avoid giving them sugary food or drinks** 3-4 hours before bedtime. Sugar can make them hyperactive.

7 **Address any underlying issues**: If your toddler is experiencing discomfort or other issues that are disrupting their sleep, such as teething or a cold, address these first. The regular routine might get affected but this is a rare exception when it is okay to go off-schedule. It is important to make sure they feel better first.

8 **Do not try to scare your child** with stories of how ghosts, witches, police officers will visit them if they don't sleep. Sometimes these fears stick with them long after they have become adults.

Figure 20: Strategies for Handling Night-time Woes

a massage from their father, story time and finally, prayer to express gratitude before switching off the lights. When they started preschool, they added preparation for the next day, such as picking out clothes and putting school library books in their bags, after taking a bath. These habits helped as they started going to elementary school.

Changing sleep habits takes time, so be patient and stick to your chosen approach consistently.

6. What are some ways to handle aggressive behaviour such as hitting, biting or throwing things?

Toddlers usually act out aggressively when they are frustrated. Their brains are still developing, and the emotional centres responsible for the freeze/flight/fight response are well-developed.

On the other hand, the frontal lobes—the seat of impulse control and emotional regulation—are still a work in progress.

Limited Verbal Skills

With their limited verbal skills, physical expression becomes their primary mode of communication when they are overwhelmed or frustrated. It is not easy to experience, but as parents, we need to lower our expectations that they will behave like rational, calm adults. They haven't yet learnt emotional regulation, so guiding them with patience and understanding will shift the focus to supporting their development rather than expecting perfection.

Helping Them Verbalize

Each time your toddler acts out aggressively, gently intervene to stop the behaviour without resorting to yelling or threats. Verbalize their emotions and explain why their actions are not acceptable, all while maintaining a gentle, reassuring tone. For example, if your toddler hits you, calmly hold their hand and say, 'I see you're upset, but I won't let you hurt me. Let's find another way to show your feelings.'

Understanding Triggers

Take a moment to consider what might be triggering their frustration. Could it be hunger, fatigue, overstimulation or a desire for attention? Are they feeling left out? Is their behaviour a response to changes in their environment or routine? By empathizing with their perspective and understanding what has caused the aggression, you can either change the situation or

Strategies for Managing Aggressive Behaviour

1. **Model positive behaviour:** Toddlers learn by observing adults and older children. Show them healthy ways of managing frustration such as taking a few deep breaths, drinking a glass of water, and using words to express their feelings. Demonstrate patience when faced with challenges.

2. **Use simple language:** Teach them simple words like "mad," "sad," or "angry" to express how they're feeling. Encourage them to use these words when they're upset.

3. **Offer validation and empathy:** Say things like, "I see that you're feeling frustrated because you can't find your toy. That must be tough. Shall we look for it together?'" This helps toddlers feel understood and supported.

4. **Provide alternative outlets:** Encourage activities like stomping their feet, squeezing a stress ball, or engaging in physical play to help them release pent-up energy and tension.

5. **Encourage problem-solving:** Encourage them to think about what will make them feel better or solve the problem. Praise their effort and persistence, even if they don't find an immediate solution.

6. **Practise deep breathing**: Encourage them to take slow, deep breaths, in through their nose and out through their mouth to help them relax and regain control of their emotions.

7 **Use play to teach:** Use dolls or stuffed animals to enact scenarios where characters feel frustrated and demonstrate how to handle the situation calmly and respectfully.

8 **Be patient and supportive:** Be patient with them as they learn, and offer plenty of support and encouragement along the way. Celebrate their progress, no matter how small, and continue to reinforce positive behaviour.

Figure 21: Strategies for Managing Aggressive Behaviours

teach them how to navigate it. For instance, if your toddler is throwing toys, you might say, 'I see you're upset because you can't build the tower. Let's take a break and try again later.'

Remember, you cannot control your child's behaviour, but you can help them learn and grow. Instead of forcing them to do whatever caused the outburst, such as asking them to share their toys, focus on redirecting their attention. Offer an alternative activity or toy to diffuse the situation.

Teaching toddlers acceptable ways of expressing frustration is essential for their emotional development and social interactions. Understanding and addressing aggressive behaviour in toddlers requires patience, empathy and a willingness to meet your child where they are developmentally.

7. How can I help my child adjust to changes, such as starting a new school or welcoming a new sibling?

These are big events in a child's life, and you should be aware that they may experience a range of emotions, including excitement, anxiety or jealousy. Give them a chance to express these feelings by talking about them or reading books on the topic. Prepare them for what's to come by using simple language and age-appropriate explanations.

For example, 'Starting at a school can feel a bit scary, and it's okay to feel that way. I feel nervous when I start new things too.'

'I heard that they have a really cool playground at your new school! You'll get to run, jump and play games with your new friends. How fun is that?'

Concerning the arrival of the new baby, you can say 'You know how Mommy's belly is getting bigger? That's because there's a baby growing inside. I can see that you are excited, and also a little nervous about having a new brother or sister. When the baby comes, things will be a little different around here. The new baby will need a lot of attention and care, but we'll still play together every day.'

To get them excited, you should involve them in preparing for the change, such as choosing a special backpack or lunchbox for preschool or involve them in setting up the baby's crib. This gives them a sense of control and ownership over the changes.

While change is inevitable, try to maintain consistency in other areas of your child's life. Stick to regular routines and schedules as much as possible. Just as you talk to them to prepare them for the change, also use that time to reassure them that certain things will stay the same, 'At school, your teacher will have lots of fun things for you to do! You'll get to play, eat yummy snacks, and listen to stories. You'll even have a nap, just like at home. And guess what? After school, we'll go to the park, like we always do!' You could also try saying, 'Remember when you were a baby and we cuddled together? We'll get to do that with the new baby too! It will be so much fun to play together as a family.'

Listen to how they react and understand if they have any concerns. Let them know that you're there for them. Offer plenty of hugs, cuddles and quality time together to strengthen your bond. These conversations will help you later as well, when they actually go through the change. If your child hasn't been able to verbalize their feelings, you can offer them the chance to express their feelings through art or play too.

8. My child touches their own or other children's private parts. What should I do to stop this inappropriate behaviour?

It's essential to approach these situations with an understanding and awareness of what constitutes normal behaviour in young children, particularly those between the ages of three and six years. At this age, it's not uncommon for children to exhibit behaviour that may seem sexually motivated but is actually rooted in curiosity and exploration of their bodies. Children may comment on differences they observe, such as referring to genitalia as 'tails' or noting variations in appearance.

When you observe such behaviour in your child, it's crucial not to overreact or respond with alarm. Avoid yelling, shouting or forcefully stopping them. Stay calm and redirect their attention to another activity, such as playing with toys or engaging in creative play. Avoid threatening or shaming them or calling them 'dirty child'—this will only make them fearful and self-conscious about their body and sexuality.

Refrain from shaming or labelling your child as 'bad.' Negative reinforcement can lead to self-doubt and a negative self-image. Use opportunities to educate your child about body parts, appropriate touch and personal boundaries in a gentle and age-appropriate manner. This is crucial for their safety and well-being. Initiate age-appropriate conversations about body parts, emphasizing the importance of respecting personal boundaries. Engage in role-playing scenarios with your child to teach them about 'good touch' and 'bad touch,' empowering them to recognize and assert their boundaries. Encourage open communication within the family and create a supportive environment where your child feels comfortable expressing concerns or discomfort.

While a lot of childhood sexual behaviour is normal and harmless, some behaviour may indicate potential abuse. Watch out for sudden changes, such as increased aggression, withdrawal or reluctance to participate in certain activities. Also, observe if they display any discomfort or distress when discussing certain individuals or situations. Physically, all parents should watch out for unexplained injuries, discomfort or pain in the genital area.

A government-sponsored survey conducted in India in 2007 across thirteen Indian states reported the prevalence of Child Sexual Abuse (CSA) as alarmingly high, with a rate of 53 per cent.[5] These findings underscore the urgent need for awareness and proactive measures to protect children from abuse and exploitation. It's essential to recognize that boys are also at risk of sexual abuse, and perpetrators are often individuals, both men and women, known to the child or in positions of trust and responsibility. Many of our therapy clients have experienced sexual abuse from family members, their parents' friends, tutors or household help. Some of them did not tell their parents because they thought they would not be believed; even if they did tell, no action was taken by the parents to protect them from future abuse. Some were too small to understand what was happening to them.

To protect your child, never let them sleep alone with older relatives. Before they visit relatives, especially for holidays or events, make sure a trusted adult will be supervising them. Most importantly, create a safe space where your child feels comfortable telling you if anything inappropriate happens.

9. We live in a joint family. I don't believe in punishments. However, my in-laws think I am 'too soft' on my child. How should I handle this situation?

It's unrealistic to expect everyone in a joint family to do everything the same way. However, if your in-laws' advice clashes with positive parenting principles, have an open and honest talk with them. Respecting elders is important in our culture, but it's also crucial to set boundaries about parenting decisions. You can politely, but firmly, assert your role as the primary caregiver and the decisions that are best for your child.

When you are trying to do your best, a comment on your parenting style can seem unfair and hurtful. Do not view it as a personal attack on you. It's just a difference of opinion and perspective. Be respectful, yet clear and confident, in your approach. Set aside a time when you are relaxed and calm. Have a conversation with your in-laws when your child is not present.

First, thank them for everything they do for your child, such as dropping them off at school/bus stop, picking them up from the bus stop, taking them to the park, buying fruits/vegetables for the household etc. Let them know you really appreciate their wisdom and experience as parents. Then, ask about their concerns with your parenting style: 'What are you worried about? What would you do differently?' If they suggest punishing or shouting to get things done, explain, 'Punishments can work in the short term, but I've chosen a more positive parenting approach for a reason.'

'I understand that my approach might seem too lenient or permissive to you, but I'm not letting him do whatever he wants. You might think I spend too much time talking to him when a quick spanking could do the job, but I don't want him to be just obedient. I want him to grow up to be confident and compassionate, able to think for himself. Times have changed, and as he grows up, he'll face more external pressures. I want to create a safe space for him to come back to, where he can talk to me freely about anything without fearing punishment. I wish to build a strong connection with him based on mutual respect.'

Open and Honest Communication Helps

Invite your in-laws to be a part of your positive parenting approach by saying, 'I'd love for you to be involved in this too. Your support means a lot to us and to the kids. Maybe I can share some of the techniques we're using and see how they work when you're with them. I am still setting boundaries and expecting good behaviour. We're just approaching it in a way that helps him understand and respect those boundaries.'

By communicating in this way, you show respect for the grandparent's experience while also asserting your own informed choices in parenting. This approach may foster understanding and, possibly, help gain their support for your parenting style.

If it does not, that's okay, too. Accept that you cannot change or control other people's behaviour. Protect your children from outright emotional or physical abuse. Ignore the advice you don't believe in and move on. Prioritize your own well-being. Dealing with family conflicts can be emotionally draining, so it's important for you to take care of yourself, seek support when needed and carve out time for enjoyable activities.

Overindulgent Grandparents

Grandparents often love to indulge and pamper their grandchildren, especially because they did not do so with their children as they were busy being 'parents' and focusing on discipline and training. Riri's in-laws, who used to be quite strict as parents, were completely lenient with the grandkids, pampering them with cartons of ice cream and chocolates, during the one month the kids spent with them. However, long after their demise, now that the kids are adults, they fondly remember all those indulgences with love and affection. Riri recalls that when she would visit her grandfather, she would bully him into buying her an ice cream every day—something she could never get away with her parents! Those fond, loving memories remain with her. While kids need the firm upbringing of parents, they also deserve the unconditional love of grandparents, and the fear that it spoils them may not be true. Children learn to experience both types of love and it helps them navigate their adult life better—feeling loved and supported unconditionally.

Many times, grandparents become the buffering adult for the child who feels abused or neglected by the parents, and their loss becomes unbearable. Therefore, it is good for children to experience that kind of love as well, along with the parents' firm and authoritative love.

Self-Reflection for Parents

1. Who took care of you in the first six years of your life? Did you feel safe and loved?
2. What is your earliest positive memory? How old were you? Where were you? Who was there with you? What happened? How did you feel? How did it affect how you behaved as you grew up?
3. What is your earliest negative memory? How old were you? Where were you? Who was there with you? What happened? How did you feel? How did it affect how you behaved as you grew up?
4. What did your parents/other family members say about you as a child? Did they describe you as happy, cranky, curious, quiet, troublemaker etc.? How did those labels affect you or continue to affect you?
5. How did your parents discipline you when you were young? What impact did it have on your childhood and how do you feel it affects your role as a parent now?
6. Did you enjoy going to kindergarten? Why or why not?
7. Choose a difficult experience from your childhood. Close your eyes and picture yourself at that age. What did that child need? Give the child the support he needed at the time. Looking back, what did that child not know or understand, that you understand today?

6

The Middle Childhood Years: 7 to 12

> 'Discipline is helping a child solve a problem. Punishment is making a child suffer for having a problem. To raise problem solvers, focus on solutions, not retribution.'
>
> —L.R. Knost, from *Gentle Parenting*

Specific Traits and General Challenges

The years between seven and twelve are marked by a blend of childhood and adolescence. This stage is characterized by a unique combination of stability and change. Children of this age are starting to think in new ways, understand the world around them better and learn how to control their emotions. This stage is a fertile ground for growth and development.

The Athletic Years: Physical Development

Physical growth is steady during these years, with improvements in co-ordination, strength and endurance. Children become more capable of participating in organized sports and physical activities. These physical advancements contribute to increased self-esteem and confidence.

Puzzles to Possibilities: Cognitive Development

Between the ages of seven and twelve, the brain is like a nascent garden. It is growing and changing rapidly. The connections between the different parts of the brain are getting stronger, helping children think faster and learn new things. It's like building new paths in the garden. Just like plants need sunlight and water to grow, your child's brain needs experiences to grow. The more they learn and play, the stronger their brain becomes. This is why it's important to give them lots of opportunities to explore, learn and have fun. The more you plant in your garden, the more beautiful the flowers will be.

Overall, seven- to twelve-year-olds become significantly better at problem-solving. They begin exploring their interests and get engrossed in certain hobbies or things. They are also able to figure out puzzles, understand rules and think about things in different ways. Their ability to think abstractly, solve problems and understand cause-and-effect relationships expands rapidly. While they still rely on concrete experiences, they begin to grasp hypothetical concepts. They get better at remembering things and applying their skills. This newfound cognitive ability often manifests in a strong desire for independence and a tendency to question authority.

Tweens Ups and Downs: Emotional Development

While still prone to emotional outbursts, seven- to twelve-year-olds are generally more emotionally stable than younger children are. They develop a better understanding of their own emotions and can begin to empathize with others. They understand people's expressions and emotions better and start to see things from other points of view. However, they also experience more self-awareness, which can lead to mood swings and sensitivity.

Finding Their Tribe: Social Development

Children in this age group are increasingly influenced by their peers. Even though they are starting to figure out who they are, they may want to copy their friends' behaviour. They form strong friendships and begin to navigate social complexities. Co-operation, competition and conflict resolution become essential skills. They also develop a stronger sense of right and wrong and are more aware of social expectations.

Parenting Tips for Handling Specific Challenges

1. I always have to nag my child to complete the homework. What can I do so my child develops good study habits?

If your house is echoing with the daily battle cry of 'Do your homework!' you're not alone. Many parents find themselves nagging their children to complete their homework. Imagine homework time not as a chore that you must dictate, but a collaborative effort.

Owning Their Schedules

The first step to achieving this is creating a sense of ownership. Sit down with your child and discuss their schedule. What activities do they have planned? When do they feel most alert and focused? Together, co-create a homework routine that fits in seamlessly with the rest of their schedule, so they don't feel like they're missing out on the things they actually want to do. This involvement fosters a sense of control and responsibility, making them more invested in the process. Talk to them and agree on a time slot for homework completion. Keep in mind that children are often tired right after school, so give them some time to unwind and have a healthy snack. They'll concentrate better with some downtime and replenished energy.

Decoding the Homework Drama

It is also important to determine the root cause of your child's resistance. Does your child find homework boring? Or is it a simple conflict of desires? Homework competes with playtime, hobbies and screen time. Instead of giving a lecture on the importance of homework, let them know you understand the appeal of those other activities. Ask them what they'd rather be doing and create a list of fun things they can do before or after completing their homework. Show genuine interest in what they learn through their homework, letting them see that you value the process of acquiring knowledge, not just completing tasks.

It could also be that your child finds homework overwhelming. Faced with a mountain of math problems or a large project, your child might shut down. If you think your child is overwhelmed by the workload, help them plan the homework. Break bigger assignments into smaller, more manageable tasks. Work with them to create a strategy, visualizing progress piece by piece, instead of feeling crushed by the whole workload.

Frequent Breaks Help

Some children lose concentration easily. In such cases, schedule short breaks every twenty minutes to allow them to recharge. Encourage them to get up and move around during these breaks. Spot jogging, skipping, jumping jacks or even a few stretches can work wonders in refreshing their minds and boosting focus for the next round of studying. Doing their favourite activities in the break time (playing, doing art, listening to music or dancing, scribbling or doodling, making a quick snack) can help them feel re-energized and charged up to go back to studies again.

Teach Prioritizing

Children in this age group are still learning how to manage time effectively. Teach them how to prioritize tasks. Ask them to estimate how long each assignment will take, then create a schedule that allocates sufficient time for each task. This helps them take charge of their work and feel great when they finish things and mark them as done.

Create a Conducive Environment

Parents forget to consider that the home environment might be stopping their child from getting the homework done. At one of our workshops, when a participant asked her child why he does not do his homework, he said that it was because he did not have a place to study. They lived in a joint family, and space was a constraint. When she created a small study corner for him, with her child's help, homework no longer seemed like such a struggle. Constant fights between parents, stress in joint family dynamics etc. can also be quite distracting for the child.

A quiet area, free from distractions such as televisions and toys, allows children to focus on the task. Schedule homework time in the same place every day, preferably after a snack or before screen time. This routine helps them settle in and focus more readily. Consistency is key here.

Until elementary school, Anagha's children would do their homework at the dining table. It worked well for them because she could easily help them, if needed, while preparing dinner. When they were older and went to middle school, her daughter would study in her room, while her son would study in the living room with the TV playing in the background. Growing up, Anagha, too, preferred to have a quiet place to study like her daughter. Initially, she insisted that her son should turn the TV off. However, he did not think it was necessary. He told her that he didn't actually watch what was playing but the background noise helped him focus. He would study in his room only when he wanted to do some reading. She decided not to insist and the system seemed to work for him. He submitted good work on time. Each child is different. It is better not to impose your ideas about how the work should be done. Let them figure out what works for them.

Let them know when you will be available to help them. When they encounter challenges, offer help without giving them all the answers. Guide them through finding solutions on their own, fostering their problem-solving skills. This empowers them to think critically and build confidence in their abilities.

Effort Over Outcomes

Instead of nagging your child about missed work, notice their effort, focus and responsible behaviour. Did they tackle a difficult math problem without giving up? Did they stay focused for their entire study session? Acknowledge their persistence. Positive reinforcement will encourage them to stay enthusiastic about learning.

Learning from Consequences

Even after the child agrees to a system, they may not always follow it. Sometimes, letting your child experience the natural consequences of not doing their homework can be a powerful motivator. Talk to the teacher and let them know you are giving your child more ownership for their homework. The earlier children take responsibility for their homework, the easier it is when they are older. Do not make excuses for the child or write dishonest notes in the child's diary to protect your child from consequences of not doing homework. Let the child face whatever the teacher chooses to do in the matter. This might mean a lower grade or having to complete the work in school. This will help the child learn accountability and responsibility.

2. My child is bullied at school. How can I handle this?

When your child confides in you about being bullied, don't say, 'Just ignore them!' or 'You are such a crybaby. Stand up for yourself!' or 'Why can't you just ask them to stop?' It took a lot of courage for them to share this with you. They might be feeling helpless or ashamed. So, be supportive and find out what exactly is happening. It could be direct bullying, wherein they're facing physical or verbal aggression. It could also be indirect bullying and they're at the receiving end of rumours or isolation.

Some children do not even tell their parents that they are being bullied for fear of being seen as weak or because they feel that no one would believe or support them. Watch out for signs, such as torn or dirty clothes, refusal to go to school, making up excuses for skipping school or not taking the school bus. Research has shown that victims of bullying have higher chances of psychosomatic symptoms.[1] So, if your child unexpectedly starts experiencing symptoms such as headaches, stomach aches, bed wetting, sleep problems, tiredness or depression, try to ask them if they are facing any difficulties at school. Seek help from a counsellor if you are unable to communicate with the child.

When Anagha's niece was in second grade, her sister once noticed shoe marks on her skirt as she got off the school bus. When her sister asked her niece what had happened, she was reluctant to tell her at first. Her sister told her, 'I just want to know if it was an accident or if someone is deliberately bothering you so we can stop that from happening.' Her niece then mentioned that a boy, a couple of years older than her, would walk on the seats and step over her. He was much bigger, so her niece was scared to say anything.

Anagha's sister acknowledged that standing up to a bigger person can be intimidating. However, she assured her that she would help her. She taught her niece how to be assertive and made her practise saying, 'Stop jumping on the seats. Don't step on me. Stop it!' She told her to inform the bus conductor or some other adult or come back to Anagha's sister if he continued to behave that way. She also decided to let the boy's mother know what was happening and had a chat with her.

Bullying usually starts as verbal aggression. If the victim is scared and does not stand up for themselves, they become an easy target for the bully. If you realize that your child is being bullied, do not teach them to be abusive (verbally or physically) towards the bully. Instead, teach them how to talk assertively. Role-play the situation. Let the child play the role of the bully, while you become the child. Demonstrate what actions the child can take.

Find out when and where bullying happens. Talk to them about how they can avoid being alone in those situations. Being with a friend or having teachers present can make situations significantly safer. Reassure your child that it is not shameful to feel scared and walk away from someone who is trying to bully them.

Depending on the situation, you may need to get involved and inform teachers or the school principal about the bullying incidents. Keep a record of events based on what your child has told you. Let your child know that they are not alone in this and that you will always support them. Sometimes, children turn into bullies when they themselves are being bullied or when they are feeling disconnected, unseen or insecure. Instead of punishing them, it is important for adults to figure out how to help them too.

3. My eleven-year-old complains of being excluded by her friends. How can I teach her to handle this situation and not be too affected?

This question was posed to us by a mother who came to Wellness Space for a consultation. She was frustrated that, no matter what she said, it made the situation worse. Her daughter had found out through Instagram that her friends had hung out at a friend's house without her. The sting of social exclusion can be sharp at any age, but it can feel particularly brutal for an eleven-year-old navigating the complex world of friendships. Nowadays, it's very common for children to find out that they are excluded from an activity through social media. It's hard to see your child hurting, so it's natural to want to jump in and fix things. However, the most effective approach is one that validates their feelings while empowering them to navigate the situation themselves.

In our client's case, the first step was to create a safe space for her daughter to express her emotions. We spoke about resisting the urge to minimize her feelings. Phrases like 'don't worry about it' or 'they probably forgot' might come from a place of good intentions, but they can shut down communication and leave the child feeling unheard. Instead, acknowledge the hurt they're experiencing. A simple, empathetic statement like, 'That must feel awful to see your friends having fun without you. I can understand how left out and hurt you must be feeling,' can go a long way in forming trust.

After validating her feelings, we recommended that the mother give her daughter space to vent. Letting her express her frustration without interrupting or offering unsolicited advice would actually allow her to process her emotions and gain clarity on what she's feeling.

Following this, we recommended giving the daughter space to vent, allowing her to process her emotions without interruption or unsolicited advice. Once she had expressed her feelings, the conversation should gently shift towards exploring options. Rather than offering immediate solutions like, 'You should call them and ask why you weren't invited,' encourage her to think for herself with open-ended questions: 'What do you think you might like to do about this?' or 'Would you be comfortable talking to them about how you felt?'

We guided our client to help her daughter, if she chose to speak to her friends, towards honest but kind communication. Suggesting something like, 'You could tell them you were a little hurt when you saw the pictures because you enjoy spending time with them and wish you had been invited,' encourages a focus on feelings over accusatory language like, 'Why didn't you invite me?'

Sometimes, the fear of the unknown can be paralyzing. To build her daughter's confidence, we suggested brainstroming potential oucomes together. Ask, 'What's the worst thing that could happen if you talk to them?' Exploring anxieties and identifying realistic possibilities can help her feel more prepared.

While talking to her friends was one option, we stressed the importance of reminding the daughter that there were other ways to cope. Encouraging her to spend time with friends who valued her and to organize activities with them could be helpful. Distraction and self-care can also be powerful tools in managing hurt feelings.

It's important to manage expectations. The hurt might not disappear overnight. Give her time to process emotions and don't pressure her to 'move on' before she is ready. Such incidents, though painful, can be a valuable learning experience. As your children navigate friendship, there may be times when they feel excluded. By fostering open communication and offering them the tools to handle social challenges constructively, you're helping them build resilience and develop healthy coping mechanisms for the future. This incident may also make them think about what kind of friends they want, while helping develop empathy, and prevent them from excluding others.

Your role is to be a supportive sounding board, not a problem fixer.

4. My child keeps lying to me. How should I encourage honesty?

We're sure it's happened to you. You ask, '*Did you finish your homework?*' only to be met with a confident 'Yes!', followed by the discovery of a half-completed worksheet later. While this can be frustrating, it's important to understand that lying is a developmental stage most children go through. The key lies not in punishment, but in fostering an environment that encourages honesty.

Before addressing the lie itself, delve deeper. Why might your child be dishonest? Here are some common reasons and how to handle them:

i. **Fear of Punishment:** If your child feels they will get in trouble for telling the truth, lying becomes a defence mechanism. Consider your own reaction when you discover a lie. Do you immediately jump to anger or blame? This could shut down communication and discourage honesty. Instead of immediate reprimands, ask questions and try to understand why they lied. Create a safe space where your child feels emotionally and physically safe to share anything with you. Acknowledge and praise instances when your child tells the truth, even if it's difficult for them. 'I am glad that you told me what happened. It takes courage to tell the truth.' Instead of punishment, let them experience natural consequences.

ii. **Avoiding Embarrassment:** Lies can shield them from vulnerability. Maybe they are embarrassed about their poor grades. To encourage honesty, let children know that it is not okay to lie just to get out of a difficult situation. Let them know that it can be embarrassing to get a poor grade, but you are willing to work together to sort things out. Do not label your child a 'liar' or a 'cheater'. If you know that your child is lying to you, instead of trying to get a 'confession' out of them, let them know you are aware of the situation, and are willing to support them to improve the situation.

iii. **Seeking Something:** Maybe they lied about how they just started playing an online game, when, in fact, they have been playing for a while. If you already know that they have been playing for a while, do not ask yes/no questions like 'have you been playing for a long time?' just to catch them telling a lie. Instead, state what you have noticed and follow up with a request. 'I noticed you have been playing for an hour. Looks like a super exciting game.' Have a little chat about the game and remind them about the agreement. 'You had agreed to play for thirty minutes. You can certainly play again tomorrow. Now it's time for homework.'

iv. **Preserving Harmony:** Sometimes, children lie to avoid hurting someone's feelings. As children get older, they sometimes tell 'social lies' or 'white lies'. They might praise a friend's new outfit or a gift they received, saying it looks good, or they love it, even if they don't actually think so. This shows that your child has an emotional intelligence to think about how the other person might feel. He may have even learnt this behaviour from you, watching you tell little white lies to avoid conflict. For example, turning down a lunch invitation by saying you have alternate plans when you just want to relax at home on the weekend. The message he might get is that honesty is not good since it creates conflict. You might appreciate your child for being kind and not hurting the other person. However, this could lead to other kinds of lying. Dr Victoria Talwar, a professor at McGill University in Canada and a leading researcher on the development of lying in children, recommends that parents model and teach 'strategic honesty', which she describes as being honest without hurting others with the harsh truth.[2] For example, instead of saying the dress looks great on her friend, she could point out what she actually liked about it—perhaps, the colour or texture—and being truthful about how she feels that some other outfit suits her better.

v. **Lies to Protect Others:** While commendable, ensure that they understand alternative solutions. Maybe they lied about seeing their friend break a window while playing because they're afraid their friend will get in trouble. Help them understand that honesty is usually the best policy, and that they can always come to you for help in such situations.

One of the best things you can do in this situation is to lead by example. Be honest in your interactions with your child and with others. Don't ask your child to lie for you to get yourself out of a situation. Books and stories that explore the consequences of lying and the value of truthfulness can also be good teaching tools.

When you create a safe and trusting home, your child will find it easier to tell the truth.

5. Morning times during school days are chaotic as my child doesn't get up on time and gets late to catch his school bus and I always lose my cool. How do I handle this?

Before you have a conversation with your child, be clear about how you feel about the situation. Also, recognize how your actions might be contributing to the problem. Do you feel annoyed because you have to wake them up multiple times? Do you feel resentful that you have to waste your time in making alternate arrangements if they miss the school bus? If you have been dropping your child off, they have no incentive to wake up on time.

Find a time and place where both of you feel relaxed and calm. Share how you feel about the situation:

'When you don't wake up on time in the morning, I feel annoyed and anxious. Annoyed because breakfast prep is interrupted. Anxious because you might miss the school bus. I end up nagging. I don't want to do that. I need my mornings to be hassle-free and smooth.'

Make sure the child understands the problem you are facing. Ask, 'Can you tell me what you just heard me say?'

Even though you have not blamed your child, they might still become defensive. Let your child know that your intention is not to blame them, rather, you need their help to find a solution because the current situation is not working for you.

One of our clients made a list of all her morning tasks and shared it with her son. This helped him see all the tasks his mother had to do in the morning. It gave him some perspective about why she might feel stressed and annoyed.

Don't assume that your child is being late on purpose. Consider what is causing them to rush in the first place. Is it because he gets up late? Does he start homework late or keeping playing games in the night and end up sleeping late? Does he have to rush because he packs his backpack at the last minute and can't find things in the morning? Together, create a checklist of things that need to be done the night before.

Most children do not have a good sense of time. They might think it takes ten minutes to get ready when, in reality, it could be twenty minutes. They may lack organizational skills too. A routine chart or schedule goes a long way in such situations.

Example of Schedule after School

2:00-3:00 pm	Come home from school Have lunch/snack
3:00-4:00 pm	Free time/extracurricular activity/reading/hobby (including some screen time and physical activity like jumping jacks)
4:00-5:00 pm	Homework with breaks in between
5:00-6:00pm	Play with friends/physical activity
6:00-6:30 pm	Shower/change clothes
6:30-7:00 pm	Prepare for the next day
7:00-8:00 pm	Dinner prep (set the table etc.), Dinner with family
8:00-9:00 pm	Reading/chatting & gratitude practice
9:00 pm	Go to bed

Figure 22: Example of an After-School Schedule

Nightly Checklist & Morning Schedule

Nightly Checklist:

- [ ] Put dirty clothes in the hamper.
- [ ] Check the next day's class schedule. Pack notebooks textbooks accordingly.
- [ ] Pack sports/music/art supplies as necessary.
- [ ] Pencil box, ruler, calculator, etc.
- [ ] Pack homework assignments.
- [ ] Take out the lunch box.
- [ ] Wash and fill the water bottle.
- [ ] Polish shoes.
- [ ] Charge laptop.
- [ ] Set an alarm.
- [ ] Brush teeth.

Create a schedule for morning tasks:

Example:

6:00 am	Wake up, brush, shower, get dressed
6:30 am	Breakfast
6:50 am	Pack lunch box, water bottle
7:00 am	Leave for school

Figure 23: Example of Nightly Checklist and Morning Schedule

Use post-it's to write down activities that need to happen once they come home from school until they go to bed. Put time blocks along with the activity so they become more aware of how much time they actually need to complete each activity. Let the child decide the sequence of these activities and make a schedule. Create a weekly calendar if the activities are different for each day. Make a similar schedule for morning activities.

Invest in a standalone alarm clock and teach your child how to set it so that they can wake up on their own. Avoid overwhelming them by introducing all the changes together. Once they are to the checklist, introduce the alarm clock and so on. Building new habits takes time, so be patient. Gentle reminders like 'Please check your schedule' or 'what's next on your list?' can be helpful without resorting to nagging. As mornings become smoother, express your appreciation for their effort and co-operation.

6. I am tired of acting like a referee when my children fight. What is a better way of handling their fights?

It can be very annoying when children fight over trivial things and come to you complaining about what their sibling did or didn't do.

- *'She is not letting me use the computer. I want to play the game too!'*
- *'He took my ruler and now I can't find it!*
- *'I want the window seat!'*
- *'She got a bigger slice of the cake!'*

First, recognize the motivation behind the bickering. Sometimes, children fight to get your attention. A well-timed 'Look at me, I'm being wronged!' act can be more effective than quietly playing alone. To counter this, carve out individual time with each child daily. Even ten to fifteen minutes of focused attention on each child goes a long way. Additionally, acknowledge positive sibling interactions. When they share nicely or play co-operatively, let them know that you noticed. Say, 'I saw how well you were playing together. It was so nice and peaceful while I was reading.' This reinforces positive behaviour and reduces the need for attention-seeking squabbles.

When faced with minor disputes, resist the urge to jump in and solve the problem for them. Instead, coach them through conflict resolution. Try a simple, 'Hmm, I'm sure you two can work this out together,' to nudge them towards finding a solution. This fosters independence and problem-solving skills that will benefit them throughout life.

Establish clear ground rules for all siblings. 'No hitting,' 'No name-calling' and 'Use kind words' are essential starting points. Fairness doesn't equate to identical treatment. Older children may have more privileges, such as different bedtimes or their own phone. You can explain the difference based on age and needs. If the younger one complains, explain that the older child had similar rules at their age. Consistency, clear communication and setting expectations is key.

For more complex situations, role-playing can be a valuable tool. Enact scenarios to help them navigate tricky situations and practise communication skills using emotional honesty. Additionally, be mindful of power imbalances between siblings. A physically stronger older child can intimidate younger ones. If this is the case, ensure the younger child feels safe while expressing their needs and intervene decisively if things get physical. You may find yourself reiterating the 'No hitting' rule and separating them for a cool-down.

The best way to handle sibling fights is to stay calm and treat both children the same way. You might think you know who started the fight, but you will never know the whole story. If you end up taking one child's side and scolding the other, who you thought was the aggressor, the other would feel it's unfair. Many times, parents blame the older child and ask them to be more understanding. The younger sibling may develop a victim mentality if you take their side all the time. The older child may start resenting the younger sibling and make the situation worse. Whenever Anagha's seven-year-old twins would get into fights, she tended to take her daughter's side, which annoyed her son. He would become angrier at his sister. Anagha's daughter did not like her interference either because that made her feel as if she was not capable of defending herself. It was a lose-lose situation.

Luckily, in a parenting training at their school, she learned about the NVC (Non-Violent Communication) technique for conflict resolution mentioned earlier. She started using it when her kids were upset. Instead of starting to solve the problem, she started asking them to take a break and calm down first. 'I see that you are angry right now. Let's take a few deep breaths.' Once they were calm, she would ask each of them what happened without taking anyone's side. She let them talk about how they were feeling, what they needed and what they wished would happen. She encouraged them to listen without interrupting the other person. Asking them to imagine how their sibling might be feeling was also a way of teaching them empathy and helped resolve the conflict sooner. When both felt heard and understood, she asked them how they could solve the problem together. With consistent coaching and patience, her children started developing the skills to manage their conflicts independently.

Usually if this is handled by parents without taking sides, in most cases children grow out of it by the time they become adults and even joke about it. But if a parent has been particularly partial towards one child or always compared one to the other, this rivalry can result in hostility among the siblings even into adulthood.

Non-Violent Communication (NVC)
Developed by Marshall Rosenberg

When your needs are not met, such as having peaceful mornings, it is best to have a conversation with your child. The 'Non-Violent Communication' (NVC) model, developed by Marshall Rosenberg, helps in resolving conflicts with others. If you use it with children from a young age, you will be teaching them valuable communication skills to carry forward into adult life. This model has four parts:

- State what you observe/experience without judgment, criticism or blame.
- State how you **FEEL**.
- State what you **NEED**.
- Formulate a **REQUEST**, speaking kindly but clearly and firmly.

It all neatly fits into one sentence like this,

"When I see that ________, I feel ________ because my need for ________ is not being met. I would like you to ________."

Figure 24: Non-Violent Communication (NVC) Model

7. My child gets very upset when he loses a game. What can I do to encourage sportsmanship?

It's natural for your child to feel discouraged when they lose at anything because they're still learning how to handle disappointments. In such moments, you must first validate their feelings before dismissing, trivializing or mocking their feelings with statements such as 'there you go again. Don't be a crybaby.' Your instinct might be to give them tips to improve their game. However, refrain from giving advice. After all, you're not trying to improve their skill. You want them to have better sportsmanship.

If you watch sports on TV together, use it as an opportunity to discuss different players' attitudes and tell them great examples of sportsmanship. Explaining the different customs of sportsmanship, such as shaking hands before and after the game, being honest or showing kindness to an injured player on the opposite team will pique their interest and be a subtle nudge in the right direction. Discuss what fair play looks like. Remember that they are curious and eager to learn at this stage, so showing them lots of positive examples will also shape their mindset accordingly.

It is also necessary for you to show, through your actions, that you value sportsmanship over winning. If your first question to your child, when they come back from a game or from practice, is 'Who won?' you give them the message that winning is the most important thing.

Instead, ask open-ended questions such as, 'how was the game?' Ask how they are feeling about the outcome. Try to identify underlying feeling. 'Your team and you had practised so hard. It must be so disappointing!'

When your child has had the time to process the day, ask about their plans for the next game. Help them evaluate what needs to improve. Is it skills or the mindset? When Anagha's daughter started playing badminton in school, she would accompany her to practices and matches. The school had great coaches who emphasized sportsmanship at every session and laid out clear expectations. At one of her inter-school games, students were made referees as multiple matches were being played simultaneously, and there weren't enough adults available to referee. Halfway through the game, Anagha's daughter lost a few points in a row. Players from the opposite teams were making comments, and some wrong calls were made. She was losing her concentration and getting frustrated. During a break, she came to Anagha and told her how frustrated she was. Anagha agreed with her, saying, 'I saw that. That's unfair.' She, however, didn't try to give her advice or tell her to focus on her game. In the moment, all her daughter wanted was to be heard.

When her daughter went back on the court, she was a completely different person. Her face was calm. Her posture showed she was steady. Her concentration was back. She shut out all the noise around her and gave it her best. Anagha doesn't even remember whether her daughter lost or won that game. All she remembers is her internal shift—as if a switch had been flipped. They talked about it later. Her daughter said that she realized that she couldn't do anything about the unfair calls and the comments. All she could do was focus on what was in her control; her own strengths and finding her opponent's weaknesses, and just go for it. Her inner voice was telling her, 'You got this!' Anagha learnt that she had to trust her daughter to tap into her own inner strength.

When your child comes home disheartened, saying things like 'It's not a big deal' or 'You'll win next time' are least helpful. Instead, let them know it's okay to feel disappointed. 'I see you're feeling down. It's tough to lose a match, especially when you gave your all on the court.'

Then, shift the focus to their individual progress, 'Did you improve your net play or land any powerful smashes?' Celebrate any small victories and the effort they put in. Be careful not to compare them to other players; instead, focus on their own growth.

Role-playing is helpful here, too, as winning and losing scenarios can prepare them for both outcomes. 'Let's pretend you just landed a winning smash! How would you celebrate? Now, let's pretend your opponent wins the final point. How would you congratulate them?'

Finally, losing can be a valuable learning experience. If they lost because of lack of practice or effort on their part, be honest and share your observation. Help them identify areas for improvement and encourage them to come back stronger the next time. By helping your child focus on improvement and the joy of the game, sportsmanship will follow.

8. My child gives up when faced with a challenge. How can I motivate him?

It's tough to watch your child struggle. When they shy away from challenges, it's natural to feel frustrated or disappointed. However, understanding why they're hesitant is the first step to helping them build resilience.

Often, kids develop a fear of failure. They might believe their abilities are fixed, that is, they're either good at something or not, and that's it. This is called a fixed mindset. If they don't succeed, they might think it proves they're not capable. This can make them avoid challenges altogether.

Some examples of a fixed mindset are:

'I'm not good at math, so I'll never be good at it.'
'I'm not a natural athlete, so why try?'
'If I can't solve this puzzle quickly, it means I'm not smart enough.'

On the other hand, a growth mindset, as popularized by psychologist Carol Dweck, emphasizes the belief that abilities can be developed through dedication, hard work and effective strategy. People with this mindset see challenges as opportunities to learn and grow. They understand that mistakes are a normal part of the learning process, not proof of their worth or a reflection of their inherent abilities.

Some examples of a growth mindset are:

'I might not be good at math yet, but I can improve with practice.'
'I can develop my athletic skills through training and practice.'
'I learnt from my mistakes, and I'll do better next time.'

You play a crucial role in shaping your child's mindset. Instead of just focusing on the outcome, highlight the effort and learning process. Celebrate small wins and turn setbacks into opportunities for growth. For example, if they struggled with a math problem and you had to help them out, instead of criticizing, ask what they learnt. This helps them see challenges as learning experiences, not failures.

Resist the urge to solve hard puzzles for your child. It might be quicker to do a jigsaw puzzle for them or complete a LEGO set for them but allowing them to figure it out on their own builds problem-solving skills and independence. Instead, for a seven-year-old, you could offer hints or break it down into smaller sections. For an eleven-year-old, struggling with a complex LEGO set, help them understand the manual or suggest different building approaches without taking over the construction.

Also, be mindful of your words. While you want the best for your child, too much criticism or a constant push for perfection can create unnecessary pressure. They might feel like they always have to please you, which can lead to a fear of disappointment. Let them know you value their effort more than the outcome. This creates a safe space where they can make mistakes without fear of judgement. Offering encouragement and support throughout the process can boost their confidence.

When Anagha's son was twelve, he once abruptly quit a practice run, frustrated by his perceived failure to meet his self-imposed time goal. In academics, he was used to achieving high standards he set for himself. This setback on the running field bothered him. Recognizing his underlying worry about failure to excel combined with worry of disappointing his dad, her husband intervened. He gently reminded his son that setting high standards was commendable, but that setbacks were inevitable. He emphasized that their family valued progress over perfection. He encouraged him to focus on finishing the run and to celebrate his own milestones rather than comparing himself to others. This simple conversation proved transformative. Her son never quit another run, consistently striving for small improvements and giving his all. He continued to challenge himself throughout high school too, becoming the captain of his cross-country running team in his final year, a testament to the power of cultivating a growth mindset.

Inspiring stories can ignite your child's motivation, too. Exploring the lives of admired personalities can offer invaluable insights. By understanding their journeys, children can grasp that even their heroes faced obstacles.

Sometimes, children may simply feel overwhelmed by a challenging assignment. Breaking down large tasks into smaller, manageable steps can make the challenge less daunting. Visual aids, like checklists or charts, can help them track their progress. For example, a school art project, which is due in three days, can be broken down into smaller, manageable tasks.

First, provide the framework: PLAN—DO—SUBMIT.

On Day 1, PLAN: Create a rough sketch of the concept based on the project requirements. Collect all necessary supplies.

On Day 2, DO: Create the artwork.

On Day 3, SUBMIT: Make final corrections, if required, and submit the project on time.

Lastly, before you look to change your child's attitude, turn inwards. Be mindful of how you react when faced with an everyday challenge like a hard-to-open jar or a tangled string of lights. Do you show patience and perseverance? How you overcome small challenges shapes your attitude and helps you overcome bigger challenges in life. For example, when Anagha decided to take up running to improve her fitness, she couldn't run for even five minutes continuously. Rather than letting this deter her, she saw it as a starting point. She set an ambitious goal of a half-marathon in three months. Her children witnessed her adherence to a training plan she had developed with the help of her brother who had run many marathons. She openly shared her struggles with her nine-year-old children, demonstrating that learning and growth involve vulnerability. She managed to achieve her goal, demonstrating that with a growth mindset, right resources and persistent effort, significant progress is possible. Share such relatable examples of dealing with challenges in personal life or at work with your children.

9. I am tired of constantly arguing with my child over screentime. What should I do?

There are a few reasons why children nowadays are getting increasingly addicted to the mobile phone. Of course, because of COVID-19, all forms of education and activities had gone online. There were no physical games or outdoor activities and hence, it became a new routine for kids. Moreover, the parents themselves are using a lot of phones and devices at home because of work-from-home and because of COVID situations. Peer pressure also plays a role. When children see their friends owning and playing games on mobile phones, they feel left out. For the new generation, mobile gadgets, devices and electronics are very much a part of their life, existence and activities as opposed to the generations who came before. More parents are also working now. They have very little time to spend with their own children. There are no other alternatives and thus, children get addicted to mobile phones.

The seven to twelve age range is a whirlwind of growth and independence for your child. They venture out socially, their brains develop rapidly, and technology becomes a big part of their world. This can make managing screen time feel like a constant battle.

A child's brain is like a sponge, soaking up new experiences that shape its development. That's why setting clear boundaries around screen time is essential. It is crucial to minimize screen time and prioritize intentional digital experiences.

The best approach is a family effort. Talk openly with your child about the pros and cons of screen time. Involve them in creating a 'family media plan' that outlines screen-free zones (bedrooms, dinner table) and daily or weekly limits. This fosters a sense of shared responsibility and empowers your child to take ownership of their tech use.

The guidelines on screen time, as per the Indian Academy of Pediatrics, are as follows: screen time is defined as the total time spent on watching screens like computers, laptops, tablets, smartphones, television and handheld video games, in a day.[3]

Age group	**Max. Screen time**	**Physical activity**	**Night-time sleep**
Less than 24 months	None		
24–59 months	Max. 1 hour of supervised screen time; each session should not be more than 20–30 minutes.	Min. 3 hours (at least one hour of physical activity of moderate to vigorous intensity)	10–14 hours (Younger the child, greater the sleep duration)
5–10 years	Max. 2 hours	Min. 1 hour of physical activity of moderate to vigorous intensity	9–12 hours

Age group	Max. Screen time	Physical activity	Night-time sleep
10–18 years	Balance screen time with other activities that are required for overall development. If screen time interferes with playtime, sleep, schoolwork, meals, hobbies, peer interaction or family time, it must be reduced to accommodate other activities.	Min. 1 hour of outdoor physical activity	8–9 hours

Guidelines on Screen Time by Indian Academy of Paediatrics

Kids are great imitators. If you're constantly glued to your phone, it sends mixed messages about your screen time rules. Put your phone down during family time and find ways to unwind offline. Let them point out when you're not following the rules; it can be a good reminder for everyone!

The more time your child spends online and playing computer games, the more they get addicted to a rush of dopamine and excitement. Make sure that they have access to screen-free alternatives. It could be outdoor sports, storytelling, board games or even art and craft hobbies.

Do not use fear, coercion, punishment or force to stop the child from using a phone or other screens because this could backfire. Your child may look for ways to secretly find more screen time. Instead, introduce screen-free alternatives over a few days or weeks.

While computer games can be a convenient way to spend time with your child, they often create a passive form of interaction. While enjoyable, they may not foster the same level of connection as shared experiences that require active engagement. Consider replacing screen time with activities that encourage communication, co-operation and skill-building. Physical activities like biking, hiking or sports or indoor activities like boardgames, baking or cooking, provide opportunities for conversation. These shared experiences will create lasting memories and help strengthen your bond with your child. Talk to other parents and form a community of like-minded adults. Have the same rules so that children get a consistent message from all parents. Consider hiring a coach together for the children in the community. Encourage children to play outside or join a sports team.

When Anagha's son was nine, the allure of online gaming, fuelled by his friends' enthusiasm, was hard to resist. While Anagha shared his excitement, she was hesitant to introduce gaming at such a young age. Instead of simply denying his request, she shared her concerns with him. By discussing the potential impact on his brain development and sleep patterns, she empowered him to make an informed choice. His own experience with feeling tired and irritable after excessive gaming became his most compelling teacher.

Over time, he learnt to balance his social life with other activities. This journey reinforced the importance of mindful decision-making and the value of delayed gratification. She waited until he was sixteen, when he had developed strong study habits and could effectively manage his time between school, hobbies and family life, to buy him a PlayStation.

Not all screen time is equal. Prioritize educational content, interactive games or watching movies together, as a family. This can be a great way to bond and spark meaningful conversations. You can even let them choose the content you watch together to increase their interest and sense of ownership.

Colourful screens stimulate visual senses, producing dopamine and activating reward centres in the brain. It keeps the user engaged with screens longer. By changing the screens to greyscale, after game time is over, kids can focus better on other activities, such as homework, music practice etc. Switching screens to greyscale also reduces the temptation of using devices. Research done with college students has shown that greyscale settings reduce screen time.[4]

Most devices and platforms offer parental control features—a valuable tool for managing screen time and online safety. Use them to filter content, set time limits and monitor your child's online activity. Remember to create strong passwords for these controls and update them regularly as your child grows and explores different platforms.

The key to success is sticking to the plan. By combining clear guidelines, engaging alternatives to screen time and open communication, you'll empower your child to develop a healthy relationship with technology.

10. My child is upset because his teacher scolded him in front of the whole world and called him 'lazy'. How should I deal with this situation?

First, have a chat with your child and understand the complete story. Refrain from jumping to conclusions about the teacher's attitude or teaching style based on this one incident. Gather more information about the incident from your child. Ask specific questions, such as, 'What exactly happened? How are you feeling about the situation?' Sometimes, he may not have the words to express how he is feeling. Help him identify the emotion. 'Sounds like you were embarrassed or humiliated.'

You will have to make the call about whether or not to address the issue directly with the teacher. It depends on your child's response to the situation. If your child is feeling better just by talking to you, let the matter go.

If your child is scared and refuses to go to school, you will need to talk to the teacher. If your child is repeatedly getting such treatment from the teacher, you should certainly address the issue. When you decide to talk to the teacher, approach the situation tactically. Make an appointment to talk. Take a collaborative approach. Say that you need their help to understand exactly what happened. Explain how your child is feeling. Rather than blaming the teacher, see what can be done to help the child. For example, 'he feels he is targeted' or 'he feels it is unfair when some other students were not working either.' You can explain how it's affecting your child and discuss what can be done differently. If the situation does not improve even after talking to the teacher, you could contact the principal.

Sometimes, you have to trust that your child is strong enough to handle such situations. You cannot protect your children from every mean remark or every uncomfortable situation. As long as the child knows he has a safe space to vent his feelings, and that you will understand him without judgement, he will have courage and inner strength to face such situations in the future.

When her children were in the third grade, Anagha and her family moved to India for three years. This was the first time she wasn't working full time, so she would be at home when they would come back from school. Recognizing that they needed some alone time after a long day at school, she would give them a snack and let them be. Instead of asking them many questions, she would just listen if they were in a mood to share. However, one day, when her son got home from school, he wasn't his usual self. So, she asked him if everything was okay because he seemed agitated.

'Hey, is everything okay? You seem a bit upset.'

'Everything is not okay! My Hindi teacher tore my essay in front of the whole class today!'

'What! She tore your essay in front of everyone!'

'Yes! She could have just told me to rewrite it. Why did she have to tear it? It had taken me TWO DAYS to write the essay. It was so hard!'

'I would be mad, too, if that happened to me.'

'She just hates Indian students who don't know much Hindi. It's not my fault that I have never learnt Hindi before.'

'You think it's unfair?'

'Yes! It's SO unfair.'

'You were working on it for two days. You had put in so much effort into it. That must have been so frustrating. Also, she tore it in front of everyone. Did you feel embarrassed?'

'No, I am not embarrassed, I am just mad! She is always praising the non-Indian students for the smallest things!'

'You feel like no matter what you do, she will never be happy with your work?'

'Yes, exactly! She is unfair to all Indian students, not just me.'

'Looks like she has very high standards for Indian students. Maybe she doesn't know that you haven't lived in India. Would you like me to talk to her about it?'

'No, she wouldn't like it. I'll get in trouble. It's okay. I guess I will have to be extra careful when I write my essays.'

'Let me know if you need any help. If she tears your work again, I'll figure out how to talk to her. Don't worry about getting in trouble.'

'Okay, I will. Thanks, Mom!'

'Thanks for sharing what was bothering you.'

Anagha shares:

Even my daughter was annoyed about the unfair treatment by this teacher. But, before talking to the teacher, I would have asked other Indian parents about their children's experience in this class. If it was a serious issue, we could have taken some collective action. In this case, I did not pursue it further because I felt that my children were learning to deal with the situation. They had accepted that this teacher was different, and they had to adapt to her style. Both continued to love school. If they had complained about going to school or had started making excuses for not going, I would have taken some action. Since they still went to school happily every day, it became a joke between us. 'How many essays turned into jigsaw puzzles today?'

Parents love to jump in to protect their children, but they need to first let the child learn how to handle the situation which helps the child build resilience. Only if the child's efforts are not showing results or the teacher is very abusive and it starts affecting the child's mental health, should you take matter in your own hands. It sometimes helps to let the child learn to navigate around such adults who will keep presenting themselves in your child's life even in adulthood.

Self-Reflection for Parents

1. How would you describe yourself as a school-going child? What were your interests? What were you good at? How did you feel about yourself? What belief did you have about yourself as a learner?
2. What was your home environment like (peaceful/tense/predictable/unpredictable)? How did it affect you?
3. What did your parents value? How did you know what they valued (family/relationships, education, money, status, material things, learning, social responsibility, excellence, treating people with respect etc.)?
4. Were you stressed about anything during those years? What was the reason? How did you cope with it?
5. How was your relationship with your siblings? What role did your parents/other adults play in making it healthy or unhealthy?
6. How were your friendships? Did you feel accepted by your peers?
7. Is there a memory when you felt confident and capable? What had happened? What impact did it have on you moving forward?
8. Did you have an experience that completely changed how you felt about yourself/others in a positive or negative way? What was it?
9. Think of a memory when you were sad, fearful or angry. What had happened? How did you deal with it? How did

your parents/teacher/other adults respond? Did it help you feel better or worse?

10. Choose a difficult experience from your childhood. Close your eyes and picture yourself at that age. What did that child need? Give the child the support he/she needed at the time. Looking back, what did that child not know or understand, that you understand today?

7

The Teen Years: 13 to 18

'Parents can only give good advice or put them on the right path, but the final forming of a person's character lies in their own hands.'

—Anne Frank (1929–45)

Teen development is a complex period marked by significant changes in the brain. These changes can lead to behaviour that may seem impulsive or irrational. However, it's important to understand that this is a normal part of teen development as they form their identity and prepare for adulthood.

Teenagers experience a range of emotions and go through an intense period of experimentation and self-discovery. It's a crucial period of brain development that shapes who teenagers become as adults. Here's a breakdown of the key traits teenagers exhibit, based on the research of Dr Daniel Siegel, a renowned neuropsychiatrist.[1]

The Teenage Brain: Under Construction!

Just like toddlers, teenagers experience a dramatic shift in brain development. The prefrontal cortex, responsible for rational thinking, planning and impulse control, goes through major construction. This explains why teens might act impulsively or struggle with long-term planning. The amygdala, the brain's emotional centre, matures faster than the prefrontal cortex. This imbalance leads to intense emotions and mood swings.

Driven by the developing brain, teenagers crave autonomy and a sense of identity separate from their parents. This can lead to them forming strong opinions, exploring new interests and spending more time with friends. This is a way for them to explore their identity and develop their own sense of style. Expect that arguments about curfew or homework will happen. Recognize their desire for autonomy and independence.

Friendships become a top priority during adolescence. Teens seek acceptance and belonging within their peer group. Sometimes, this can lead to a desire to impress friends, even if it means taking risks or making impulsive decisions.

The risk-taking is not just an expression of rebellion. The teenage brain seeks novelty and is wired for exploration. This can manifest as rule-breaking or arguing; it's part of their developmental need to push boundaries and test their independence. Teenage behaviour is a result of a brain under construction, not simply bad choices. By understanding the science behind these actions, parents can be more supportive and provide guidance during this crucial stage.

Supporting Your Teenager

i. **Offer guidance, not control:** Teens need to feel like they have some control over their own lives. Recognize their need for autonomy while still providing support and setting boundaries.

ii. **Focus on connection:** First, repair connection, if it is broken, and continue to build it via non-judgemental, open communication. Create a safe space for them to express themselves.

iii. **Communicate openly and honestly:** Set clear expectations, but be willing to negotiate. Teens need to know what is expected of them, but they also need some room to make their own choices. Let them know your concerns and reasons behind setting expectations. Make agreements, wherever possible, in advance. Decide on the consequences of actions. Refrain from punishment and instead, help your teen reflect on what they learnt from the experience and offer opportunity to fix the problem they have created.

iv. **Be a positive role model:** Teens learn by watching the adults around them. Make sure you're modelling the behaviour that you want to see.

v. **Embrace change:** Their evolving interests and desire for independence are normal and healthy.

Teenagers typically need space from their parents. The child, who once shared everything with their parent, might barely talk to them now. You may notice that they want to spend long hours alone in their rooms. They will not want to share their social media passwords or phone passcode any more. This is normal. If a parent tries to be too friendly and keeps asking questions about school and friends, they might get irritated, roll their eyes or shut down further.

This is also an age where they are easily impressed by role models on social media or in their school or college. A person, who is a few years older, and whom they admire, can help your teen through this time. Make sure you trust them though. Lack of mentoring might make teens vulnerable to wrong role models at this age.

They also face immense peer pressure, through social media, about body image, sexuality, drugs, alcohol and sexual encounters. Parents need to have open, honest communication about these with their teens to ensure they have some idea, as these are topics not commonly discussed in Indian families. Parents have to prepare themselves to talk about sex, sexual orientations, safe sex, sexually transmitted diseases, teenage pregnancy etc. with their children. Boys, in particular, need to be educated about respecting girls, accepting 'no' as an answer and maintaining safe boundaries. Girls need to be educated on safe sex, having the courage to say 'no' and setting clear boundaries when it comes to respect.

Remember that all teens will grow at their own pace and have unique problems. Make sure you take enough time for yourself to deal with this period.

Parenting Tips for Handling Specific Challenges

1. We used to be close. But since my daughter has become a teenager, she doesn't want to talk to me. How can I rebuild a close relationship with her?

The teenage years are a time of immense change, not just for your child, but for you as well. It's important to remember that this withdrawal is a natural part of her development. Teens are craving independence, forging their own identities and navigating a complex social world. Here are some steps you can take to bridge the gap and rebuild a strong, supportive relationship:

The first step is to consider your own communication style. Here are some questions to ask yourself:

- What are your typical conversations with your daughter? Are they filled with instructions, reminders or criticisms? Teens crave connection, not lectures. Instead of focusing on chores, deadlines or her appearance, try to weave in genuine questions about her day, her interests and her feelings.
- Do you praise her efforts and accomplishments? Instead of focusing on choices or outcomes, compliment her hard work, talents or character strengths like leadership and kindness. Show genuine interest in things that are important to her.
- Are you an active listener? When she does talk, do you give her your full attention, put your phone away and avoid interrupting. Make an effort to create a dedicated listening space, whether it's a short chat before bed, a short walk after dinner or simply letting her know you're available to talk whenever she wants, without distractions.

Once you've considered your communication style, it's time to rebuild the bridge:

i. **Be open about your feelings:** Let your daughter know that you miss spending time together. This simple act of vulnerability, like saying, 'Hey, I miss our chats before bed.

Would you be interested in doing that again sometime?' can open the door for conversation.

ii. **Offer options, not demands:** Suggest ways to connect that are low-pressure and enjoyable for her. This could be a weekly walk, a movie night, playing a board game you both used to enjoy, cooking dinner together or even a comfortable silence while doing activities side-by-side. Think back to the activities you used to enjoy together and see if there's a way to adapt them for their teenage interests. Perhaps, you could watch her favourite show with her or try a new recipe that she's been wanting to make.

iii. **Respect her boundaries:** Teenagers value their independence and respecting her privacy is crucial for building trust. Don't take her need for privacy personally. It's a normal part of her development. Show you value her boundaries by simple acts such as knocking before entering her room and not reading her diary. Teens crave privacy, especially after school. School can be mentally and emotionally draining. Teens need time to unwind and recharge on their own terms. This might involve relaxing in their room, listening to music or spending time online. School day may be stressful due to friendship troubles, academic challenges, constant social interactions or activities. Having some space after school allows them to reflect on these experiences and process their feelings without feeling pressured to talk to someone about it.

iv. **Mind your comments:** Avoid criticizing her clothes, appearance, likes and dislikes. Instead, look for ways to offer sincere compliments about her character strengths and abilities such as her generosity with friends, her keen eye for design and style, or her kindness towards pets.

When your child does talk to you, this is how you can do a good job of listening to them:

- Pay attention to her words and body language. Don't interrupt or jump to conclusions. If she seems withdrawn or sighs a lot, acknowledge it and ask if something's bothering her.
- Instead of asking 'How was your day?' try 'What was the highlight of your day?' or 'How was recess today?' 'How did the (drama/sports) practice go today?' These questions encourage elaboration and show you're genuinely interested.
- Show empathy. Let her know her emotions are valid, even if you don't agree with them. Phrases like 'It sounds like you're feeling frustrated about this teacher/class.' or 'It must be tough when you were the only one who wasn't invited to the party' can go a long way. Try to see things from her perspective. Acknowledge that her experiences are important and valid.
- Sometimes, teens just need a listening ear. You could say, 'I'm here to listen if you want to talk about it, or if you'd rather just vent for a while, that's okay too.'
- Your primary role is to listen and understand her perspective, not solve her problems. Avoid lectures or unsolicited advice.

By following these steps, you can bridge the gap and build a stronger and supportive relationship with your daughter during her teenage years. The most important thing is to show her you love, respect and support her unconditionally, even when there's distance.

Here's a great example of how implementing just two tips changed my client's communication with her fourteen-year-old son:

Every day after school, this mother would bombard her son with questions about school, homework etc. He would often be reluctant to share. On rare occasions, when he did share a problem, she would immediately give suggestions or lecture him on what he should do. He would then stop talking and withdraw. After attending one of our parenting workshops, she decided to try two simple tips: First, do not ask your children any questions right after school. Let them be for some time. Second, when they do share, ask them, 'Do you want me to just hear you or help you?' If they ask you to just listen, respect their wish.

This helped him eventually open up. He shared what was happening with his friendships. He was a sincere student, and he felt that his teachers and friends' mothers liked him more than his friends did because he was responsible and a 'teacher's pet'. Instead of saying that he should ignore his friends and lecture him on how being focused on academics would help him in the future, his mother simply listened attentively. Then, he admitted that it was okay for them to comment on his study habits, and that he knew what was important for him. Her non-judgemental listening made him feel comfortable to share more.

2. How can I address my son's disrespectful and rude behaviour towards me?

In Anagha's practice, she often meets families struggling with a widening communication gap during teenage years. Many parents describe their teenager as irresponsible, self-centred and disrespectful. This perception creates a tense and strained atmosphere at home.

Unfortunately, the ways parents try to address these concerns often have the opposite effect. The stress and frustration they feel can lead to nagging and micromanaging. Teenagers, unsurprisingly, interpret this as constant criticism and judgement. It pushes them further away, making them more defensive and rebellious. It becomes a frustrating cycle for everyone. To break this cycle, parents can begin with self-reflection and prioritizing connection over control. A shift in perspective on parents' part is the starting point for restoring respect. Therefore, before addressing your son's behaviour, consider how your own behaviour might be influencing his.

Recognizing your part in your teen's defiant behaviour is the key to restoring lost connection. As a parent and an adult, it is your responsibility to initiate the process of repairing the connection. Apologize to your teen if you have hurt them in the past and express your sincere wish to repair the relationship. Moving forward, ensure that your teenager feels comfortable seeking help and communicating openly, without fear of judgement or criticism. A calm and relaxed atmosphere at home is essential. A stressful environment only exacerbates tension.

Restoring Respect

Questions for Self-reflection

- [ ] **Is your tone respectful?** Even if you're upset, avoid yelling, nagging, or using sarcasm.

- [ ] **Do you listen actively?** Give your teen your full attention when they talk and avoid interrupting. Acknowledge how they must be feeling. Try to understand their perspective, even if you disagree. Some parents dismiss how teens feel all the time. 'Oh you are such a drama queen!' 'You fuss over nothing.' 'Why do you worry about what your friends think about it? It's not important.'

- [ ] **Do you over-advise?** Teens are forming their own identities and want to make their own choices. Offer guidance when they ask for it, but avoid constant advice.

- [ ] **Do you criticize excessively?** Avoid harsh judgment or comments about their appearance, interests, or abilities. Respect their privacy regarding clothes, music, hobbies, etc. Start noticing positive behavior and compliment your teen. Do not compare them with their friends, siblings, or cousins.

- [ ] **Do you micromanage their lives?** Do you demand or expect perfection in every area of their life? When you talk to your teen, do most of your statements begin with "You should or should not…". "Your room should be spic and span", "You should always take bath in the morning." "You should do guitar practice every day." and so on.

- [ ] **Are you overprotective?** It's natural to feel protective towards your children. But is this fear dominating your parenting decisions? Are you so afraid of your teen getting hurt or disappointed that are you not allowing them to fail or learn from their own mistakes?

- [ ] **Do you respect their privacy?** Invading a teen's privacy by reading their diary or entering their room without knocking can be harmful. These actions erode trust and lead to resentment. While it's natural to feel concerned about your teen, it's essential to approach the situation with respect for their boundaries.

Figure 25: Restoring Respect - Questions for Parents

When your teenager is angry, upset or lashing out, do not indulge in power games or feel the need to have the last word. It also helps to change your physical position from being opposite to the teen to quietly sitting next to the teen and doing some deep breathing. By taking the position next to the child, the child feels you are not against them but you are with them. If they speak rudely, encourage them to go to their room to calm down.

When Anagha's son was thirteen, he began taking drums lessons after school. His lesson would start one and a half hours after school finished. The solitary wait was challenging for him. One afternoon, he texted Anagha feeling frustrated and tired. She made a conscious effort to understand his perspective. Instead of dismissing his feelings or lecturing him about the commitment, she focused only on his experience. In Anagha's words:

'Mom, I have been waiting for so long. I finished my homework. Still half an hour to go!' he texted.

Rather than jumping to solutions, I said: 'It sounds like you're feeling bored and lonely waiting by yourself.' This simple acknowledgement validated his emotions and encouraged him to share more.

He continued, 'I wish I could go home. Why didn't you give me an extra snack?'

Instead of getting irritated by his accusatory tone and reacting with 'It's not my job to remember to pack extra snacks.', I responded with empathy, 'It must be frustrating to be hungry and tired while waiting. Wish you had something to eat.'

'Yes, I am so hungry. Can't wait to have dinner as soon as I get home. I will listen to some music for some time.' Once he felt heard and understood, he was able to let go of his negative emotions and come up with some solutions himself. Later that day after dinner, I asked him to carry extra food with him on such days.

Once trust has been established and communication has improved, you can share your feelings too. Have a calm conversation with your teen when emotions aren't running high. Explain how their disrespectful behaviour makes you feel, using 'I' statements. Do not use accusatory statements such as, 'You always talk back.' Instead, use 'I' statements, such as 'I feel disrespected when you raise your voice.'

Outline what respectful behaviour looks and sounds like in your household. For example, you could say, 'We take time to calm down before engaging in a conversation. We show respect for each other by refraining from yelling, name-calling, cursing or banging doors. We are open and honest about how we feel. We also listen without interrupting the other person and try to see things from their perspective. We are willing to compromise. We find solutions together that would work best for our family.'

Explain to them what happens to their brain when they are angry and the importance of taking a break to calm down so that they are ready to reason and think about the situation rationally. Model this behaviour yourself when you are frustrated. Avoid escalating the situation with anger or threats.

When it comes to correction, collaboration is key. Work together to find solutions rather than placing blame. Offer help, but don't dictate solutions. Ask them how you can best support them. Instead of micromanaging and overprotecting, respect your teen's need for autonomy. Give your teen space to make their own decisions. In the process, mistakes may happen. Discuss what they can do differently next time and trust them to make responsible choices in the future.

Through consistent respectful communication and honouring your teen's autonomy, you can see a positive change in your teen's behaviour.

3. How can I help my child avoid the body shaming that I went through?

As a parent, it's natural to want to protect your child from this pain. However, it's important to address your own pain and anxieties first. Many of our Indian clients felt they were flawed or inferior growing up, because of comments about their looks or dark skin tone by their own family members. It affected how they interacted with others. Many felt invisible in front of their "better looking" siblings. If you are still struggling with your own experiences of body shaming, consider seeking out a professional.

From Self-doubt to Self-love

Self-love is one of the best ways to overcome negative feelings and to prepare children for the criticism and negativity they may face. To help them develop healthy self-esteem, start recognizing their strengths. While you encourage them, watch out for how you speak about yourself, your body and your appearance in front of your child. Model self-love by taking good care of yourself. Your child may be less conscious about their body until they notice your anxiety. Many girls think they take after their mothers. If they see their own mother doubting herself or being unhappy with her body, she may start developing a negative body image.

Don't let your own anxiety about body shaming rub off on your child. If your self-worth is tied to your weight or your appearance, you might feel anxious when your child gains weight. Do not dwell on this, as it is normal for kids to gain some weight during puberty. Instead, you should focus on ensuring that they are fit and eating a balanced diet suited to their nutritional needs. Avoid keeping junk food in the house and replace it with healthier options. Encourage regular physical activity and adequate sleep to help your child feel good, physically and mentally. Talk to your child's sports coach or other adult your child admires and trusts, who might be in a better position to influence your child.

In India, body shaming may be normalized in many families. Calling someone *motu* (fatty) or *golu* (for someone who is overweight) is considered normal. Extended family members, such as uncles, aunts or grandparents, may comment on a teenager's weight, skin, pimples etc. The situation is made worse when they comment about these things in front of a group of people because that makes the teen extremely self-conscious and uncomfortable. Even parents tend to do it unintentionally, at mealtimes or when their child dresses up. Riri remembers doing the same thing until her teenager told her, '*Mom, I know I have put on weight. I see myself in the mirror every day. So, telling me about it is not helping at all. It's only making me feel worse.*' That's when she realized her mistake—she quickly apologized and backed off.

We must understand that teenagers, who look at themselves in the mirror, know that they may be overweight. They are already struggling with their own body image issues. By constantly telling them about it, we are not helping. Instead, talk to your teen and ask how they feel about it and what you can do to help. People can gain weight not just due to overeating, but also because of hormonal imbalances, a lack of sleep and chronic stress.

The same factors play a role in skin issues. So, help your teen with solutions to resolve the root cause, instead of pointing out the problem repeatedly, as that will only antagonize them. Because of these reactions and behaviour, many teens hate going to family functions and events. If required, consider consulting a specialist, but remember that despite all efforts, the most important thing is to support your teen to build confidence. In Riri's words:

> *As a young teen, my son used to eat a lot of junk food, and at some point, I gave up correcting him because he just didn't understand my point. So, I told him honestly that I would not nag him about food any more, and he could choose to eat whatever he wished to and face the consequences. But, just before he started college, he began to get severe skin breakouts, and he realized his folly. He changed his food habits and became the healthiest eater in the entire family! He also started coaching us on making healthy food choices. He started following a regular skin care regimen (which we never had!). He had always been very thin, and we never made a big deal about it, but once he started college, he started going to the gym regularly to build his physique. We were both amused by and proud of this transformation. It is best when it comes from them organically vs parents constantly nagging and pushing for such things.*

Body Image and Self-Esteem

Engage in open and honest discussions about body image and self-esteem. Encourage your child how they feel about themselves. The content your child is exposed to on social media will play a large role in how they perceive themselves and others. Educate your child about the unrealistic body standards often portrayed in the media and help them develop critical thinking skills to analyse these images. If your child does experience body shaming, help them develop skills to respond assertively with phrases such as, 'What you just said is completely unacceptable. Stop saying it.' 'I didn't ask for your opinion. I am happy with the way I am.' It is also important to assure your child that it's okay to seek help from trusted adults, like teachers or school counsellors, if they experience body shaming.

Anagha's daughter experienced 'skinny-shaming' from a young age. Comments like 'Eat more, you are so thin,' or 'Is that your twin brother? He looks so much bigger than you!' were common. She was even told, 'You don't look like a high-schooler!' Sometimes, these remarks would upset her, while at other times, she could ignore them. No matter what, she always came to Anagha to share her feelings. When she felt better, she would say, 'I don't know why people keep commenting on my body! I am fit and healthy.' From the time she was little, Anagha had consistently assured her that she had a strong body. In Anagha's words:

> *I had never forced her to eat more than she wanted to and supported her when others asked her to eat by saying, 'She knows when she is full. Please don't force her.' My daughter rarely fell ill, and when she did, I would encourage her by saying she would recover quickly.*
>
> *I would also share stories of her great-grandmothers, whose petite frames didn't stop them from being fearless. Once, I told her a story of how my grandmother had hit a gold chain snatcher with a sugarcane and defended herself. Now, as a young adult, my daughter tells me that she could ignore the negative comments because she felt completely accepted by me and my husband, and, later, by her supportive circle of friends.*

You cannot protect your child from other people's judgemental remarks, but you can help the child develop a healthy body image. It is important for both parents to be careful of their words, tone and actions. Teenagers are at a crucial stage of identity formation. How we view them affects their self-esteem. Refrain from making comments about other people's bodies or appearances, as children can pick up these habits. Instead, teach your child that everyone is unique, and that diversity in body shapes, sizes and appearances is something to be celebrated. Emphasize the importance of inner qualities like kindness, hard work and creativity rather than focusing solely on physical appearance.

4. Why do I get so anxious about my child's exam?

Take a moment and reflect on your own experience of writing exams. Were you a bundle of nerves just before exams? What did you say to yourself? 'I am not good at taking exams.' Maybe your parent's comments, like 'Don't make silly mistakes in the exam', made you anxious. Did their well-intended comments, like 'You are smart. I am sure you will do well', which were meant to boost your confidence, ended up making you feel even more nervous? It could be that you carry this anxiety even today and it rears its ugly head every time your child is about to take an exam.

Another reason you feel anxious could be that you have tied your self-worth and success as a parent to your child's academic success. Since you cannot do anything about how your child actually performs on the test, you might feel helpless and hence, worried. If your child feels nervous before exams, know that it is normal to feel that way. It's important that you manage your anxiety, otherwise, your child will sense it and become even more anxious. Practise self-regulation techniques described later in this book. Teach them to your child, too.

Many clients, who come for therapy, have experienced exam anxiety due to undue expectations put on them by their parents, teachers or other family members. Rather than prioritizing the learning process and encouraging children's innate talents, many felt unseen and unappreciated for who they were. Some were physically punished or berated for not meeting their parents' standards of excellence. Others were compared to their cousins or siblings.

Even when some did extremely well, their parents only asked about the couple of points they had lost out on. These clients put high expectations on themselves and felt unworthy without accomplishments. Parents either became hyper-anxious about their kids' performance or had a hands-off approach to their kids' studies. Neither is beneficial. As you become aware of your own triggers, make sure you work on them so that your child does not have to go through what you did.

5. My teenager keeps procrastinating while working on his school projects. Many times, he asks for help at the last minute. How do I teach my child to manage time better?

The last-minute scramble for help can be stressful for both you and your teen. Before diving into solutions, it's crucial to identify why your teen procrastinates. Here are some common reasons:

i. **Feeling overwhelmed:** Too many assignments, poor grades or a looming deadline can be paralyzing. Your teen might feel demotivated and opt to avoid starting at all.

ii. **Too many commitments:** Balancing schoolwork with extracurricular activities, hobbies and social life can be challenging. Is your teen overbooked?
iii. **Disorganization:** Poor planning and a messy study environment can make even small tasks feel daunting.
iv. **Unsure how to start:** Complex projects with unclear instructions can lead to procrastination. Your teen might not know where to begin.
v. **Lack of interest:** Some subjects might hold little personal interest, leading to a lack of motivation.
vi. **Social media distraction:** The constant lure of notifications and online interactions can easily derail focus.
vii. **Overconfidence:** Some children keep pushing things till last moment because they believe that they can manage to do it under pressure. Many have the belief that they work best under pressure. In the past if they have managed to get things done at last minute and got appreciation for it, they become overconfident about that approach. In such cases its best to let them face consequences of their procrastination or delay.
viii. **Fears:** Facing consequences of a decision made can be fearful and so they become indecisive and procrastinate. Usually, procrastination is a coping mechanism for fear that they have relating to the outcome of the action or the decision. Fear can be due to past experiences of parents being too harsh, critical or punitive about the child's decisions or actions – especially related to grades, behaviour, choices etc.

If it has become a pattern that your child frequently asks for last minute help, it is time to stop helping them. If he knows that you end up helping anyway, you are not helping the situation. Find a time to talk to your teen when both of you are relaxed and calm. State your observations without judgement and help him see how his procrastination is impacting you. '*I want to talk to you about your homework. I get stressed when you come to me for last-minute help. I cannot get my work done on time. I have to stay up late to finish it. If I don't get enough rest, I feel tired the next day. This has happened four times in the last two weeks. If you need help, you will have to let me know in advance. Can you tell me what is happening?*' Check if any of the reasons stated above are causing procrastination. Help your teen prioritize and consider reducing some activities if they create undue stress.

We find it helpful to share Steven Covey's (author of *The Seven Habits of Highly Effective People*) 'Big Rocks' principle to help them prioritize their activities:[2]

Imagine you have an empty jar and some big rocks, pebbles and sand. The big rocks are the most important things you need to do, like physical activity, sleep, schoolwork and spending time with family. The pebbles are important but not urgent tasks like hanging out with friends, and hobbies. The sand represents the small stuff like checking social media, watching shows and playing computer games. If you first put the sand in the jar, there won't be room for the big rocks. But, if you first put the big rocks in, you can still fit the pebbles and sand around them. So, focus on the most important things, first, for a happier and more fulfilling life. Don't get caught up in small tasks and forget about the things that really matter.

Practically, this means working with your teen to create a daily or weekly schedule that incorporates schoolwork, extracurricular activities and leisure time. Help them learn to estimate how long tasks take and allocate realistic time slots. Next, develop a system to keep track of assignments and submission dates. This could be a digital planner, a paper calendar or a bullet journal. The key is to have a system they will use consistently and one that will create effective reminders.

Large projects can feel overwhelming. Help your teenager develop a plan as soon as the project is assigned. Break down major tasks into smaller, manageable steps. For example, a science project could be tackled by listing various tasks and setting daily goals, keeping the project deadline in mind: brainstorming topics, choosing a problem, developing the hypothesis, designing an experiment to test the hypothesis, developing a plan (what/who/when/how), conducting the experiment, collecting data, analysing the results and drawing conclusions. A printout of the plan, with dates, will help your teen keep track of the tasks.

Everyone develops executive functions like time management and organizational skills at their own space. Some individuals may require more support in these areas. Acknowledge when your teen completes tasks on time. Keep in mind that setbacks are normal. Offer support when he is stressed or overwhelmed, but avoid stepping in at the last minute, if he asks for help. Show trust in his ability to figure out what works best for him and learn important life skills along the way.

6. I don't like my teen's friends and I am scared they influence him badly. How do I talk to him about this?

During adolescence, the desire for peer acceptance becomes a powerful force. This is an evolutionary drive, helping them build connections beyond the family unit and develop social skills.

They are learning to navigate the complex world of friendships and establishing their own identity separate from you. Their friendships become increasingly important. While you might not always click with their friends, it's crucial to approach the situation with understanding and open communication.

Telling your teen directly that you dislike their friends is a recipe for disaster. They might perceive it as an attack on their own judgement or even a reflection on themselves. This can lead to defensiveness and a strain on your relationship. Instead of criticizing, try building bridges. Here are some strategies:

- Invite their friends over after school to hang out at your place. This allows you to observe their interactions first-hand and get a better sense of who they are.
- Instead of asking your child for details about their hangouts, ask open-ended questions like, 'What do you enjoy doing with your friends?' or 'What qualities do you admire in them?' This fosters conversation and allows you to understand their perspective.
- Discuss your family values, such as honesty and hard work, but avoid dictating with whom they can and can't be friends.

If you have specific concerns about their behaviour, like smoking or vaping, address them directly with your teen. Instead of accusing them, ask open-ended questions like, 'How do you feel about smoking?' or 'Have you considered the risks?' Express your concerns about their health and well-being in a non-judgemental way. Encourage them to share their thoughts and feelings on the topic.

While your teen craves independence, they still look up to you. By modelling healthy relationships and responsible decision-making, you can have a significant influence on their choices. While their friends may influence them, your influence is still strong. Ultimately, your goal is to create a safe space where your teen feels comfortable talking to you about anything, including their friends. Let them know that you're always there to listen, offer support and guide them through life's challenges.

7. My teen has a girlfriend/boyfriend. How do I talk about it and share my concerns?

As your teen ventures into the world of romance, it's a good opportunity to discuss your family's values and religious beliefs. This conversation doesn't have to be about setting rigid rules, but rather about opening a dialogue about what's important to you. This can be a whirlwind of emotions for both you and your child. While you might feel a touch of protectiveness, it's important to remember that romantic relationships are a natural part of growing up. Many teens hide things from parents and do things behind their backs. They may get into serious emotional and physical trouble as a result.

Most teen relationships do not last beyond the twelfth grade, as most people transition to different colleges. However, these first relationships offer valuable lessons about self-discovery, social skills and navigating the complexities of human connection.

The first step is to make your teen's partner feel welcome in your home. Introduce yourself warmly, offer them a drink or a snack and show a genuine interest in getting to know them. This person is important to your child, so getting to know them better can help you understand and support this new chapter in their life.

Talking calmly and engaging your teen is probably the best way to broach all the important topics and questions in your mind. It doesn't have to be awkward. Ask open-ended questions like, 'What do you like about this person?' or 'What kind of activities do you enjoy doing together?' This allows them to share their feelings and experiences without feeling judged. Use the conversation as a chance to introduce key concepts like consent, honesty, trust, respect, equality, communication and boundaries. Explain how these elements contribute to a happy and fulfilling relationship. The definitions below will help you start a conversation with your teen about these ideas.

i. **Honesty:** This means being truthful to your partner about your feelings and actions.
ii. **Trust:** Building trust in a relationship requires open communication and keeping your word.
iii. **Respect:** Treat your partner with kindness and consideration, valuing their opinions and boundaries.
iv. **Equality:** A healthy relationship is a two-way street where both partners feel valued and heard.
v. **Communication:** Open and honest communication is essential for resolving conflicts and building trust.
vi. **Boundaries:** Healthy boundaries establish what behaviour is acceptable and unacceptable in a relationship. These can be physical, emotional or even digital boundaries.
vii. **Consent:** Consent is an essential part of any healthy relationship, both emotionally and physically.

While we hope for the best, it's crucial to talk about potential red flags that might signal an unhealthy relationship.

i. **Body Shaming or Name-calling:** A partner who puts you down through name-calling or criticizing your appearance is not someone who respects you.

ii. **Jealousy or Possessiveness:** A partner who tries to control who you spend time with or isolates you from your friends is a red flag.
iii. **Physical Abuse:** This includes any unwanted physical contact, hitting, shoving or any action that causes physical harm. If your teen experiences any physical abuse, seek help immediately.
iv. **Non-Consensual Sexual Relations:** Sex should always be consensual. If your teen feels pressured or forced into any sexual activity, they must know that they can come to you for help.

Talking about Sex

While your teen is exploring romantic relationships, it's important to maintain open channels of communication. Remind them that they can always come to you if they feel uncomfortable or unsafe or simply need advice. For teenage girls, especially, it is important to talk about safe sex.

Talking About It Is NOT Encouraging It

Many parents assume that talking about this topic means that they are indirectly encouraging their children; however, this is not true. Teens today have access to a lot of information, both right and wrong, online, and even if you don't have the conversation, they might be still experimenting and exploring. However, when parents talk about sex openly, the kids understand that if they are in trouble, they can reach out to their parents for help. Otherwise, they might be misguided into doing some things that could be harmful. For example, girls are sometimes forced into unprotected sex by their boyfriends. Ensure that your daughter can always talk to you about her experience.

Riri had this conversation with her daughter and son when they were fourteen. For her daughter, she emphasized how important it is to keep oneself safe and not fall for any sort of pressure when it comes to intimacy. She also educated her about protection and cyber safety—about not allowing photos or videos in intimate moments and their misuse to blackmail (though her daughter was visibly uncomfortable and embarrassed, and Riri was nervous, it went well). These days, teens know a lot more than what we like to believe, but having such conversations gives them the trust that they can talk to us if they are in trouble. With her son, she focused on the importance of respecting NO from a girl and respecting her space as well as safe sex. With her son, it was easier as she had practised with her daughter earlier!

Girls who have self-worth issues and seek love and validation outside the home are most vulnerable to boyfriends who might be abusive, physically, emotionally or sexually. It is important to educate teen girls about these issues. Here, if trust and connection are built with the teen, from childhood, and their confidence and self-worth are intact, they are better able to handle such situations. For both girls and boys, consent, or the importance of saying 'no' and respecting the consent of the other person are very important lessons.

Parents of boys also need to sensitize their teens about respecting girls and ensuring she is safe. Talking about safe sex and sexually transmitted diseases is very important. Boys also need to be coached about not taking physical or emotional abuse from their partners. If parents are not comfortable with such conversations, it is best to ask an older cousin, family friend or professional counsellor, with whom the teen is comfortable, so that they can coached and educated in this area. There are also sex educators in India now, who can help with such conversations.

In today's times, having conversations about cyber bullying and the risks of intimate videos have also become more important. Talking about the dangers of spiked drinks at parties is also required. If your teen goes to a party, warn them about not accepting drinks that are mixed by strangers and to keep their location tracking on. Riri had these conversations with both her teens. These chats were met (of course!) with rolling of the eyes and comments like 'Mom, we know all these things!' or 'You don't need to tell us all this!' Nevertheless, she did it for her own satisfaction and to indirectly let them know that she was willing to talk about these things if they needed to.

Riri believes the following points need to be covered in conversations with teens, which can be difficult for many parents (including herself):

i. Safe sex—why and how
ii. Consent and boundaries
iii. Social media posts of intimate moments
iv. Spiked drinks—dangers
v. Masturbation
vi. Sexual orientation

8. My teen is always on the phone. I don't know what she is watching. What should I do?

It is understandable to feel concerned when your teen seems glued to their phone. While it's tempting to monitor their every move, open communication is often more effective. Instead of focusing on controlling their phone usage, aim to understand the underlying reasons for their behaviour.

By fostering open communication, you can help them develop self-awareness about their phone habits. Guide them to consider the physical and emotional impacts of excessive screen time. Encourage them to reflect on how their phone usage affects their mood, sleep and relationships.

How to deal with social media usage is not something that can be learnt from previous generations, so parents need to read up and be careful about their own social media usage, too. If they cannot model behaviour for teens, they are unlikely to listen.

While social media has expanded our ability to make friends, connect with anyone, while being a source of unlimited knowledge and education, it comes with its share of harmful effects when it is not used properly or overused. A recent report indicates five billion people worldwide have Internet access, and a typical user now spends more than 40 per cent of their waking life online. Several studies have highlighted challenges, such as insomnia, depression and addiction, related to overuse of phones and social media. Recently, the Australian government announced banning social media for children younger than sixteen years.

At Wellness Space, we conducted a study with 258 individuals and assessed their well-being, anxiety, depression and insomnia, while trying to understand if it was linked to the number of hours they spent on the Internet. Daily Internet usage was classified into four categories: Up to two hours was classified as low usage, between two to four hours was medium usage, four to six hours was high usage and above six hours was very high usage. We found that, as the usage increases from low to medium to high and very high, the negative impact on mental health parameters also goes up. We found out that younger individuals (aged 16–25 years) were at a higher risk of experiencing poor well-being and depression as opposed to older ones. We also noticed high instances of anxiety and insomnia among high and very high usage individuals. (See Figure 26)

Overall, we found that using social media for more than four hours negatively affects mental health parameters like anxiety, depression, insomnia and well-being.

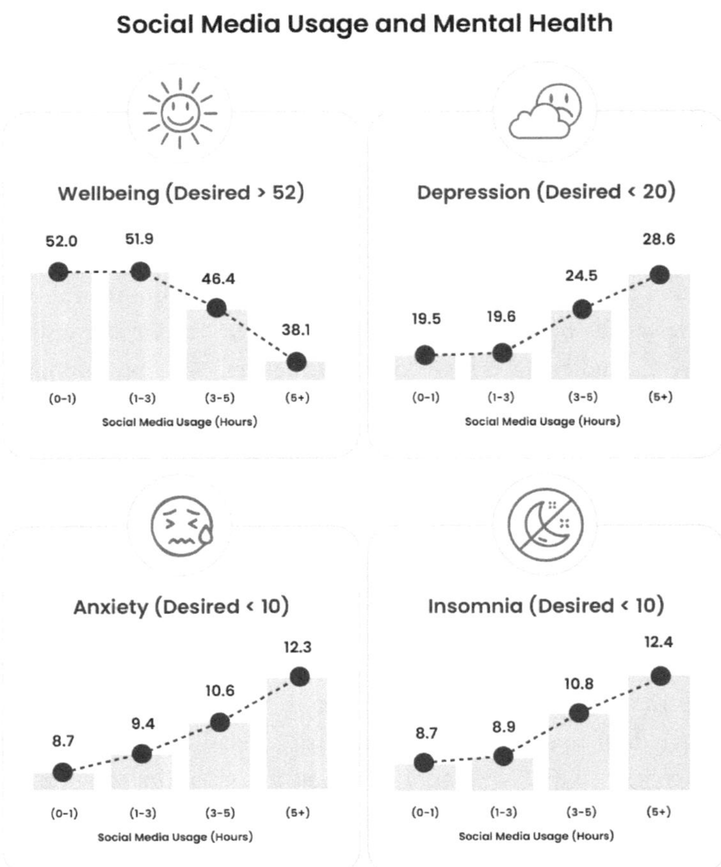

Figure 26: Social Media Usage and Mental Health
(Based on a Study Done at Wellness Space)

We see children and parents reaching for their phones at any given free moment, while waiting for the bus, during a conversation, in parties and social gatherings or while waiting for someone. It is almost a compulsive need to check their social media feeds or notifications. It has resulted in a decline in concentration and focus among individuals. We are witnessing a phenomenon known as 'popcorn' brain—a need for constant stimulation with a compromised ability to stay focused on one thing—among adults and teenagers who spend a lot of time online.

Constant scrolling on social media is like a dopamine high for the body. This is the brain's feel-good hormone, and it motivates us to do things that bring us joy and pleasure. It is also linked to addictive behaviour. The greater the release of dopamine, the more addictive the experience is. This fuels our desire to keep doing it and to keep repeating the experience. However, once that activity or experience is over, there is a dopamine dip because the body needs to regain balance. When we constantly seek instant rewards, like scrolling on our phones, it shortens our attention spans. This habit makes us rely more on the emotional part of our brain (limbic system), which focuses on immediate gratification. As a result, we don't engage the part of our brain that's responsible for thinking ahead, solving problems and making decisions.[3] When we encounter difficult or distressing situations at work or in social settings, our digital devices provide convenient distractions to avoid dealing with these issues, as the digital feed is endless, unlike in substance addictions.

When Anagha's daughter entered middle school, the allure of social media became a significant distraction. Her focus on schoolwork waned as she became increasingly absorbed in maintaining online connections. It was clear that the pressure to keep up with the digital world was interfering with her studies. Anagha initiated a conversation about her observations, expressing concern. Her daughter acknowledged the problem and the negative impact on her schoolwork. Together, they explored potential solutions. The idea of temporarily relinquishing her phone emerged as a viable option.

They agreed that she would have access to her phone only at specific times. The rest of the time, it would be kept in another room. Her daughter initially felt restless, but within a few days, she got used to not having her phone nearby. She could focus better and finish her work more quickly. She saw for herself the correlation between reduced screen time and improved academic performance. This collaborative approach helped her to take ownership of her time management.

Over time, she regained control over her phone usage. This experience taught them the importance of open dialogue, mutual respect and gradual steps towards independence. By working together, they found a solution that balanced her social needs with her academic responsibilities. Today, as a young adult, Anagha's daughter acknowledges the value of those early conversations.

To prevent excessive screen time, continue to communicate your concerns and expectations. Be curious and genuinely interested in hearing your teen's perspective before enforcing rules. Ask them how many hours they think they use the phone. Invariably, they will underestimate the duration. They might even be surprised when they find out the actual number of hours. To gain a clearer understanding of their phone usage, consider a joint analysis of their screen time.

Start by expressing genuine curiosity about their online life. Ask about their favourite platforms, the content they engage with and their thoughts on what they see.

Phone Ready Questionnaire

developed by Dr. Megan Moreno in collaboration with AT&T and AAP (The American Academy of Pediatrics)

You could use the free "Phone Ready Questionnaire" developed by Dr. Megan Moreno, an adolescent medicine physician and researcher in collaboration with AT&T and AAP (The American Academy of Pediatrics). Based on your answers to the questions below, the online tool will tell you whether or not your child is ready for a phone.*

Is your child ready for phone?

Q. In your family, who is starting conversations about getting your child a phone?

Q. How often do you feel your child needs a cell phone for their safety? For example, do they travel on their own to school, for after school activities or to visit family and friends?

Q. How often would having a phone help your child connect with family or friends whom they can't see in person?

Q. How often does your child act responsibly, such as finishing things that they are assigned at school?

Q. How often does your child follow rules about other media in the home such as limits on TV, tablets, or video games?

Q. How often does your child successfully keep track of things like their backpack, hats or gloves?

*To use the online interactive version, visit https://screenready.att.com/digital-parenting/

Q. How often do you trust your child's judgement when they make decisions when you're not there?

Q. How often is your child able to handle impulses (for example, can they resist talking during class, avoid interrupting others, or handle disappointment without overreacting)?

Q. How often does your child admit to you when they make a mistake and then work to make things better?

Q. Are you prepared to take steps such as setting parental controls, creating a family media plan, and talking with your child about what they see and do online?

Figure 27: Phone Ready Questionnaire

This approach fosters trust and opens the door for deeper conversations. By understanding their perspective, you can collaboratively address potential concerns and establish healthy boundaries.

Acknowledge the benefits such as connecting with friends and family, accessing educational resources, learning skills, pursuing hobbies etc. Talk to them about the potentially negative consequences of excessive phone use and ask if they are experiencing any of these issues:

i. Not able to fulfil responsibilities: Falling behind in schoolwork, chores or social commitments.
ii. Isolation: Spending increasing amounts of time alone in their room, avoiding family or friends.
iii. Sleep disturbances or deprivation:[4] Difficulty falling asleep, staying asleep or feeling unrested. Sleep deprivation is known to cause many issues such as tiredness, difficulty

concentrating, problem-solving and learning, and a weakened immune system.

iv. Decreased physical activity.

v. Mood changes: Increased irritability, mood swings, disruptive behaviour[5] or signs of depression or anxiety.

vi. Physical symptoms: Eye strain, headaches or back pain related to excessive screen time.

vii. Withdrawal symptoms: Anxiety, difficulty concentrating, irritability or even phantom vibrations when separated from the phone.

Assure your teen that your objective is to help them achieve a balance so that they are physically and mentally healthy and safe. To balance screen time, encourage offline activities. Explore options that combine physical activity with social interaction, such as joining sports teams, dance classes or outdoor clubs. Suggest hobbies, like art, music or cooking, to foster creativity and relaxation. Encourage them to read physical books rather than e-books as these may be on devices that have other distractions too.

Set clear expectations about phone-free zones. Ideally, they should not be allowed in the bedroom, while sleeping and at the dining table. Charge phones in a common area instead of bedrooms. This small change in habit helps improve sleep quality. Create phone-free times such as before going to school, study time and family time. Having agreements in advance creates a sense of responsibility. Teens are more likely to adhere to rules they have helped create.

Respect the family rule about phone-free zones yourself. By demonstrating mindful phone usage, you can guide your teens towards a balanced relationship with phones. Technology is a tool, not a master. It's about teaching our children to use it effectively rather than being consumed by it.

Creating a Family Media Plan

Establish some guidelines before giving your children a phone or social media: to create a Family Media Plan, visit the link: https://www.healthychildren.org/english/fmp/pages/mediaplan.aspx#/priorities

- Keep notifications off to avoid distractions.
- Stop using the phone one hour before going to bed.
- Keep the phone on 'night mode' to turn blue light off, which interferes with sleep.
- Include physical activity in daily schedule.
- Do not share any personal information such as address, phone number etc.
- If an unknown person messages, do not engage, and block them.
- Do not post photos with other people in it without their permission. Ask your friends to do the same.
- Your digital footprint is the online trail you leave behind. Every post, like, comment or search contributes to this digital identity. It includes everything from your social media profiles to your online shopping history. Your digital footprint can affect your future. Colleges, employers and even potential friends and romantic partners might look at your online presence. It's essential to be mindful of what you share and how it might be perceived.

- Treat online interactions with the same respect as face-to-face conversations. Avoid posting anything hurtful or offensive. Your words have consequences, both online and offline. If you are angry with someone, wait for a day before responding. Talk to the person instead of sending messages to resolve the conflict.

9. I just found out that my teen is cutting herself. I am panicking! How do I handle it?

At the outset, it is important to understand that self-harm is not the same as suicide. Teens practise self-harm not with the intention to end their life but usually to deal with difficult emotions. This practice is common among pre-teens and teens, and is done by usually cutting the skin on the arms or thighs with a blade, scissors, knife or other sharp objects. It also includes harmful behaviour like scratching, biting, burning, picking on wounds, pulling out hair, picking at scabs, overdosing on drugs or medicines, banging the head or body parts against a wall or a hard surface in order to get injured and indulging in harmful behaviours like addictions etc.

There are several reasons why young people self-harm, each linked to how the individual handles their emotions, challenges and environment. Some common motivations include:

- Managing extreme emotions like hurt, pain, anger, frustration or grief
- Reducing tension
- Providing physical pain to distract from emotional pain

- Actually 'feeling' the pain when the teen is numb or feeling lifeless
- Making an effort to regain control over feelings or problems
- Punishing themselves or others
- Getting attention and love from others
- Identifying with their peer group

In addition to these causes, there may be some deeper factors that can make teenagers want to self-harm. These include:

- Mental health challenges like depression, anxiety, low self-esteem, hopelessness, anger, extreme stress, eating disorders, bullying, addictions, etc.
- Childhood trauma, which causes the mental health challenges listed above, including but not limited to a having dysfunctional family; witnessing domestic violence; being subjected to physical, emotional or sexual abuse, isolation, or emotional neglect; having a stressful relationship with their parents; enduring excessive punishments or authoritarian parenting that causes rebelliousness and anger. For example, a fifteen-year-old, who started cutting herself from the age of eleven, without her parents finding out, told us, '*Every time my dad and mom would violently fight, I would lock myself in my bathroom and cut myself in order to release my feeling of anger and helplessness.*'
- A family history of self-harming behaviour: Children who see their parents engaging in such behaviours grow up normalizing self-harm. One of our clients told us, '*My mother would always slap herself out of anger and guilt every time we misbehaved and she hit us—I also do the same thing.*'
- Having poor emotional resilience and experiencing social isolation, loneliness, peer rejection and body shaming. These

experiences can intensify a child's feelings of worthlessness, shame or frustration, which may result in self-harm.

- Being around friends who self-harm: Being part of a social circle that indulges in such behaviour can increase the risk of your teen taking part in such behaviours.

It is also important to note that self-harming behaviours can also become a habit or addiction. For example, sixteen-year-old Nyra got into the habit of self-harming because every time her parents fought, she would start hitting herself so they would stop fighting and rush to stop her. Soon, this became a habit, and Nyra never learnt how to process her anger or fear, or express it in a healthy way. Even after she left home for college, she continued this habit every time she felt angry, upset, helpless or frustrated. It is critical that you try to understand *why* your child is engaging in such behaviour so that you can offer the support that they need.

If you feel your teen may be self-harming, watch out for these common signs:

- Unexplained cuts, burns or bruises.
- Keeping their bodies (especially their arms and legs) covered by wearing pants or long sleeves, even when it is hot.
- Avoiding swimming or changing clothes around others.
- Being withdrawn or isolated from their friends or isolating themselves from family as well.
- Constantly experiencing a low mood, lack of interest in life or suffering from depression.
- Experiencing and engaging in intense feelings of self-blame, failure, hopelessness, poor self-worth or anger.

What Parents Can Do

Finding out that your child is engaging in self-harming behaviours can be a very upsetting and stressful experience. You may feel anger, helplessness, sadness, shame or guilt, and indeed, all of these emotions as well. Remember that it is normal to feel this way, but before talking to the child/teen, it is important to work on yourself, ensure that your emotions are well-regulated so that you don't pass any negative emotions on to your child.

Before you speak with your child, you may first need to administer them first aid and make sure that they are not in any physical danger. For example, if your child has cuts and wounds from self-harming, ensure that they are treated at once and not allowed to be infected. If your child has suffered burns, use cold water to treat the wound and consult a medical doctor at once.

When you talk to your teen, don't bring up the topic straightaway. Have the conversation when both of you are in a more relaxed and neutral environment like on a walk or drive. Start by asking if anything is bothering them. Let them know you are not judging them or putting them down, and that you are always there for them. Allow and help your teen feel safe about talking to you. If you find that your teen can't talk and express themselves in a conversation, ask them to write you a note or an email about how they feel.

In case they are unwilling to share their feelings with you, check if they would prefer to speak to a professional therapist, counsellor, coach or mentor. If your child/teen begins to tell you about their self-harming behaviour, do not overreact. Instead, calmly work with them to understand the reasons. Help the child navigate the feelings or emotions that are leading to self-harm. Work with the teen as a partner to solve this problem together—it is critical that you do not blame, shame or criticize them. Check if your child/teen has suicidal thoughts or ideas. Take any mention of suicide seriously.

In terms of the family environment, do not let self-harm become a topic of discussion around the house and do not let it become the most important event for the family. Try to deal with the situation in a matter-of-fact manner. Let your teen know that your connection with him/her is the most important thing to you and their emotions are important and valid. Ensure that your teen knows that you are there to help and that you will work together to find a solution. Do not treat this as a disease that your child has or let your child feel that he/she is flawed and damaged because of this behavior. Tell them it could be a passing phase or a temporary situation, which they can overcome.

In conversations, remind the child of their strengths and unique traits. Assure them that they are not a failure and that this experience does not define them as a person. While supporting your child to move beyond these behaviours, work out ways with them to make it difficult for them to self-harm. For example, remove sharp objects or things that might remind them to do it or make it easier to do it.

If you feel you need a professional opinion, especially if the child has mental health issues like anxiety, depression, trauma etc., you could consult a therapist and work with them to best support your teen.

Moving Forward and Prevention

To help your teen move forward and prevent further self-harm, you can try some of the following strategies:

1. Teach the child self-regulation techniques to manage difficult emotions such as coherence breathing, pranayama, humming, EFT tapping, self-hypnosis, guided imagery (described in Chapter 8) etc.
2. Use creative activities, like art, music, dance etc., to divert their mind and provide an outlet for their emotions.
3. Take them out in nature. You could go for walks, runs and spend time outdoors, listening to the sounds of nature.
4. Consider getting a pet. Having a pet will give your child a companion who will lower stress and increase feelings of comfort and connection.
5. Encourage them to journal to express their emotions or talk to non-judgemental friends.
6. Teach them how to use physical techniques, like punching a pillow, kicking, jumping, shaking etc., to release difficult emotions.
7. Encourage them to seek therapy for past traumas.
8. Help them stay busy with constructive and fun activities.
9. Encourage them to incorporate activities, like sports, gym, yoga etc., into their daily lives, boosting their mood and providing a sense of well-being.

10. How Do I Discuss Sexual Orientation with My Teen?

As Indian parents of Gen Z or Millennials, we have not grown up normalizing such conversations, and yet today, young children are exposed to discussions on sexuality and sexual orientation at very early ages—especially children growing up in the West. Indian parents struggle to have these conversations due to a lack of any relevant experience in the area and due to their own feelings of shame and discomfort around such topics. Yet, there is also a lot of fear of children and teens being misguided. Most parents are extremely uncomfortable, ashamed or fearful to touch upon such conversations. Many think that by discussing these topics, they will put the ideas into the teens' minds and that such discussions might normalize being homosexual. All this is far from truth.

In India's culturally rich, yet often conservative society, discussing sexual orientation with teenagers can feel like walking in the dark. However, parents are responsible for creating a nurturing space where their children feel safe expressing their true selves. This journey begins with self-awareness—parents must recognize their own biases and seek to educate themselves about the spectrum of sexual orientations. Indian history and mythology offer potent examples of diversity that can guide these conversations. The *Ardhanarishwara*, a deity combining Lord Shiva and Goddess Parvati, symbolizes the unity of masculine and feminine energies, celebrating the fluidity of identity. Similarly, the story of Shikhandi from the Mahabharata—born female but living as male—shows that gender and identity have long been recognized as complex and diverse. These themes also resonate with other mythologies: in Greek mythology, the figure of Tiresias, who experienced life as both a man and a woman;

in Norse mythology, Loki's shape-shifting to both male and female forms. These examples help make the topic of sexual orientation and identity more relatable and less intimidating for both parents and children.

Creating a safe and supportive environment at home is crucial for fostering open discussions. Parents should aim to normalize conversations about sexual orientation, ensuring their teenagers feel comfortable exploring and expressing their identities without fear of judgement.

In our experience, in most cases, by the time parents are ready to talk about this, teens have already discussed it with their friends and have quite a lot of information about it—right or wrong!

The best way to approach this area is to start by asking the teen what his/her thoughts are on the subject. Share your own views or concerns. Let them share what they have understood and learnt. Usually, teenage years are very confusing and since the brain is undergoing major changes, it can be a period of extreme confusion about sexuality, too. It is best to tell teens to not come to any conclusions and just stick to whatever they are feeling around this topic. If the teen has genuine confusion about orientation or questions about feelings around it, it is best to take help of a counsellor or sex educator. There are professionals who can guide and help your teen navigate the confusing years without feeling the need to hide or be afraid. If taking professional help is not an option, it is best to tell your teen to wait and not jump to any conclusions till he/she becomes an adult.

If your teen is sure about their orientation and if they happen to relate to being bisexual or gay/lesbian, it is best to help them embrace their identity with confidence and courage.

Sometimes, once they are out of their teenage years, they might finally figure out who they are or wish to be—sometimes, it can take much longer. By fostering inclusivity at home, parents can guide their children towards a society that values diversity, love and dignity for all. Real-life examples, such as Prince Manvendra Singh Gohil, the first openly gay royal in India, or Bollywood figures like Karan Johar and Sushant Digvikar, or athlete Dutee Chand, can inspire teens to not be ashamed about themselves but excel in their fields and create a name for themselves—irrespective of their sexual orientation. For this, parents also need to work on themselves, accept their own prejudices and overcome mental blocks in accepting their children's choices.

Among Indian families, gays and lesbians are forced to get married. Parents and grandparents also believe that marriage can change their orientation or make them heterosexual again. This is far from the truth. Such marriages ruin not one, but many lives, and such adults are forced to live a life of toxic shame, deception and falsehood. This further causes stress in relationships. Bringing children into such marriages also does not 'fix' or change the adult's orientation. Indian parents need to understand this and accept it as a part of a changing world.

11. How Do I Discuss My Concerns around Porn Addiction?

In today's digital age, early exposure to pornography is an uncomfortable reality many teenagers face, often stumbling upon it through a friend's phone, a pop-up ad or sheer curiosity. In fact, many kids accidentally come across porn content while using the phones of their cousins, grandparents or parents.

As parents, we must approach this topic with empathy rather than disgust or judgement, recognizing that such exposure can confuse and overwhelm teenagers. If you notice your teen spending excessive time online, approach them gently, saying, 'I've noticed you've been online more often recently. Is there something you're curious about or need help understanding?' This keeps the conversation open and non-confrontational. You might also explain, 'You know how advertisements sometimes show perfect-looking food that's nothing like what we eat? Pornography works the same way—it's exaggerated and doesn't reflect real relationships or emotions.' This analogy can help your teen understand that what they see is not a healthy standard but a distorted portrayal of intimacy.

Porn addiction among youth is not a sign of moral failure but a by-product of unfiltered access to digital content and natural curiosity. To help them navigate this challenge, explain how overexposure can affect their mind, much like how eating too much junk food affects their body: 'Just as relying on chips for every meal can make you sick, relying on these videos for understanding relationships can harm how you see yourself and others.' Encourage healthier outlets—suggest they join a sports team, learn a musical instrument or spend time with friends. Share relatable examples like how athletes or artists stay focused on their goals by avoiding distractions. If the issue feels overwhelming, consider seeking professional help with the same care you'd take them to a doctor for a persistent fever. By addressing pornography exposure with compassion and relatable examples, you can help your teen develop a healthier understanding of relationships and make thoughtful decisions for their future.

We have worked with a few teens and adults struggling with porn addiction, and when we work on building their self-confidence, overcoming past traumas and working on building motivation towards some goal, they are able to significantly reduce the addiction or get over it. Like all addictions (drugs, alcohol and social media), porn addiction is also most commonly seen among teens who have severe childhood trauma and porn helps them feel numb from that pain. It is also seen among teens who are lonely and isolated from parents and peers. Teens, who are socially isolated, not connected to their parents or siblings and have poor coping skills, are most vulnerable to porn and other addictions. For most teens, it starts with curiosity and eventually, once the novelty is gone, they are out of it. Very few remain addicted—they might need therapy or professional help.

Self-Reflection for Parents

1. How was your relationship with your parents in this phase of your life? Were they supportive and understanding? How did they encourage/discourage you to follow your interests and passions?
2. What expectations did your parents have of your behaviour? How did they set those expectations? Did you meet them? Why or why not? What happened when you did or did not meet them?
3. How was your relationship with your siblings? What was it that your parents/other adults did or did not do that influenced such relationships? Is your relationship with your siblings different now? In what way?
4. Did you feel accepted by your peers? Did you feel you had to change yourself, in some way, to fit in?
5. Is there anything you did that was out-of-character for you?

6. Who were your idols? What did you admire about them? How did they influence your actions?
7. What is your most empowering memory?
8. What was most challenging for you about being a teenager?
9. What was the biggest mistake you made? Did you tell your parents? What was their response? What did you learn from it?
10. If you did not have a supportive home environment, how did you cope with it? Were there any other adults (relatives, teachers or coaches) who supported you? How did you benefit from those relationships?
11. Choose a difficult experience from your childhood. Close your eyes and picture yourself at that age. What did that child need? Give the child the support he/she needed at the time. Looking back, what did that child not know or understand, that you understand today?
12. What values did your parents pass on to you? Which of those values are you passing on to your children and why? Which ones are you not passing on to your children and why? Are there ways in which you try to be like/unlike your parents? What do you feel your parents could have done differently?

8

Self-Care and Self-Regulation for Parents

> 'Between stimulus and response, there is a space. In that space lies our freedom and power to choose our response. In our response lies our growth and freedom.'
>
> —Victor E. Frankl,
> Austrian neurologist and psychologist

It is unrealistic to expect parents to always feel calm, balanced and positive while taking care of their children. It is hard to focus on showing children love and compassion when they are acting difficult or triggering you in certain ways. Instead of feeling guilty about this, be compassionate towards yourself as it will help you be a good parent. Accepting our own emotions frustrations, stress, fear and anxiety allows us to be kind and accepting of our children too.

Parents' unhealed traumas tend to dictate their reactions and behaviour. They logically know what is right and wrong, but when faced with triggering situations, their adult brains and responses go into fight or flight mode and get hijacked with stress and painful memories. Becoming aware of these and working on healing them is an important part of the parenting journey. If we are too harsh and judgemental about our challenging situations and distressing reactions, we also prepare our children to be harsh and unaccepting of us. We've seen instances where a parent's guilt or regret can create more distance in the relationship with the child than the actual lapse.

Children tend to unknowingly trigger their parents more than anyone else, so it becomes even more important for parents to love and accept their inner children. Only when we heal our own wounded parts can we truly and deeply connect with our children.

Parents Are Also Learning and Healing!

While you embark on this journey, understand that not every day of parenting will be the same. There will be good days and not-so-good days. The challenge is to embrace our humanity and frailty with openness and kindness, with humour and patience so we can treat our children's mishaps and errors with the same attitude. It is important to note that, as parents, we are constantly learning, making mistakes, correcting them and relearning, just like our children. We should not expect perfection from ourselves as parents just as we should not expect perfect children. It is important to take responsibility for our actions, but not to condemn ourselves just because we could not live up to the 'ideal parent' image we created for ourselves. In spite of doing everything right, some days will be rough, when communication fails and nothing works. It is a part of life and of being human.

Parents Are Not a 24x7 Concierge Service

It is perfectly acceptable and even necessary for a parent to need time alone, and to take time to de-stress. Children also need to understand that parents need time for themselves and cannot be present 24x7 for them. This is as important for the child to learn and understand, as it is for the parents to practise this guilt-free. Child has to understand that a parent may not be available all the time at beck and call—they have to learn to wait patiently till the parent is available. Sometimes a parent has to teach the child to wait—even if the parent is available—so that they can learn the valuable lesson of patience and consideration. This trait seems to be missing in todays kids because parents are hypervigilant and often hovering over the child trying to meet all their requirements as quickly as possible. This makes the child entitled. The child also gets used to this and starts taking it for granted. It burns out the parent and spoils the child as well.

It is better to tell your child that you need fifteen minutes before you can play with them instead of being stressed, resentful or not being present. When you tell them gently, they learn that your need for time alone is not about them or their behaviour but about your own needs. This way, they learn to accept the needs of others too, and do not grow up believing that the world revolves around them.

In the time that you carve out for yourself, it is not easy to disconnect instantly from the stressors in all parts of your life. To make sure that you have the best chance to de-stress and calm down, we have put together some techniques that will help you train your nervous system to respond more effectively to triggers. These techniques will make you more aware of what stimulates you and how you can bring down stress levels so that you respond more calmly when you are overwhelmed. Research shows that when self-regulation is practised regularly, people can benefit from lowered stress, anger and violent outbursts in as soon as four weeks.[1]

The first chapter of the book helped you recognize any trauma you may have experienced or baggage you may have carried into adulthood. This section helps you understand how to rewire your brain to have different reactions to the same kind of stimulus. The techniques mentioned here are crucial of bringing together all you have learnt in this book. Without learning to parent your inner child and reclaim the fragmented pieces of yourself, the advice in this book will be of no use. It will be an interesting read merely, rather than practical changes that can improve your relationship with your child.

When we introduce these evidence-based self-regulation techniques with parents and children in our workshops and clinical practice, we always see steady and positive impact.

The videos of all these techniques are available on the website (www.wellness-space.net) as well as Riri Trivedi's YouTube channel. You can use these videos to learn these or experience them as well. These are also taught by Riri and Anagha in their parenting workshops—Basics of Positive Parenting and Pathways to Positive Parenting as well as their The Journey Within workshop.

You can access all online parenting resources and self-regulation technique videos by scanning this QR code:

Self-Regulation Techniques

There are two aspects of self-regulation:

- To balance and regulate the nervous system that is dysregulated due to stress or trauma.

- To create a positive state of mind that helps you have a balanced and empowered response to difficult situations.

Both these can be achieved through the following practices:

1. Humming/Simple Bhramari
2. Abdominal breathing
3. Guided relaxation with autosuggestions
4. Guided imagery for healing inner child of parents
5. Emotional Freedom Technique
6. The SEE Protocol for Self-hypnosis

All these techniques are also explained in detail in the parenting section of our website. They are also available as English and Hindi videos on YouTube, which demonstrate the techniques and explain the process. Before that, let's understand each of them a little more.

1. Humming/Simple Bhramari: The Ideal Stress Buster

Humming is the simplest of all self-regulation techniques. A daily humming routine can help enhance the parasympathetic nervous system and slow down sympathetic activation. People enjoy lower stress levels due to a reduced heart rate, improved heart rate variability and better sleep quality. Humming for ten to fifteen minutes, twice a day, also improves lung parameters and focus. It is so simple that it can be a family activity where children benefit from it as well. It involves the following steps:

i. Sit down with your spine erect. You can sit on a chair, sofa, cross-legged on the floor or even on the bed with your legs stretched. Pick whatever is most comfortable for you.

ii. Close your eyes. For those who feel anxious or uncomfortable keeping their eyes closed, keep them open and stare at a blank wall in front of you.
iii. Take a deep breath from the nose, counting slowly until five. Make sure you are inhaling deeply for three to four seconds.
iv. As you exhale from the nose, make a humming sound, with your lips sealed shut. For three to four seconds of inhalation, you should typically be exhaling for six to eight seconds, while humming.
v. Do not hum too loudly or too softly. Keep it at a pitch that allows you to feel the vibrations of the sound in your body.
vi. Do this for ten minutes, or twenty-five rounds, in the beginning. Build up to twenty minutes once you get used to it.
vii. It is not recommended to follow this practice lying down.

The beauty of the practice lies in its simplicity. People of any age, above three years, can practise it. You can even do it while you're waiting for an appointment, during lunchtime at office, at night before going to bed, as a family, just before meals, etc.

	Physical body	Energy body	Emotional state	Focus	Nervous system	Reduces anxiety, depression	Improves mood (positive)
Humming	HRV, HR, lung function, heart function	Optimizes energy	Influences emotional regulation	Increases focus	Improves autonomic function	Helps	Yes
Guided relaxation	Yes	Restores energy	Significantly	Enhances	Improves autonomic function	Helps	Yes

Figure 28: Benefits of Humming and Guided Relaxation

Note: Simple Bhramari (humming) is an effective stress buster [2]

2. Deep Abdominal Breathing

Abdominal breathing or diaphragmatic breathing is a yogic practice that is known to reduce stress by activating the PNS and reducing SNS activation (refer to Chapter 2).

Diaphragmatic breathing involves contraction of the diaphragm, expansion of the belly and deepening of inhalation and exhalation, which consequently decreases respiration frequency and maximizes the amount of blood gases.[3]

Here is how you can do it at home:

1. Sit down in a comfortable position on a chair or on the floor, ensuring a straight back. If you want, you may also do it while lying down.
2. Place one hand on your abdomen, near the navel. For a small child you can place a rubber duckie or toy on the child's navel.
3. As you inhale, imagine your breath travelling all the way to your belly and feel your abdomen expand like a balloon.
4. As you exhale, feel the abdomen deflate.
5. As you inhale and exhale, focus on the abdomen. During inhalation, the hand should move up as the belly inflates, while move the hand down and the belly inwards. Kids may enjoy doing this with a rubber duck or paper boat on their abdomen. You can ask the child to imagine the duck or boat are moving up and down in the waves – the deeper the breath, the higher the boat goes!
6. You can do deep breathing at any time of the day. Start with ten minutes and build up to twenty minutes.

3. Guided Relaxation with Autosuggestions

The practice of guided relaxation is as old as yogic texts. The ancient practice of *yoga nidra* is based on this. There's growing scientific evidence supporting the benefits of guided imagery. Studies show it can be effective in managing pain, anxiety and other mental health conditions.[4] It's also used to improve athletic performance and emotional regulation.[5] The use of imagination and imagery in a relaxed state is known to bring about changes in the mental and physiological processes of the body.[6] It is also effective in children and young adults.[7]

Guided relaxation, combined with autosuggestions or affirmations, is a very powerful tool that helps in many situations where therapy is not the first option. Autosuggestions, or affirmations, are powerful positive sentences about the end state or the behaviour you wish to see in yourself. For example, 'I am a calm parent', 'I am handling my child's tantrum with a calm and balanced mind', 'I am enjoying my parenting journey' etc. While making these suggestions, it is important to keep the following points in mind:

1. **Use positive sentences only**. Say 'I am calm when my child is upset' or 'I talk to my child with a relaxed energy' as opposed to 'I do not get angry' or 'I do not yell at my child.'
2. **Use the present tense** even if it doesn't feel natural. So, if your current challenge is to stay calm when you get triggered very easily, your autosuggestion needs to be, 'I am calm and relaxed in my interactions with my child.' The brain will feel it is a lie, but when the body starts believing and living this reality, the actions and thoughts will follow, too.
3. **Use the language of the subconscious mind**, such as images, emotions, sensations and sounds in the suggestions. Do not use long, complex words that do not make sense to the body. Instead, use a few words that create an experience for the body, preferably in the language you are most comfortable in.

4. **Make suggestions suited for yourself** and not for others. So do not make suggestions about your child doing something or spouse behaving in a certain way. This process is for you to reprogram yourself with new behaviours so keep suggestions focussed on the changes you wish to see in yourself.

To start your guided meditation, follow these steps:

1. Lie down in a relaxed position with your eyes closed.
2. Starting from your toes, focus on a particular part of your body and begin to relax it. Alternatively, listen to the guided imagery for relaxation from the website or Riri's YouTube channel.
3. Breathe in and imagine your breath is travelling to that body part. As you breathe out, imagine that the part is starting to feel relaxed.
4. Start with the toes, then, slowly move up to your feet, ankle joints, shins and calf muscles, knee joints, thigh muscles, hip joints, pelvic muscles, abdomen, chest, spine and all the muscles in the lower, middle and upper back. Continue relaxing the fingers, thumb, palms of the hand, wrist joints, elbow joints, entire arms and shoulder joints, followed by the neck, throat, back of the head, scalp, forehead, eyebrows, eyeballs, eyelids, nose, cheeks, lips, tongue, chin and jaw.
5. Once the entire body is deeply relaxed, do the affirmations and autosuggestions for positive change.
6. The suggestions must be repeated like a mantra, while visualizing the end state or goal to be achieved. The imagery needs to be as detailed as possible and the body needs to experience that end state as if it is happening right now. While repeating the suggestions try to use active

visualization of images including sound, smell, sensation in order to experience the suggestion with all senses.

Some positive suggestions that you can use for the practise are given below. You can pick the ones that resonate the most with you and your challenges as a parent:

1. I am a calm parent.
2. I stay calm and balanced in all situations around my child.
3. I respond to my child with kindness and compassion.
4. I stay firm, kind and empathetic while disciplining my children.
5. I listen to my child and respond from my upper brain that is calm and rational, and my heart that is filled with love and compassion.
6. I create a safe space for my child to express herself/himself freely.
7. I am very patient around my child.
8. I am present and attentive when I spend time with my child.
9. I have the ability to choose my response with my child.
10. I have open and honest communication with my child that builds a strong bond of trust between us.
11. I release my need for perfection in parenting and I celebrate the progress that we make together.
12. I release my need for seeking perfection in my child and I accept my child the way he/she is.
13. My calm and composed attitude builds connection with my child.
14. I love myself and I show kindness towards myself.

15. I take care of my needs and I respect my needs so my child also learns to do the same.
16. I take care of my needs so that I can also take care of my child's needs.
17. I am able to use all the positive parenting tips I have learnt and read about.
18. I practise self-regulation techniques, daily, that help me stay balanced and calm in the most challenging situations.
19. I am a happy parent and I love myself as a parent.
20. I enjoy my parenting journey.
21. Parenting is fun, joyful and fulfilling.

4. Guided Visualizations

Imagery is a very powerful tool for the mind to reprogram itself. Memories are also stored as images, sounds, sensations etc. Hence creating positive imagery with some auto suggestions also help the parents and child to stay calm, work towards some goal or challenge or even simply use it to overcome some blocks.

Guided imagery can be used for children also in order to reprogram their subconscious mind. The best time to do this is just before they go to bed while they are in half awake-half asleep state. This is when their mind is most receptive to guided imagery and suggestions we give them. So before they fall into deep sleep, they can be encouraged to visualize themselves doing those things they wish to do or change. This needs to be repeated in the morning also just before they wake up fully.

One student's niece who was three would cry while going to kindergarten every day. They tried everything to convince her or soothe her—from changing the bus stop to changing the school! But nothing worked and one day she tried to jump out of the moving van! She asked the girl's parents to just whisper in her ears before she should fall asleep (in her native language) '*Mayra loves going to school every day, Mayra goes to school happily every morning*' about fifteen to twenty times. Lo and behold, in two weeks the girl started going to school happily! After this, many parents have tried this method to inculcate good habits or teach the child a new skill and it has worked. Some kids take a bit longer than others, but it always helps!

Rules for making suggestions are mentioned in the previous section.

You can use this technique to overcome your child's fear or blockage like fear of exam or fear of a subject or fear of speaking in front of a group—the suggestions have to be formed using positive sentences and words that can create an image. For e.g.,

'*I am writing my exams calmly and confidently. I remember everything I have studied.*'

'*I love maths. It is fun to do maths. Maths is easy.*'

'*I am speaking confidently in front of the class.*'

Asking the child to imagine doing all this with all the senses will help create positive programs in the child's mind and body. This technique is based on Hypnotherapy principles and works well with children.

Guided visualization and repeating positive suggestions is a powerful tool for parents and children alike. When used properly it can give very good results. We have used it with our kids and also for learning Japanese!

5. Emotional Freedom Technique

Emotional Freedom Technique, or EFT, has been very popular among the parents we have worked with, for regulating their own emotions and for teaching their children. This technique is deceptively simple and hence, many are sceptical of its effectiveness.

However, EFT has moved, in the past two decades, from a fringe therapy to widespread professional acceptance.[8,9] New evidence from emerging fields, such as epigenetics, neural plasticity, psychoneuroimmunology and evolutionary biology, confirms the central link between emotion and physiology, and points to somatic stimulation as the element common to emerging psychotherapeutic methods. EFT is also safe when administered by a therapist or life coach or even self-administered. It can be easily learnt and also taught to children as young as four to five years old.

Scientific evidence provides several conclusions about clinical EFT including:

- It reduces symptoms for a variety of psychological conditions such as phobias, PTSD, anxiety and depression.
- It improves physical symptoms, such as pain, and autoimmune conditions such as psoriasis and fibromyalgia.
- It aids in reducing cravings and promoting weight loss.
- It produces physiological regulation of the autonomic nervous system and the HPA axis.[10]
- It can simultaneously reduce a range of psychological conditions, such as reducing anxiety and depression, along with PTSD.[11]
- It can simultaneously reduce both psychological and physiological problems, such as fibromyalgia, concurrent with PTSD, anxiety and depression.

- It is safe, both when self-administered as well as when administered by others.
- It is efficient and cost-effective, showing efficacy when delivered to both groups and individuals.

EFT may be used for managing physical aches/pains in the body or negative thoughts/emotions as an emotional first-aid tool. It helps verbalize unexpressed thoughts and emotions and, when done daily, it can help prevent the accumulation of negative thoughts and emotions. If you are doing EFT daily, do a minimum of three rounds before going to bed, on any negative thoughts or emotions going on in the mind. Stop when the mind goes blank or nothing else comes up.

EFT may be used as an emotional first aid—whenever a triggering situation arises—to prevent further trigger or to recover quickly after being triggered. It is not meant for positive reinforcement but for acknowledging, processing and releasing negative emotions, thoughts and pains. The good thing about this practice is that it can be easily taught to children. It is also easy to integrate into a busy schedule. For example, you can do the short method in public places or when there is no time for the entire process.

The short method includes only doing steps 2 and 5, for a few rounds, until the emotional charge is resolved, or the pain is gone.

For a child, you can call it 'Magic Tapping' or 'Tapping to Taming' or some creative fun name and teach the child the method in a simple format. Depending upon the age of the child the steps can be simplified, or short cut can be used. Children are very receptive to such processes as they are not as cynical as teens or adults, and they can easily switch their emotional states with such processes.

EFT Procedure Steps

	**Think of a very strong negative emotion, negative thought, or physical pain,** and get in touch with the sensation in your body.
	**Give it a number between 1 and 10 (SUD),** depending on the severity of the emotion or pain.
	Repeat the following affirmation three times while tapping at the **karate chop** point.
	'Even though I have this… / I feel ________________, I choose to deeply and completely love and accept myself, and let it go right now.' **Repeat three times.**
	**Tap the 12 given points** while focusing on the key core word of the feeling or sensation in the body (e.g., this headache, this anger, this discomfort).
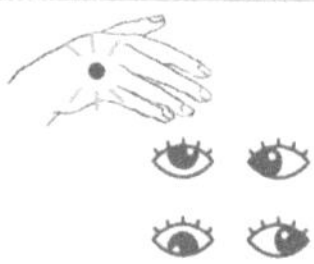	Move to the **gamut point** and, while pressing it, **look up, look down, move your eyes to the extreme left, then the extreme right.** Roll your eyes clockwise and counterclockwise, then say: **1-2-3-4-5, 5-4-3-2-1.**
	**Hum** a song or tune
	Place both hands on your heart center/solar plexus and breathe in through your nose, then out through your mouth. **Repeat this seven times.**
	This completes **one round.**
	**Check the SUD.** It should have either reduced by half or disappeared completely. Keep doing more rounds until the SUD decreases to 0 or 1.

Figure 29: EFT Steps

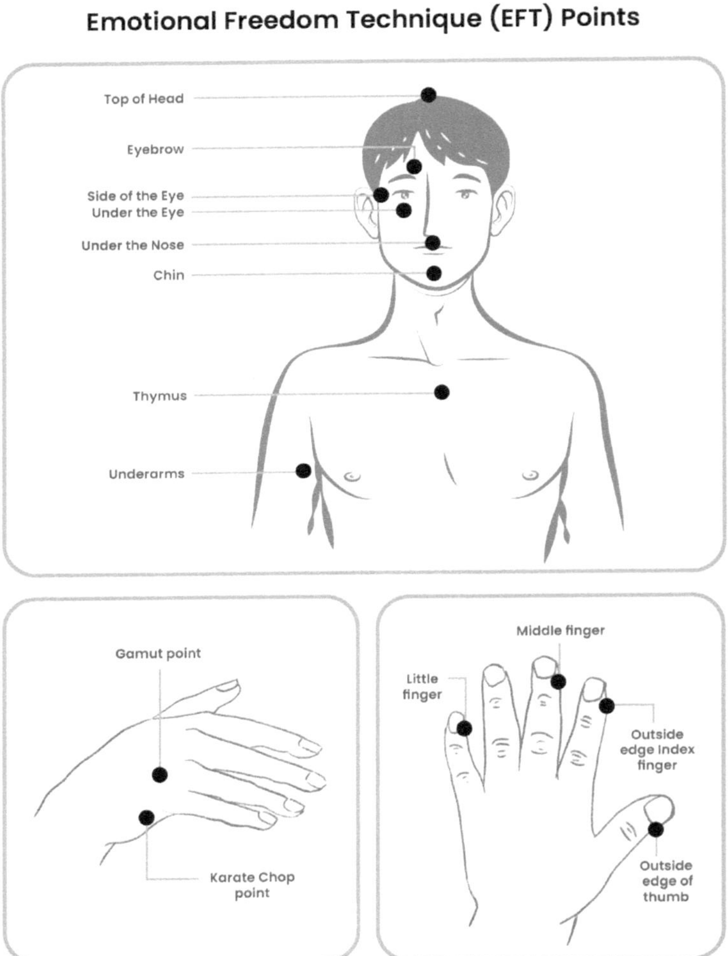

Figure 30: EFT Tapping Points

6. The SEE Protocol for Self-Hypnosis

This is a twenty-minutes process that can help you calm your nervous system, slow down your thoughts and relax your body. It can also be used for reprogramming the subconscious mind with positive suggestions for habit change, overcoming negative emotions or working on fears or blockages. It not only helps bring down stress but also prepares the mind and body for the positive changes that you wish to see in your life.

The Society for Energy and Emotions (SEE), run by Riri and Gunjan Trivedi, along with Wellness Space, has developed a self-hypnosis protocol that is a part of the Evidence-based Psychotherapy Programme taught by Wellness Space.[12] There are many different variations of self-hypnosis or meditative protocols available. Sitting down in silence and focusing on your breath is also a common approach for meditative practices

The SEE protocol for self-hypnosis is the outcome of several experiments that tried to understand how each activity affected the mind and the body and consists of series of steps that use breath, sound and imagery. These have a profound impact on the mind and body.

The study of the impact of this protocol on the mind and body (i.e. positive and negative affect/mood and heart rate variability or coherence) was published in 2022 in the International Journal of Yoga. The findings confirm the hypothesis that the SEE Protocol (active meditation) provides significant impact in terms of a positive effect (mood) and a reduction in negative effect (mood), as compared to silent meditation, where the reduction in negative affect was statistically significant. The changes in coherence (heart rate variability) were also consistent with these changes in mood.

SEE Protocol Steps

	ACTIVITY	DESCRIPTION	DURATION (MINUTES)	OBJECTIVE
1	Simple humming	Comfortable sitting position with spine erect and eyes closed (avoid if vertigo.)	25 counts or 5 minutes	Calms down the nervous system. Slows down the mind. Regulate the breath in a rhythmic pattern.
2	Coherent breathing	10 seconds (5 seconds inhalation, 5 seconds exhalation) as per the comfort level. Focus on heart centre and feel breath going in and out of the heart centre while maintaining the rhythm.	30 counts or 5 minutes	Coherence established between heart and brain
3	Invoking positive emotions (e.g., gratitude and love)	Focus on the heart chakra/centre, maintain coherent breathing and experience a positive emotion (e.g. love, gratitude, joy, peace)	About 5 minutes	Facilitates coherence and invokes positivity
4	Guided imagery	While repeating positive auto suggestions, experience the goal or desired state using images, feeling, sensations and emotions	About 5 minutes	Guided imagery with affirmations. Living the 'desired' state with your body to work on habit change, a goal or positive emotion.

Figure 31: The SEE Protocol for Self-Hypnosis Developed by Wellness Space

To practise the The SEE protocol for self-hypnosis, follow these guidelines:

- Practise the protocol once a day for eight weeks.
- Do this preferably on an empty stomach.
- Follow the recommended sequence.

For those who have never meditated before, you can start small by first doing the steps for 3 minutes each and then gradually increase the time duration of each step to 5 minutes.

Therapy Helps!

Last, but not the least, healing one's own past traumas helps. After you have used all or some of the self-regulation techniques and you still feel that you have triggers that push you off balance sometimes, consider going for personal therapy sessions. Childhood trauma can be the reason for many unexpected and impulsive parenting behaviours. Even the most logical, sharp, successful and intellectually sound parents may become helpless victims of their deep-rooted, unconscious triggers arising from past traumas. In such situations, instead of feeling guilty or being in denial, it is best to take professional help and heal your traumas, so that, as parents, you can feel more empowered and positive as opposed to feeling hijacked by your reactive outbursts. Many parents who come to us for 'fixing' their children, actually realize that by healing themselves, they are able to improve their relationship with their child and the child subsequently doesn't require therapy at all!

Parents, who use self-regulation techniques but are still unable to manage their triggers due to severe childhood trauma, may need therapy to address their deep-rooted wounds from childhood. For such parents, therapy definitely helps. Mere counselling may not help with deep-rooted trauma responses and PTSD. However, Trauma-informed therapies, such as Inner Child Integration Therapy,[13] Reconsolidation of Trauma Memories[14] (RTM), EMDR or Clinical Hypnotherapy,[15] based on research, might help. The healing journey of such parents is long and intense, so one needs patience and time to notice the gradual benefits.

As parents, if we are open to working on ourselves and healing ourselves, we realize we are able to connect more deeply with our children, understand their challenges with compassion and without judgement, and have the patience and courage to help them heal, too!

Riri has encouraged both her children to seek therapy once she embarked upon the journey of healing herself, and both her kids have immensely benefitted. Their relationship only has become better and both her teens have been vocal about their therapy journey on social media to normalize conversations around mental health.

Here, we share the words of a few parents who healed their inner child wounds and transformed their parenting journeys:

> *'This therapy has been a game-changer for me as a parent. I've gained a deeper understanding of myself and my daughter. I've learnt effective communication skills, conflict resolution strategies and how to manage my own emotions, allowing me to respond to my daughter's needs more thoughtfully. Therapy has helped me. I'm grateful for the support and guidance I've received during therapy. It's been an invaluable investment in my personal growth and my daughter's well-being.'*—Shalaka

> *'I took this therapy mainly because of my son. I wanted to handle him in a better way by handling my own emotions in the right way. Therapy with you has helped me immensely to stay calm during his tantrums. Seeing me calm has changed the way he communicates during tantrums, and it has also helped me improve my relationship with my husband so my son can witness happy parents. Overall, the best thing I have done is to take therapy, and I feel proud of myself that I am a better mom now . . .'*—Navya Puttanna

> *'Going for therapy . . . Earlier, I was sceptical whether to take therapy or not. But now, I can confidently say I took the best decision. Therapy really helped me in many things like understanding from my child's perspective, staying calm and dealing with children in a balanced way. Before, I had a lot of confusion in parenting, as I'm a mother of three children. But after therapy, I got more clarity about my relationship with all three of them. My gap with my kids has also reduced to a large extent after attending the sessions. I hope to become a better parent with the knowledge I gained from the therapy sessions.'*—Shruti Kosuri

For more such conversations on mental health by ordinary people tune in to Riri Trivedi's YouTube channel where she has a podcast series called 'Real People, Real Stories'. People from all walks of life include parents, young adults and mental health professionals have come forward and shared their own mental health journeys in order to normalize conversations around therapy and taking help.

Conclusion

'There is no such thing as a perfect parent. So just be a real one.'

—Sue Atkins,
author of *Raising Happy Children for Dummies* and *Parenting Made Easy*

There are many similarities between parenting and 'growing a tree'. In both, we work on several areas and increase the probability of better outcomes. First, you plant the seed with love, care and guidance and nurture with patience. With growth, you provide the right environment or ecosystem—since there would be obstructions to deal with during the course. You prune when necessary while allowing the room for growth and transformation. Over time, the tree stands tall with strong roots deep in the value system, and the branches expand, creating a unique journey. Parenting is like growing the tree, it is not about controlling the outcome, but about consistently nurturing the process!

As parents, it is critical to recognize that childhood experiences shape the adult mental health, behaviours and resilience. There are several evidence-based insights that parents can incorporate into their parenting journey.

1. **Childhood shapes adulthood:** Parents need to be aware of the link between adverse childhood experiences and adulthood depression, anxiety, insomnia and resilience. This can help them become more aware of their role in (a) encouraging positive childhood experiences; and (b) ideally preventing or addressing the adverse childhood experiences.
2. **Warmth matters:** The research supports that warmth and supporting environment from parents, caregivers and teachers can reduce the negative influence of adverse childhood experiences. Hence, irrespective of whether parents have control over the adverse events or not, they have an important role in providing warmth and social support to the child. This requires complete awareness of the role of adverse childhood experiences, their behavioural implications and the ability to recognize and address the implications.[1,2]
3. **The importance of adult psychological resilience:** Our work with hundreds of individuals over the past decade has identified that adults with stronger psychological resilience are able to cope with life's stress (including the long-term influence of childhood trauma) much better. Even adults, who were exposed to very high levels of repeated trauma during childhood, come to us for help with much lower levels of depression if they had higher levels of psychological resilience, compared to individuals with low resilience.
4. **Parenting builds resilience:** Parents need to understand how to build resilience in their children. Research has shown

that warm, supporting and child-centred parenting style is associated with the development of resilience. Balanced or authoritative parenting style (sufficient control and warmth) could be regarded as a protective factor that may increase the ability to overcome negative life events and crisis.[3]

5. **Parenting style and adolescent depression:** Extensive research supports that parental warmth, behavioural control and autonomy granting reduce the risk of depression in adolescents. Alternatively, strong psychological control by parents increases the risk of adolescent anxiety, depression and suicidal ideation.[4] Evidence supports the linkage of authoritarian parenting style with several types of adverse childhood experiences.[5] Therefore, building warmth along with control (or authoritative parenting) is likely to reduce such risk. More recently, the insights from our work of over 200 parents' assessment confirms that if parents feel they don't have social support, it is likely to result in "permissive" parenting style.

To summarize, parenting is all about creating positive childhood experiences full of warmth and control and addressing the long-term risks of adverse childhood experiences. Parenting style plays a key role in shaping the child's mental health, resilience and overall well-being during adulthood. By providing a nurturing environment, warmth and taking a balanced approach (control and warmth), parents can facilitate resilience in children and even reduce the risk of adverse childhood experiences. While the key is a balanced parenting style, the challenge is in applying that 'balance' to delicate situations, which require patience, perseverance and resilience.

Despite the above evidence, it is important to realize that parenting doesn't come with a fixed formula, because every family, child and situation is different, which makes parenting a fluid and evolving process. Hence, understanding ourselves and our unresolved pain, fears or emotional blocks is core to healthy and balanced parenting. When we become aware of what holds us back, we begin to see the patterns shaping our behaviour. By taking steps to address our limitations, through addressing the footprints of our childhood experiences, we gain power and can break the unhealthy patterns. This increases the probability of conscious and balanced parenting.

We hope the self-reflection exercises helped you identify some of your unhealed wounds, triggers and parenting habits that may not be helping you or the child. With honesty and care, even deep rooted hurts can be addressed, resulting in better relationships, and this power is available within us, as parents. It is ok to make mistakes, we all do. The key is to see them, say sorry when needed and reach out for help if you are struggling. Similar to what Riri shared about hear learnings, we all can learn from our own parenting mistakes and grow.

This book is **not a manual but a guide** to help you on your own unique parenting journey. It's about self-discovery, healing and creating a loving and supportive environment for your children to thrive in. Ultimately, the goal is to raise children who are emotionally resilient, compassionate and capable of navigating life's challenges with grace and strength.

Finally, there are **no perfect parents and there are no perfect children**! Expecting either means setting ourselves up for a life full of regrets or guilt. Let us not strive to be perfect in anything. Accepting our imperfections as humans, first, and then as parents, with grace and authenticity goes a long way in building honest connections with our children. Let our children see our honest efforts, our struggles and our intentions, and let them also learn to accept and forgive us just like we accept and forgive ourselves. In the challenging times (early years and teens), taking one day at a time helps and learning to see each day as a fresh start is a good way to keep the journey light and meaningful. Ultimately, the reality is that parenting is a journey where both child and parent learn—from each other and through each other. Let the journey be filled with joy, connection and contentment!

Compiled by Gunjan Y Trivedi, PhD

Annexure 1

ACE Table

Type of Abuse/ ACE/Trauma	Adult Behaviour that Qualifies as Abuse	Research-based Health and Behavioural Outcomes
1. Physical abuse	All forms of physically violent behaviour, including, but not limited to: shaking, pushing, choking, painful grabbing, kicking, slapping, beating, pinching and caning	• Severe anxiety disorders, depression, PTSD, sexual dysfunction and borderline personality disorder • Vulnerability to health conditions related to the immune system and cardiovascular function[1] • A higher probability of attention-deficit hyperactivity disorder (ADHD), PTSD and bipolar disorder[2] • Research also indicated that physical abuse often co-occurred with other childhood adversities, such as sexual abuse and parental psychopathology.[3] • Marital breakdown in adult life[4]

Type of Abuse/ ACE/Trauma	Adult Behaviour that Qualifies as Abuse	Research-based Health and Behavioural Outcomes
2. Sexual abuse	• Incest, rape, molestation • Inappropriate touching • Exposure to porn, sex talk and exposing body parts at an inappropriate age	• People who have experienced sexual abuse tend to be more prone to self-sabotaging behaviours, like high-risk behaviours, unprotected sex or drug addiction.[5] • Exposure to risky situations[6] • Significant consequences for the child's academic, social and emotional functioning.[7] The impact varies on the severity and frequency of the abuse, the child's age and developmental stage and the child's support network.[8] • Anxiety, borderline personality disorder, PTSD, depression, compulsive behaviour, eating disorders, self-harm, suicidal behaviour, addictions, sexual dysfunction or confusion about sexual orientation. • Prone to sexual promiscuity, victim–perpetrator cycle and poor academic performance.[9] • Impairments in multiple domains of sexual functioning, including desire, satisfaction, orgasmic functioning and sexual pain.[10]

Type of Abuse/ ACE/Trauma	Adult Behaviour that Qualifies as Abuse	Research-based Health and Behavioural Outcomes
3. Emotional abuse	• Name-calling, insulting, taunting, nagging • Threats of violence and abandonment and intentional frightening[11] • Making the child fear that they will not get food or the care they need • Socially isolating the child • Constant criticism • Allowing the child to witness the physical or emotional abuse of another • Withholding love, support or guidance • Threats of committing suicide, running away etc. • Constantly comparing the child to siblings, cousins, friends etc. • Making the child a caretaker of a sibling or sick parent • Making the child a confidante of a parent or mediator in marital problems	• A study found that emotional abuse was the strongest predictor of emotion deregulation. Especially women with history of emotional or sexual abuse, face greater emotional dysregulation.[12] • Other effects include: Loneliness,[13] depression, dissociation[14] and the perceived lack of social support, which makes them vulnerable to self-harm and suicidal behaviour.[15] • Emotional eating • Being clingy and possessive in relationships • Low self-worth,[16] poor confidence and self-doubt • Hampered development of socio-emotional and interpersonal skills in adulthood through dysregulation of emotional response[17] • Toxic shame, leading to feelings of worthlessness, undeserving of love, self-criticism and also PTSD • Increased vulnerability to affective disorders in adulthood • Irrational fears and phobias • Low self-esteem[18] • A comprehensive meta-analysis of 3,37,185 individuals demonstrated that physical abuse, emotional abuse and emotional neglect were significantly associated with higher suicide attempts.[19]

Type of Abuse/ ACE/Trauma	Adult Behaviour that Qualifies as Abuse	Research-based Health and Behavioural Outcomes
4. Emotional neglect	• Not meeting the child's emotional needs • Not being available for them	• Hostile and aggressive physical behaviour toward others • Social withdrawal • Poor academic performance • Impulsivity and hyperactivity • Depressive and anxiety disorders • Somatic complaints • Low self-esteem and hopelessness • Addictions and eating disorders • Teenage suicide. • The rates of dysthymia (persistent depressive disorder), alcohol dependence and prevalence of antisocial personality disorder is higher in people who have faced abuse and neglect.[20] • Oppositional defiant disorder, panic attack, major depression, and dysthymia[21]
5. Physical neglect	• Not meeting the child's physical needs for timely food, clean clothes, safety, medical treatment etc.	• Loneliness[22] • Depression[23] • Worthlessness[24] • Perceived lack of social support[25] • Self-harming and suicidal behaviour[26]
6. Peer isolation 7. Peer victimization	• Peers isolating the child • Peers verbally abusing the child • Body shaming by peers • Humiliation by and in front of cousins, friends or classmates • Child being the victim of pranks by peers	• Social anxiety[27] • Loneliness[28] • Depression, self-doubt[29] • Irrational fear • Low confidence • Toxic shame • Eating disorders[30] • Body image issues[31]

Type of Abuse/ ACE/Trauma	Adult Behaviour that Qualifies as Abuse	Research-based Health and Behavioural Outcomes
8. Domestic violence 9. Community violence	• Witnessing parents fight • Seeing a parent being physically injured • Hearing the screams of a parent who is being beaten	PTSD symptoms were predicted by victimization, witnessing or hearing about community violence or domestic violence.[32]
10. Constant fighting between parents	• Parents fighting in front of children	Adolescents who experience the divorce of their parents and destructive, chronic co-parent conflict experienced: • Increased emotional dysregulation • Behavioural problems • Psychological difficulties • Insecure parent-child attachment • Adjustment issues, leading to high levels of distress and internalization • Less satisfaction in life • Anxiety and depression[33]
11. Parent's mental health challenges	• Experiencing emotional neglect, household dysfunction or growing up with an authoritarian parent as a result of one or both parents' mental health issues	• Stress, anxiety[34] and constant need to take care of others • Co-dependency on older sibling • Need for validation by over-caring as adults[35]
12. Parent struggling with addiction and substance abuse	• Experiencing material neglect due to one or both parents' addiction or substance abuse • Exposure to drug use and drug dealing • Risk of violence and physical abuse	• High tendency of criminal behaviour[36] • Family break-up[37]

Type of Abuse/ ACE/Trauma	Adult Behaviour that Qualifies as Abuse	Research-based Health and Behavioural Outcomes
13. Family incarceration	Violent family environment or emotional neglect due to the incarceration of a family member	• Children live in denial or shame.[38] • Experiencing ambiguous loss and stigma[39] • Living in constant fear of reprisal from the victim's family[40]
14. Death of a parent/primary caregiver	Witnessing the death of a parent or primary caregiver due to natural disasters, illness or accident	• Higher grief distress[41] • Abandonment issues[42] • Fear of relationships[43] • Cautious about getting close to anyone else[44] • Clingy and over-possessive as adults—with their spouse, child or friends[45]
15. Divorce	Experiencing divorce and separation of parents	• Anger towards both parents[46] • Trust issues[47] • Sense of not belonging anywhere[48]
16. Socio-economic condition	Peer isolation, peer victimisation, physical neglect or emotional neglect due to family's socio-economic conditions.	• Shame[49] • Low self-esteem[50]

Annexure 2

Spotting Signs and Seeking Support

What is the difference between a psychologist, a psychiatrist and a psychotherapist? Who do we go to for mental health problems or parenting issues?

A **psychiatrist** is a medical doctor (MD), specializing in mental health, who is qualified to diagnose mental illnesses and prescribe medication. Their expertise is often sought for managing severe conditions such as schizophrenia, bipolar disorder or major depression. While psychiatrists may provide therapy, their primary focus is medical treatment. Usually, we go to a psychiatrist when there is a severe mental health crisis like suicide attempts, severe depression or irrational behaviour.

A **psychologist** or **counsellor,** holds a master's degree in Psychology and specializes in addressing mental health issues through therapeutic interventions rather than medication. They utilize evidence-based approaches, like cognitive-behavioural therapy (CBT), and are skilled in psychological assessments. They may also have additional training in coaching or techniques in managing stress, relationship conflicts etc. Unlike psychiatrists or psychologists, counsellors are not trained to diagnose or treat severe mental health disorders but are instrumental in fostering emotional resilience and personal development.

A **psychotherapist** is a broad term that encompasses professionals who offer various types of therapy to address emotional, behavioural and psychological concerns. This role can be filled by psychiatrists, psychologists or other licensed practitioners, such as clinical social workers, Certified Hypnotherapists, Inner Child Therapists, Trauma Informed Therapist, Regression Therapist etc. Psychotherapists often focus on deeper, long-term issues, helping clients uncover and address thought patterns and behaviours affecting their well-being. Life coaches can also help with many behaviour-related issues. It is important to check the certifications and accreditations of any practitioner you go to for your or your child's therapy.

There are also parenting coaches, Child Psychology experts, Intimacy Coaches and Sex Educators. Depending on your requirement, you can choose to go with whomever you feel confident to work with and are comfortable sharing your problems with.

We believe that if a problem that can be managed by non-intrusive therapies, taking psychiatric medicines should be the last resort since medicines have side effects that may be harmful to the developing brain of a child or teen. It is alarming to see how many young children, who have anxiety, exam fear or panic attacks before exams, are taken to psychiatrists and medicated. This can also become a habit. In our experience, such things can be easily worked on and resolved through psychotherapies prescribed by certified practitioners.

However, in extreme conditions, when the child is completely dysfunctional, suicidal or experiencing severe conditions like psychosis etc., psychiatric intervention, along with therapy, is necessary.

Who to consult for Neurodevelopment Disorders? How do I know if my child has learning disabilities or a mental condition?

This section has been put together by our team of psychologists—Neha Pandya, Parishi Thakore and Sayan Bannerjee.

In our journey as mental health professionals, we've found that everyone may not have the exposure and access to resources to understand when they need to reach out to a doctor. Not only with adults, but with children, too, developmental conditions and challenges that they may be experiencing might go undiagnosed for years. Having the right information and tools to handle special challenges can change your child's life. Here, we have put together a table and some questions you should ask if you believe your child may need more help than others of their age. However, the information in this table is indicative and should not be used as a diagnosis or assessment of any condition. Guidance from a certified professional is necessary before concluding anything.

Neuro-Developmental Disorders	Symptoms	To whom should we reach out?
Intellectual or developmental disorder *If child is less than 5 years, then Global Developmental Delay	• Taking more time to learn new things compared to others • Difficulty in achieving independence in self-care activities such as eating, bathing, dressing etc. • Difficulty in understanding and following instructions. • Difficulty in coping with academic demands • Finding it hard to think through problems and make sense of things • Problems with judgement and critical thinking • Finding it challenging to figure out solutions to problems	Paediatrician or psychiatrist, clinical or rehabilitation psychologist
Specific learning disability *If child is less than 5 years, then Global Developmental Delay	• Difficulty in understanding and using language • Difficulties in comprehending, speaking, reading, writing, spelling or performing mathematical calculations	Paediatrician, paediatric neurologist, developmental paediatrician, psychiatrist or clinical psychologist (RCI-licensed)

Neuro-Developmental Disorders	Symptoms	To whom should we reach out?
Autism Spectrum Disorder (ASD)	• Difficulty making friends and talking to people • Repetitive movements of hands, limbs and body (hand flapping, rocking etc.) • Repetition of words and phrases; repeating questions instead of answering them • Being extremely sensitive or not sensitive enough to things like sights, sounds, touch and taste	Paediatrician, psychiatrist, clinical/ rehabilitative psychologist (RCI-licensed)
Attention Deficit Hyperactivity Disorder (ADHD)	• Consistently having trouble paying attention, sitting still or acting without thinking for (at least 6 months) • Getting easily distracted, losing interest in one task and frequently shifting from one activity to another • Difficulty in awaiting turns, interrupting or intruding on others activities, acting or speaking without thinking about consequences	Psychiatrist, clinical psychologist (RCI-licensed)

These questions will help you determine if you need to reach out to a professional for your three- to six-year olds' behaviour to check for intellectual or developmental conditions:

- Does the child experience any delays in speaking, sitting, standing or walking?
- Is the child's speech not clear?
- Does the child have difficulty seeing or hearing?
- When you tell the child something, do they seem to have a problem understanding it?
- Does the child sometimes have fits or lose consciousness?

- Does the child have difficulty in learning to do things like other children of their age?
- Does the child seem slow, dull and not responsive?

If any of the answers to these questions is 'Yes', please consult the concerned professionals mentioned in the table.

These questions will help you determine if you need to reach out to a professional to check for intellectual or developmental conditions if your child is over the age of seven years.

- Does the child have difficulty in speaking, sitting, standing or walking?
- Can the child not do things for themselves like eating, drinking, dressing, bathing and grooming?
- Is the child's speech not clear?
- Does the child seem to have problems understanding and following instructions?
- Does the child have difficulty in expressing and relating to events happening around them, on their own?
- Does the child have difficulty in understanding and learning new things?
- Does the child have difficulty in reading, writing, monetary transactions or understanding time?
- Does the child sometimes have fits or lose consciousness?
- Does the child seem slow, dull and not responsive?

If any of the answers to these questions is 'Yes', please consult the concerned professionals mentioned in the table.

These questions will help you understand if your child may have autism spectrum disorder:

- Does the child not make and maintain eye contact?
- Does the child make repetitive movements like hand flapping, nodding and rocking?
- Does the child bang their head, bite or hit themselves?
- Does the child laugh, cry or get agitated and excited for long periods, without any apparent reason?

- Does the child have difficulty in initiating or engaging in conversations or social interactions with family members or peers?
- Does the child repeat words or phrases multiple times or repeat the questions asked instead of answering them?
- Does the child stare at a place and remain aloof for long durations?
- Does the child close their ears to certain noises like cooker whistle or mixer-grinder?

If any of the answers to these questions is 'Yes', please consult the concerned professionals mentioned in the table.

These questions will help you understand if your child may have ADHD:

- Is the child restless and unable to sit in one position for a required duration?
- Does the child disturb other children without any reason?
- Does the child leave a task incomplete and switch to doing something else?
- Does the child cry often and easily?
- Does the child's mood fluctuate frequently and drastically?
- Does the child fidget constantly?
- Does the child exhibit tantrums and unpredictable behaviour?

Acknowledgements

Riri G Trivedi

This book is a testament to the incredible support and love that surrounds me. First and foremost, to my husband, Dr Gunjan Y. Trivedi, my deepest gratitude. Your unwavering support, insightful guidance, and gentle challenges were the bedrock of this journey, from the initial spark of an idea to the final page. Your contributions to the research, intertwined with my six years of doctoral studies, have enriched this work immeasurably.

To my children, Tvishi and Ansh, thank you for being my greatest teachers. You've shaped me into the parent I am today, and your willingness to share your stories, even the most personal ones, has given this book its heart. Your experiences, my 'hits and misses,' have been invaluable, and your encouragement to share my insights, both online and in these pages, has been truly inspiring.

My parents, the late Prof. P.A. Trivedi and Mrs M.I. Patel, instilled in me a deep understanding of nurturing and respectful parenting. Their unwavering encouragement and belief in me have been a constant source of strength. Growing up in an environment free from punishment and filled with open expression has profoundly shaped my perspective on childhood and trauma. Though my father's physical presence is missed since 2013, his legacy lives on in my love for teaching. My mother, with her boundless positivity, remains my guiding light, always there to bolster my confidence and authenticity.

To my dedicated team of therapists at Wellness Space, thank you for your invaluable contributions to the case studies and data analysis. Your expertise and support have been essential.

I extend my heartfelt thanks to my students and clients, whose encouragement and belief in this project helped me overcome my self-doubt and bring this book to fruition. Your questions and engagement on social media confirmed the need for this resource.

A special thank you to Niyati Dhuldhoya and Roshini Dadlani, whose expertise in structuring and refining my writing was indispensable.

To Gurveen Chadha, Areeb Ahmad and the entire Penguin Random House India team, especially Akangksha Sarmah, for the beautiful graphics, thank you for your belief in this project and for guiding us through the publishing process.

Most importantly, to Anagha, my co-author, this book which would not have existed without you, stands as a testament to our remarkable partnership. From our social relationship that started in Japan in 2003 which transitioned to teacher and student equation, to finally this shared project, your unique perspective and complementary talents were absolutely essential.

This book is born from our conviction that conscious parenting, equipped with the right tools, can significantly mitigate the mental health challenges we face today.

Anagha Nagpal

This book is a reflection of the values of those who have shaped me. I am deeply grateful to have been born into a progressive family where girls were treated with respect and love, a stark contrast to the experiences of many of my clients who felt unwanted, unseen or unloved because of their gender.

My parents, late Prof. Dr. Anil D. Mokashi and Mrs. Neelima A. Mokashi, both educators, instilled in me a lifelong love of learning, appreciation for excellence, importance of family bonds and a sense of responsibility towards society. Their teachings consistently guide my decisions. I admire my mother for her quiet strength and resilience. She is an inspiration to many. My father always made me feel special. Losing him during my pregnancy 21 years ago was a deeply challenging time. I am forever indebted to my husband, mom, in-laws, siblings and friends; their care provided a secure and nurturing start for my twins, a gift I cherish.

To my husband, Samir Nagpal, my fellow empty nester, thank you for being an amazingly involved and caring father since Day One! I am grateful for your enthusiasm and shared commitment to parenting. Your unwavering support has given me the courage and freedom to pursue my passions. It means the world to me!

To my beloved twins, Aryaman and Simran, the light and joy of my life! Writing this book allowed me to revisit your precious childhood and I realized how few truly "tough" moments there were to recount. You have gifted me with a profound understanding of unconditional love, a wisdom far beyond the pages of any book. Thank you for always being my biggest supporters. God bless you both.

I am grateful to my elder brother, Mr. Nikhil A. Mokashi for always being my steadfast ally and a positive influence in my children's lives. Thanks to all my nephews and nieces, my energy boosters, for (willingly) hanging out with me!

In addition to my family, my approach to parenting has been profoundly shaped by the teachings of Rabindranath Tagore and Dr. Maria Montessori, whose philosophies of holistic education, respect for children's dignity, connection with nature, and appreciation for diverse cultures resonate deeply with me. When my children were six, I transitioned from engineering to early childhood education, driven by a desire to contribute to shaping the next generation. I received invaluable coaching from my Montessori mentors, Martha and Donald Monahan. A few years later, thanks to the Positive Discipline Association's Parent Educator course, led by Dr. Jane Nelsen and Lynn Lott, I could more effectively guide parents in nurturing their children's well-being.

I am immensely graetful to Riri and Gunjan for being exceptional teachers, guides and friends. It's been so rewarding to use all my skills and experience to help others live fulfilling lives and spread the message of positive parenting to a wider audience. I am so thankful for all my clients whose commitment to their personal growth is a constant source of inspiration.

Finally, this book would not exist without the guiding presence of my elder sister, Late Mrs.Tanuja A. Kulkarni who continues to influence me from beyond. Her unexpected passing in 2018, shortly after her 53rd birthday, left a void that can never be filled. A psychic reading prompted by my work with Riri to address unresolved grief, revealed my sister's encouraging message for me to write. This revelation, just a month before Riri's invitation to collaborate on this parenting book, felt like a divine nudge. I had to say yes!

The timing of this book's release, on my sister's birthday, June 1st, which also coincides with the United Nations' Global Day of Parents, feels like a profound sign of her enduring presence.

This book is for all parents who strive to do what's best for their children. Thank you for reading!

Notes

Introduction

1 Post-traumatic stress disorder (PTSD) is a mental health condition that is caused by an extremely stressful or terrifying event—either being part of it or witnessing it. Symptoms may include flashbacks, nightmares, severe anxiety and uncontrollable thoughts about the event.

2 A psychotherapy technique that involves recognizing and healing childhood trauma, not just acknowledging those events, emotions and impact. It may involve the use of hypnotherapy or regression methods.

Chapter 1: The Shadows of Childhood

1 K. Hughes et al., 'The Effect of Multiple Adverse Childhood Experiences on Health: A Systematic Review and Meta-Analysis', *The Lancet Public Health*, 2(8) (2017): 356–366.

2 V. Naik et al., 'Navigating Generational Patterns: How Childhood Trauma Shapes Authoritative Parenting Practices in Indian Families',

International Journal of Indian Psychology, 12(2), (2024): pp. 4179–4189, DIP:18.01.372.20241202, doi:10.25215/1202.372.

3 G. Trivedi et al., 'A pilot study to understand the presence of ACE in adults with post-traumatic stress disorders at a well-being centre in India', *European Journal of Trauma & Dissociation*, 7(4) (2023): 100355.

4 R.G. Trivedi et al., 'The Insidious Nature of Childhood Emotional Abuse', *International Journal of Indian Psychology*, 11(4), (2023).

5 R.E. Norman et al., 'The Long-Term Health Consequences of Child Physical Abuse, Emotional Abuse, and Neglect: A Systematic Review and Meta-Analysis', *PLoS Medicine*, 9(11) (2012), https://doi.org/10.1371/journal.pmed.1001349

6 M.D. De Bellis and A. Zisk, 'The biological effects of childhood trauma', *Child and Adolescent Psychiatric Clinics of North America* 23(2), (2014): 185–222, vii. doi: 10.1016/j.chc.2014.01.002. Epub 2014 Feb 16. PMID: 24656576; PMCID: PMC3968319.

7 Society for Energy & Emotions, Wellness Space, India data (N=950).

8 G.Y. Trivedi et al., 'Adverse Childhood Experiences & mental health – the urgent need for public health intervention in India', *Journal of Preventive Medicine and Hygiene*, 62(3) (2021): 728–735, doi: 10.15167/2421-4248/jpmh2021.62.3.1785. PMID: 34909501; PMCID: PMC8639107.

Chapter 2: The Neuroscience of Childhood Trauma and Parenting

1 D. Cross, Fani, N., Powers, A., & Bradley, B. (2017). Neurobiological Development in the Context of Childhood Trauma. *Clinical Psychology: A Publication of the Division of Clinical Psychology of the American Psychological Association*, *24*(2), 111–124. https://doi.org/10.1111/cpsp.12198.

2 Ibid.

3 M.D. De Bellis and A. Zisk, 'The biological effects of childhood trauma', *Child and Adolescent Psychiatric Clinics of North America*, 23(2) (2014): 185–222, vii. doi: 10.1016/j.chc.2014.01.002. Epub 2014 Feb 16. PMID: 24656576; PMCID: PMC3968319.

4 B.A. van der Kolk, 'The neurobiology of childhood trauma and abuse', *Child and Adolescent Psychiatric Clinics of North America,* 12(2) (2003): 293–317, ix. doi: 10.1016/s1056-4993(03)00003-8. PMID: 12725013; M.D. De Bellis and A. Zisk. 'The biological effects of childhood trauma', *Child and Adolescent Psychiatric Clinics of North America,* 23(2) (2014): 185–222, vii. doi: 10.1016/j.chc.2014.01.002. Epub 2014 Feb 16. PMID: 24656576; PMCID: PMC3968319.

Chapter 3: The Parenting Compass

1 B.R. Sahithya et al., 'Parenting Styles and Its Impact on Children–A Cross-Cultural Review with a Focus on India', *Mental Health, Religion & Culture,* 22(4), 2009: 357–383.
2 Ibid.
3 Ibid.
4 Alison L. Barton and K. Hirsch Jameson, 'Permissive Parenting and Mental Health in College Students: Mediating Effects of Academic Entitlement', *Journal of American College Health,* 64(1), 2006, pp. 1–8, doi:10.1080/07448481.2015.1060597.

Chapter 4: Guiding Principles of Parenting

1 D.J. Siegel and T.P. Bryson, *The Whole-Brain Child* (London: Constable & Robinson Ltd., 2011).
2 Ibid.

Chapter 5: The Early Years: Birth to 6

1 Mary Gregory, 'What does the 'still face' experiment teach us about connection?' *Psych Help,* https://psychhelp.com.au/what-does-the-still-face-experiment-teach-us-about-connection/
2 UMass Chan Psychiatry & Behavioral Sciences, 'The "Still Face" Experiment by Dr Ed Tronick', YouTube video, 11 July 2022, https://www.youtube.com/watch?v=FaiXi8KyzOQ

3 Guidelines for Normal Sleep and Physical Activity, *Indian Academy of Pediatrics* (IAP), 2020-21, https://iapindia.org/pdf/Guidelines-for-Normal-Sleep-and-Physical-Activity.pdf
4 A Montessori classroom is a learning space designed to help children develop independence, curiosity and a love of learning. Montessori classrooms are known as 'prepared environments' because they are intentionally structured to support children's learning
5 S. Tyagi and S. Karande, 'Child sexual abuse in India: A wake-up call', *J Postgrad Med* 67(3) (2021): 125–129, doi: 10.4103/jpgm.JPGM_264_21. PMID: 34380802; PMCID: PMC8445113.

Chapter 6: The Middle Childhood Years: 7 to 12

1 As, & Durmishi, Lindita & Ibrahimi, Silva & Ibrahimi, Ervin & Mazzarini, Giorgia & Rexha, Labinot, 'School Bullying and its Influence on Psychosomatic Symptoms and Health', 2003, doi: 10.33422/6th.shconf.2023.06.115.
2 V. Talwar and K. Lee, 'A Punitive Environment Fosters Children's Dishonesty: A Natural Experiment', *Child Development* 82(6) (2011): 1751–1758, https://doi.org/10.1111/j.1467-8624.2011.01663.x
3 P. Gupta, 'IAP Guideline Committee On Digital Wellness And Screen Time In Infants, Children, And Adolescents. Indian Academy of Pediatrics Guidelines on Screen Time and Digital Wellness in Infants, Children and Adolescents', *Indian Pediatrics.* 59(3) 2022: 235–244, epub 2021 Dec 29. PMID: 34969943.
4 Alex Holte and F. Ferraro, 'True colors: Grayscale setting reduces screen time in college students', *The Social Science Journal* 60 (2020): 1–17, 10.1080/03623319.2020.1737461.

Chapter 7: The Teen Years: 13 to 18

1 D.J. Siegel, *Brainstorm* (Tarcher/Putnam, 2015).
2 S.R. Covey, *The 7 Habits of Highly Effective People* (Simon & Schuster, 1989).

3 Jamie Waters, 'Constant Craving: How Digital Media Turned Us All Into Dopamine Addicts', *Guardian*, 22 August 2021 https://www.theguardian.com/global/2021/aug/22/how-digital-media-turned-us-all-into-dopamine-addicts-and-what-we-can-do-to-break-the-cycle.

4 R. Preety et al., 'Sleep deprivation and cell phone usage among teenagers', *Drug Invention Today*, 10(10) (2018): 2073.

5 Meghna Sharma et al., 'Human Behaviour in Digital Bubble: Relationship between Mobile Phone Dependency and Disruptive Behaviour among Teens', *Indian Journal of Health and Wellbeing*, 14(2) (2023): 248–251.

Chapter 8: Self-Care and Self-Regulation for Parents

1 A. Adithy, 'Understanding and Addressing Stress and Trauma, with a Focus on Interventions for Users and Providers of Mental Health Services in India', 2022.

2 G. Trivedi, K. Sharma, B. Saboo, S. Kathirvel, A. Konat, V. Zapadia, P.J. Prajapati, U. Benani, K. Patel, and S. Shah, 'Humming (Simple Bhramari Pranayama) as a Stress Buster: A Holter-Based Study to Analyze Heart Rate Variability (HRV) Parameters During Bhramari, Physical Activity, Emotional Stress, and Sleep', *Cureus*, 15(4) (2003): e37527.

3 Shu-Zhen Wang et al., 'Effect of Slow Abdominal Breathing Combined with Biofeedback on Blood Pressure and Heart Rate Variability in Prehypertension', *The Journal of Alternative and Complementary Medicine* 16(10) (2010): 1039–1045, doi:10.1089/acm.2009.0577.

4 J. Hart, 'Guided imagery', *Alternative and Complementary Therapies*, 14(6) (2008): 295–299.

5 D. Feltz and D. M. Landers, 'The effects of mental practice on motor skill learning and performance: A meta-analysis', *Journal of Sport Psychology* 5 (1983): 25–57.

6 H. Benson and W. Proctor (2010). *Relaxation Revolution: The Science and Genetics of Mind Body Healing*. Simon and Schuster, 2010.

7 S.A. Lambert, 'The effects of hypnosis/guided imagery on the postoperative course of children', *Journal of Developmental and Behavioral Pediatrics* 17(5) (1996): 307–310.

8 D. Church, 'Clinical EFT as an Evidence-Based Practice for the Treatment of Psychological and Physiological Conditions', *Psychology* 4 (2013): 645–654. doi: 10.4236/psych.2013.48092.

9 Mahnaz Hajloo et al., 'Investigation on Emotional-Freedom Technique Effectiveness in Diabetic Patients' Blood Sugar Control', *Mediterranean Journal of Social Sciences* 5 (2014), 10.5901/mjss.2014.v5n27p1280.

10 The Hypothalamus-Pituitary-Adrenalin Axis manages the body's stress response.

11 D. Church et al., 'Emotional Freedom Techniques to Treat Posttraumatic Stress Disorder in Veterans: Review of the Evidence, Survey of Practitioners, and Proposed Clinical Guidelines', *The Permanente Journal* 21 (2017): 16–100, doi:10.7812/TPP/16-100.

12 G.Y. Trivedi et al., 'Comparative Study of the Impact of Active Meditation Protocol and Silence Meditation on Heart Rate Variability and Mood in Women', *International Journal of Yoga*, 13(3) (2020): 255–260, https://doi.org/10.4103/ijoy.IJOY_18_20

13 R.G. Trivedi, G.Y. Trivedi, N. Pandya & H. Ramani (2024). 'Effectiveness of "Healing the Child Within" Techniques for Well-being, Anxiety, and Depression', *International Journal of Regression Therapy*, 15.

14 G.Y. Trivedi, N. Pandya, P. Thakore, H. Ramani, R.G. Trivedi, & S. Kathirvel (2024). 'The effectiveness of Reconsolidation of Traumatic Memories for Complex PTSD–A pilot quasi-experimental study from a wellness centre in India', *European Journal of Trauma & Dissociation*, 8(4), 100480.

15 A. Valiente-Gómez, A. Moreno-Alcázar, D. Treen, C. Cedrón., F. Colom, V. Pérez, & B.L. Amann, (2017). 'EMDR beyond PTSD: A systematic literature review', *Frontiers in Psychology*, 8, 1668.

Conclusion

1 R.G. Trivedi et al., 'Association between Adverse Childhood Experiences and Internalizing Symptoms in Adults at a Wellness

Centre in India', *Indian Journal of Community Medicine,* 10 (2023).

2 J. Hall et al., 'Reducing adverse childhood experiences (ACE) by building community capacity: A summary of Washington Family Policy Council research findings', *Journal of Prevention & Intervention in the Community,* 40(4) (2012): 325–334.

3 H. Zakeri et al, 'Parenting styles and resilience', *Procedia-Social and Behavioral Sciences,* 5 (2010): 1067–1070.

4 A. Gorostiaga et al., 'Parenting Styles and Internalizing Symptoms in Adolescence: A Systematic Literature Review', *International Journal of Environmental Research and Public Health,* 16(17) (2019): 3192, https://doi.org/10.3390/ijerph16173192.

5 C.M. Lo et al., 'Prevalence of Child Maltreatment and Its Association with Parenting Style: A Population Study in Hong Kong', *International Journal of Environmental Research and Public Health,* 16(7) (2019): 1130, https://doi.org/10.3390/ijerph16071130.

Annexure 1: ACE Table

1 Rosana E. Norman et al., 'The Long-Term Health Consequences of Child Physical Abuse, Emotional Abuse, and Neglect: A Systematic Review and Meta-Analysis', *PLoS Medicine* 9(11) (2012): e1001349, doi:10.1371/journal.pmed.1001349.

2 M. Ferrer et al., 'Differences in the association between childhood trauma history and borderline personality disorder or attention deficit/hyperactivity disorder diagnoses in adulthood', *European Archives of Psychiatry and Clinical Neuroscience* 267 (2017): 541–549.

3 L. Sugaya et al., 'Child physical abuse and adult mental health: a national study', *Journal of Traumatic Stress* 25(4) (2012: 384–392.

4 P.E. Mullen et al., (1996). 'The long-term impact of the physical, emotional, and sexual abuse of children: A community study', *Child Abuse & Neglect* 20(1) (1996): 7–21.

5 J. Stuewig et al., 'Children's proneness to shame and guilt predict risky and illegal behaviours in young adulthood', *Child Psychiatry Human Development* 46(2) (2015): 217–27, doi: 10.1007/s10578-014-0467-1. PMID: 24842762; PMCID: PMC4239200.

6 Ibid.

7 T. Taj et al., 'Impact on Physical and Mental Health of Sexually Abused Children', *Child Sexual Abuse: A Public Health Problem in India* (Singapore: Springer Nature, 2024), pp. 135–143.

8 Ibid.

9 E.J. Letourneau et al., 'Comorbidity of sexual problems and posttraumatic stress disorder in female crime victims', *Behavior Therapy* 27(3) (1996): 321–336.

10 Ibid.

11 E.O. Paolucci et al., 'A Meta-Analysis of the Published Research on the Effects of Child Sexual Abuse', *The Journal of Psychology* 135(1) (2001): 17–36, https://doi.org/10.1080/00223980109603677

12 E.E. Burns et al., 'Child Maltreatment, Emotion Regulation, and Posttraumatic Stress: The Impact of Emotional Abuse', *Journal of Aggression, Maltreatment & Trauma* 19(8) (2010): 801–819, https://doi.org/10.1080/10926771.2010.522947

13 Y. Qu, 'From childhood emotional abuse to adolescent loneliness: The roles of self-compassion and rejection sensitivity', *Child Abuse & Neglect* 156 (2024): 107020, ISSN 0145-2134, https://doi.org/10.1016/j.chiabu.2024.107020.

14 V. Verrastro et al., 'Childhood Emotional Abuse and Problematic Internet Use: Trait Mindfulness and Dissociative Experiences as Mediators', *Psychological Applications and Trends* (2024): 478–482.

15 D. Kosak, *Mediator Role of Early Maladaptive Schemas Between Childhood Abuse and Suicide* (Doctoral dissertation, The Chicago School of Professional Psychology, 2024).

16 Sumiarti, A., & Puspitawati, H. (2017). 'The Relationship between Domestic Violence, Social Support, and Self Esteem Women Victims.' *Journal of Family Sciences, 2*(2), 34. https://doi.org/10.29244/jfs.2.2.34-44

17 J.C. Poole et al., 'Do adverse childhood experiences predict adult interpersonal difficulties? The role of emotion dysregulation', *Child Abuse & Neglect* 80 (2018):123–133, doi: 10.1016/j.chiabu.2018.03.006. Epub 2018 Apr 5. PMID: 29604503.

18 P.E. Mullen et al., (1996). 'The long-term impact of the physical, emotional, and sexual abuse of children: A community study', *Child Abuse & Neglect* 20(1) (1996): 7–21.

19 M.D. De Bellis and A. Zisk, 'The biological effects of childhood trauma', *Child and Adolescent Psychiatric Clinics of North America*, 23(2) (2014): 185–222, vii. doi: 10.1016/j.chc.2014.01.002. Epub 2014 Feb 16. PMID: 24656576; PMCID: PMC3968319.

20 A.V. Horwitz et al., 'The Impact of Childhood Abuse and Neglect on Adult Mental Health: A Prospective Study', *Journal of Health and Social Behavior* 42(2) (2001): 184–201, https://doi.org/10.2307/3090177

21 G.Y. Trivedi et al., 'Adverse Childhood Experiences & mental health – the urgent need for public health intervention in India', *Journal of Preventive Medicine and Hygiene* 62(3) (2021): e728–e735, doi: 10.15167/2421-4248/jpmh2021.62.3.1785. PMID: 34909501; PMCID: PMC8639107.

22 Ai-shu Liu, 'Child Neglect, Resilience and Loneliness', *Chinese Journal of Clinical Psychology* (2009).

23 Wei-Bo Zhang et al., 'Explaining how childhood physical abuse and physical neglect influence adult depression: An analysis with multiple sequential mediators', *Child Abuse & Neglect* (2024), doi: 10.1016/j.chiabu.2024.106771.

24 M. William et al., 'Physical neglect in childhood as a predictor of violent behavior in adolescent males', *Child Abuse & Neglect* (2018), doi: 10.1016/J.CHIABU.2018.03.008.

25 Jennifer Pierce et al., 'Perceived social support partially mediates the association between childhood abuse and pain-related characteristics', *Frontiers in Pain Research* (2022), doi: 10.3389/fpain.2022.1075605.

26 Cheng Fang et al., 'The relationship between childhood traumatic experience and suicidal tendency in non-suicidal self-injury behavior patients', *BMC Psychiatry* (2023), doi: 10.1186/s12888-023-04863-0.

27 P. Morgan et al., 'Mitigating the impact of adolescence isolation on the development of social anxiety: A potential role for oxytocin', *Frontiers in Behavioral Neuroscience* (2022), doi: 10.3389/fnbeh.2022.1038236.

28 J.V. Carney et al. 'Peer Victimization and Loneliness: The Moderating Role of School Connectedness by Gender', *Journal of School Counselling* 18(8) (2020).

29 S.M. Cheek et al., 'Social rejection, popularity, peer victimization, and self-injurious thoughts and behaviors among adolescents: A systematic review and meta-analysis', *Clinical Psychology Review* 82 (2020): 101936, ISSN 0272-7358, https://doi.org/10.1016/j.cpr.2020.101936.

30 N.A. Akhator-Eneka, 'The Impact of Adverse Childhood Experiences on Body Image Dissatisfaction in Adolescents: A Narrative Review', *Journal of Advances in Medicine and Medical Research* (2024).

31 Ibid.

32 P.J. Fowler et al., 'Community violence: A meta-analysis on the effect of exposure and mental health outcomes of children and adolescents', *Development and Psychopathology* 21(1) (2009):227–259, doi:10.1017/S0954579409000145.

33 S.A. Kumar and J.F. Mattanah, 'Interparental conflict, parental intrusiveness, and interpersonal functioning in emerging adulthood', *Personal Relationships* 25(1) (2018): 120–133.

34 M. Bilalli, E. Bilalli and V. Iseini, 'The Impact of Anxious and Non-Anxious Parents on the Mental Health of Children', Journal Human Research in Rehabilitation, 13(2) (2023): 343–351. https://doi.org/10.21554/hrr.092317

35 Manning Cressida and Gregoire Alain, 'Effects of parental mental illness on children', *Psychiatry MMC*, (2006), doi: 10.1016/J.MPPSY.2008.10.012.

36 Sandoz Vania et al., 'Children of parents with substance abuse: assessing impacts and available support', *Revue médicale suisse*, (2024), doi: 10.53738/revmed.2024.20.862.405.

37 N. McKeganey et al., 'Paying the Price for their Parents' Addiction: meeting the needs of the children of drug-using parents', *Drugs: Education, Prevention and Policy* 9(3) (2002): 233–246. https://doi.org/10.1080/09687630210122508.

38 Kim Yeonjae and Kang Dahyeon, 'Silent Suffering: Secondary Stigma on Children of Incarcerated Parents and Strategies for Mitigation—A Systematic Review', (2024), doi: 10.31235/osf.io/98qpy.

39 Ibid.

40 R. Condry, A. Kotova and S. Minson, Social injustice and collateral damage, Routledge eBooks pp. 622–640, 2016. https://doi.org/10.4324/9781315797779-36

41 Ana Vera Costa et al., 'Growing in the shadows of suicide', *Nascer E Crescer - Birth and Growth Medical Journal,* (2020), doi: 10.25753/BIRTHGROWTHMJ.V29.I1.18631.

42 M. Molinié, 'L'enfant orphelin et sa famille face à la violence de la mort', *Soins, 66*(858) (2021): 46–50. https://doi.org/10.1016/j.soin.2021.07.010

43 Ana Vera Costa et al., 'Growing in the shadows of suicide', *Nascer E Crescer - Birth and Growth Medical Journal,* (2020), doi: 10.25753/BIRTHGROWTHMJ.V29.I1.18631.

44 Ibid.

45 Kelvin James, 'Transference, Countertransference and Mourning the Death of a Parent', *Contemporary Psychoanalysis* (2022), doi: 10.1080/00107530.2021.1997479.

46 Zhou Yanyu, 'Review of the Impacts of Parental Divorce on Outsprings', *Journal of Education, Humanities and Social Sciences* (2023), doi: 10.54097/ehss.v22i.12423.

47 B.A. Knight, *Holding their words: Children's experiences of parental separation and divorce*, 2019, https://doi.org/10.26199/5ce03fdcb8d6b

48 Z. Rejaän, I.E. Van Der Valk, W.M. Schrama, I. Van Aalst, A. Chen, C.G.J. De Boer, J.M. Houtkamp and S. Branje, 'Adolescents' Post-Divorce sense of belonging', *European Psychologist, 27*(4) (2021): 277–290. https://doi.org/10.1027/1016-9040/a000444

49 L. Brandts, H. Bosma, A. Simons, D. Groffen and M.A. Van Den, 'The socioeconomic roots of shame and perceptions of social inadequacy', *MaRBLe, 2,* 2016, https://doi.org/10.26481/marble.2014.v2.318

50 Guo Shijing, 'The Psychology of Social Class: How Socioeconomic Status Impacts Self-Acceptance and Self-Esteem', *Lecture Notes in Education Psychology and Public Media,* (2024), doi: 10.54254/2753-7048/37/20240545.

Scan QR code to access the
Penguin Random House India website